MW01378145

THE MAN WHO LIVED MY LIFE

A Neurosurgeon's Trials of Job

Yisrael Bernstein, MD

The Man Who Lived My Life: A Neurosurgeon's Trials of Job

Published by Aliyah Publishing
Tucson, Arizona

ISBN: 978-1-0878-0037-0 (paperback)
ISBN: 978-1-0878-0038-7 (bw hardcover)
ISBN: 978-1-0878-0039-4 (color hardcover)
ISBN: 978-1-0878-0040-0 (ebook)
LCCN: 2019914025

The events described in this book are not fictitious. Similarity to persons living and dead is not merely coincidental.

The Lord gave, and the Lord took;
may the name of the Lord be blessed.

The Book of Job (Iyov) 1:21

To the blessed memory of
Robin and Maurice Bernstein.

Contents

PART II
The Story

FOREWORD

As the rabbi of Oro Valley, Arizona, I have met many individuals over the seven years I have been servicing the community. I offer advice, counsel, and inspiration in whichever way I can. Yisrael is one of the most special people I have gotten to know in my career as a rabbi, one who has offered me a great deal of inspiration.

Yisrael and I met at a High Holidays service when our congregation was just starting out. We quickly formed a close bond, and spent numerous hours studying, debating, and celebrating Shabbos and holidays together. Yisrael is a household name amongst my six children, and they eagerly look forward to his frequent visits. They know he will take the time to ask them each individually about their latest achievements and adventures.

I don't consider Yisrael a congregant of mine. Truthfully, Yisrael is a friend. He is my go-to when something comes up and I need a hand. His broad knowledge has helped me countless times, be it car trouble on the side of the road, or taking out my two-year-old's stitches. I have come to rely on Yisrael greatly, and he always comes through.

I am constantly impressed by the incredible growth Yisrael has shown in his relationship with G–d. He has taken upon himself many commitments and has shown true dedication to Torah values. Yisrael takes the time to learn the meaning behind our observances, and has studied and analyzed some deep Torah texts.

Reading the stories in this masterpiece of Yisrael's journey will give you a glimpse into his somewhat challenging, at times humorous, yet always fascinating story of his life. You will find many lessons through the pages of this book. Yisrael's intelligence has led him to perceive his many experiences and memories in a most meaningful way.

I wish Yisrael continued progress in his upward journey in *Yiddishkeit* and many more years of health and *nachas*.

To the reader: I am confident that this book and the incredible experiences described, will serve as an enjoyable read and most importantly, a message of perseverance, happiness, and inspiration.

Rabbi Ephraim Zimmerman
Director, Chabad of Oro Valley

PROLOGUE

The Hangar

For almost two years, Tao and I lived in the office of the airport hangar, a twenty-foot by thirty-foot cell with painted cement floor, cracked plaster walls, two multipaned windows facing east and two facing north, and closet commode. It was empty, save a corner desk.

After I realized that we were destined to spend more than a few nights, I ventured down to Walmart, a place I'd vowed never to set foot in, and purchased a queen-size air mattress. The mattress took up most of the floor, and Tao, a particularly large German shepherd of Nepalese descent, took up most of the mattress. During the night, his poorly manicured nails punctured little holes in the vinyl. I awoke to the incessant

Tucson sun shining through the dusty, time-glazed windows and an intractable hardness beneath me.

My cell

I bought some repair adhesive at the local sporting goods store and read through the unintelligible instructions several times. As one week turned into two, three, four weeks, and weeks leached into months, I started ordering large quantities of the adhesive online. Finally, I invested in a new air mattress. By then, the Walmart greeters knew me.

And to think, I used to do neurosurgery and own a hospital.

One thing the hangar taught me was the power of bare walls. They decimate all vestiges of well-being and are the reason prison inmates hang posters and sometimes themselves. When an email advertising a sale on photos landed in my inbox, I ordered an enlarged custom canvas print of my three children. The photo so brightened the space that I decided to stretch my Social Security income and order a second. I hung the canvases on the wall opposite the microcalligraphy I commissioned in Tzfat, Israel. My favorite always will be the photo of my daughter, Elyse, at ten years old flanked by my sons, five-year-old Michael and baby Joshua, taken when they still smiled at me every day. The other photo was of the three of them at Elyse's wedding, an event I didn't attend. I was not invited.

Mitigating loneliness

Living in the hangar was terribly frustrating. No, I take that back. It was gut-wrenchingly frustrating and lonely. The *objets d'art* mitigated only a modicum of loneliness and sometimes exacerbated it. I finally concluded that I could either wallow in melancholia or direct my energies in a more positive way. "Give me a lever long enough and a fulcrum on which to place it, and I shall move the world," wrote Archimedes. He was preceded by the great religious leader Moses, who a millennium earlier transcribed the Torah at Sinai and espoused the concept of *tikkun olam*—the acts of kindness intended to repair the world. It was time to contribute to that reparation.

For the first time in decades, I made an effort to meet my neighbors. When I was a neurosurgeon, I was busy extirpating brain tumors, stabilizing spines, and testifying as a medical expert. Who had time to become acquainted with neighbors? I arrived late to neighborhood parties, indulged in a cold drink, kibitzed with a few folks, then left. Sure, I waved to people walking through the neighborhood or working in their yards, but if I encountered them in the supermarket or at the gas pump, I most likely didn't recognize them. Tao and I, however, had plenty of hours and days to get to know folks in the airpark and listen to their stories of what was and what might have been.

I was supposed to be living in Israel, not in the La Cholla Airpark on Tucson's northwest side, but my plans had been thwarted yet again. My first trip to the Holy Land in 1967 kindled a burning desire to become a citizen of the Medinat Yisrael. My Israeli relatives convinced me to return to the States and complete my undergraduate education at the University of Chicago. Forty-five years later, I thought I was Israel bound for good. I had everything in place. I no longer owned any of my residences. The 3 Gorillas Moving and Storage Company had been hired to pack and move my belongings. I earmarked the boxes to be shipped to Israel. Everything else would be transported fifteen miles and stored in the airplane hangar.

Then the unthinkable, unimaginable, bizarre occurred: 3 Gorillas loaded box after box into huge semitrailer moving vans. We agreed to meet at the hangar to begin the unloading process. They had other ideas. Furnishings, paintings, exotic potted plants, first-edition books, Italian suits—even a Ferrari—never arrived. Not even one plate or fork or cup. Nothing.

After all the tumult that occurred with my family, my health, and my career, I never imagined that being robbed of a lifetime of belongings and nostalgia would be part of my journey. As Rabbi Zimmerman often reminds me, personal plans don't always coincide with G–d's plans. While we have free choice, the Divine orchestrates the symphony of our lives. Some movements may be easier to play than others. I love Mendelssohn's Violin Concerto in E minor, but I could only play the andante middle movement. I stumbled through the rest. Yet, no student stumbles alone. Hashem is with us through every step and every measure.

What a journey it has been. What a symphony it continues to be.

PART I

Early Years

1

Bashert: Union of Two Souls

I've loved cars for as long as I can remember. I still recall riding as a toddler in my father's new car, securely positioned on the bench seat between my parents. The car was a 1949 midnight-blue, four-door Plymouth, although I only know this from photos I've seen.

Our many cars

You know, it's funny; when you have memories, you always worry. Are you remembering photographs, or is some Leonardo DiCaprio character planting ideas and images in your dreams like in the movie *Inception*? Or are you genuinely remembering the incident? My father filmed enough home movies on his Bell & Howell 8 mm movie camera to play for a week in an IMAX theater; he even filmed me sitting in the Plymouth with that Palestinian settlers hat—or was it just a Buster Brown chapeau?

The omnipresent 8 mm camera

That's when we lived in a cramped one-bedroom apartment at 1145 W. Morse Avenue on the northern edge of Chicago, half a block from Lake Michigan. My parents, Maurice and Robin Bernstein, lived there after they married in 1945.

June 24, 1945—Bernsteins and Dorfmans

They met a few years earlier at a high school dance. I still have Mother's dance card. My father's name is listed second, after Walter, a classmate who became a gas station attendant.

Years later, when we drove by his station, we would tease my mother about Walter. I always wanted to stop and see if Walter still worked there and what my father could have looked like.

I was born on January 9, 1948, the same year that Israel became a nation. Back then, all my relatives called me Ronnie, then later Ron. Now I much prefer being called by my Hebrew name Yisrael, or the sobriquet Srully by close friends. Sometimes people address me as "rabbi" when I walk through the neighborhood on Shabbat or walk through Walmart or Costco. With my long white beard, immature peyot, kippah, and tzitzit dangling at my sides, they mistake me for an ordained rabbi. While I consider myself a religious scholar and an observant Jew, I am but a Chassidic student.

I'm named after my paternal grandfather, Israel Bernstein Z"L (may his memory be a blessing), who emigrated from Lithuania to Chicago.

Israel Bernstein

My grandmother, Ella née Yaffee, was born in Latvia and was five years younger. They married in Chicago on November 9, 1903. Sadly, my grandfather passed away when my father was sixteen. I never met him, of course, but we regularly visited my great-grandfather, Aaron Yaffee. I was almost three when he passed, and he was ninety-two. I have recovered a favorite photo of my second birthday party where I'm sitting on his knee. He's wearing his black hat and white shirt sleeves. That photo connects me to him in a special way. I also have a *Chicago Sun Times* news story about his activities as a leader of the Orthodox Jewish community. In the accompanying photo, he's wearing his tallit and old-world kippah.

Orthodox community leader

Our Morse Avenue apartment was located on the third floor of what today is a Cream City brick condominium building. Before its gentrification, however, I recall the facade being quite dingier. I slept on a cot in a closet. The apartment had very high ceilings. A huge wardrobe, which my dad built to compensate for the lack of closet space, ran the length of one wall. I'm sure my father used his grandfather's old-world tools to construct the toy chest with the color clown decals that eventually became a toolbox. I still cherish it even though it's cracked and warped, thanks to 3 Gorillas leaving it out in the rain.

A half-block east of our building, the cul-de-sac abutted an expansive grassy park with a sandy beach. Every other day, my mother and I walked to the park. During the summer, I splashed barefoot in Lake Michigan's brisk waters. I always drank from the big stone fountain with its center geyser and little surrounding faucets. One day, I put my mouth right up against the metal of one of the faucets and contracted trench mouth (thrush). My tongue was painted with a terrible tasting purple paste by my pediatrician, Dr. Benjamin Levin, at his Chicago office. That was before Dr. Gutin, the doctor with whom I became well acquainted in high school, joined his practice.

Every weekend, Auntie Anne and Auntie Ettie, my mother's older and younger sisters, both single, visited us. Auntie Ettie looked just like my mother, and the two were inseparable despite being ten years apart in age. I still marvel at their closeness. Maybe sisters are different than brothers, or at least my brothers. My aunts took the 151 CTA bus down Sheridan Road. It didn't matter if the winds were whipping off Lake Michigan, chilling us to the bone, or if they had to stomp through snow or slush or raise their umbrellas against rain. They came to visit, and it was a special day when they did. They lived on the West Side of Chicago with their parents. We walked to the corner where the bus dropped them off and expectantly waited. Auntie Anne always had Lucky Strike chocolate cigarettes for me.

Lucky Strike confectionery

Once, on the way to meet them, I happened to be carrying a glass milk bottle. Goodness knows why I was clutching a glass bottle. I was about two or three years old, and it slipped out of my hand. Somehow it shattered, and a piece of glass gashed my leg just above the ankle. My mother was pale and I was bloody when my aunts hopped off the bus. They all fussed and worried and carried me. I'm pretty sure they thought I was going to exsanguinate, but in the end, I didn't go to the hospital because my parents couldn't afford stitches. I still have a scar to this day. That accident, however, wasn't nearly as serious as the accident I endured during high school. Nothing is as serious as when you die.

Shortly after the milk bottle incident, we moved to 853 W. Gunnison Street in Uptown, a relatively new Jewish community on Chicago's North Side. Our second-floor apartment had two large bedrooms, formal living and dining rooms, and front and back porches. Since the ceilings were much lower than those on Morse Avenue, my father had to saw off the top row of cabinets from the wardrobe in order for it to fit. A narrow driveway ran alongside the six-unit brick building and dead-ended in a concrete yard with wooden garages behind it.

Our landlady, Mrs. Glasser, lived directly below us. By my standards, she appeared to be very old. Now when I think of her, she reminds me of the actress Gertrude Berg, who starred in the TV series that we watched back then, *The Goldbergs*. At times, loud jackhammering noises reverberated from her apartment, most likely the radiator sending protests through the registers during winter. Our dog, Tippy, tried to harmonize. On family trips, when our car hit a bump, a similar thumping noise emanated from the back. We said it was Mrs.

Glasser in the trunk. We all laughed. On the first of every month, I knocked on the Glassers' unlocked door and waited for a voice to reply, "Leave the rent check on the front table." Mr. Glasser, whom I don't ever recall seeing, had a fatal heart attack in their apartment. The ambulance arrived with siren blaring and lights flashing and parked in front, blocking all traffic. My first close-up experience with death was very frightening.

Not far from our apartment was Silver, Millman and Company, the accounting firm where my father worked. On weekends, he relinquished his adding machine for his carpenter tools. I always accompanied him to Walt's Workshop, the tool section inside Edward Hines Lumber Yard. There, he purchased a new hammer, special hand saw, drill, or whatever he needed to complete his current project. My favorite hand tool was the Yankee screwdriver. I still have it with all its accessories, bits, and minute parts. After he passed, I discovered boxes full of unopened tool sets. I inherited this hoarding gene from him.

One of our joint enterprises was a balsa wood airplane with a gas engine. We sat at the table in the screened-in front porch during assembly. Banana paper covered the wings. He did most of the cutting and gluing, though he entrusted me with the final task of injecting fuel into the engine using a syringe. We took the ultralight plane to the park a block away and launched it. Up it soared, right into the top branches of a nearby maple tree. Needless to say, its maiden voyage was its last.

My dad also built a Ping-Pong tabletop. Together we painted the plywood British racing green; I helped him mask the table and paint the white stripe border. He propped it on two sawhorses in the basement for all the tenants to use and taught me how to volley. Unless he let me claim victory, he usually won. After I married, I shipped that table to our first house in Tucson. When Mike and Josh challenged me, I'd hit the ball with backspin or topspin, driving the neophytes crazy. Yet, even my custom pro-paddles failed to maintain my winning streak as the boys improved. They learned to anticipate where the ball was going to land, then BOOM, they'd send it flying over my head, driving me crazy. My skills in chess and downhill skiing similarly exceeded theirs but for a short time.

The most special time with my father was walking to weekly Shabbat services at the Agudas Achim North Shore Congregation. My mother dressed me in a clean white shirt and, in cold weather, a fancy wool coat purchased from Marshall Field's. I reached up for my father's hand and off we went, even in subzero wind chills. As we approached the synagogue, fellow congregants greeted my father with, "*Gut Shabbos,* Maisch." His name was Maurice, but almost everyone called him Maisch.

Built thirty years earlier, Agudas Achim had a magnificent facade of three arches and an even more ornate interior. Inside, we climbed the steps of one of the massive curved marble staircases to the balcony, where the benches had built-in book and tallit storage racks. The cavernous sanctuary stretched beyond us. Colored light filtered through the rows of stained glass windows arching around the Aron Hakodesh (Holy Ark), the Torah scrolls within it. Even at four and five years old, I sensed its sanctity and felt the hand of Hashem.

Shabbat became the focal point of my week and remains so to this day. After I started Hebrew studies, my understanding of the Torah grew, and much, much later, so did my understanding of its Kabbalistic insights.

Three arches

The sanctuary

The synagogue's basement housed classrooms, where I made my little dreidel out of clay, and when it was dry and ready, I did play. There was also a small auditorium, complete with a stage, podium, and folding chairs. At the end of the first year, our class presented a program of Jewish historical soliloquies. My extended family applauded my recitation of Emma Lazarus's famous sonnet, "The New Colossus," adorning the base of the Statue of Liberty and still imprinted in my memory.

Grandparents, aunts, uncles, and cousins lived relatively close, at most three CTA bus transfers. We always gathered at one apartment or another for holidays. Any holiday—Jewish, Israeli, or secular—was an excuse to be together. Even if there weren't holidays, we gathered. When I turned five, Mom showed me how to visit my grandmothers via the bus. I boarded the 151 bus on Sheridan. With trepidation, I asked for a transfer, still free. A minute later, I queried, "Can you tell me when we get to Diversey?" He nodded, and I took a seat immediately behind him. Every few minutes, I anxiously asked, "Are we there yet?" Finally, he offered, "Next stop, Diversey." I then had to cross a busy intersection. Bubbe Fagela, my maternal grandmother, always made prize-winning latkes. Bubbe Gelke greeted me with hugs and kisses and mouth-watering blintzes, which I learned to make while perched on her kitchen table. After a bowl of matzo ball soup and kishke, Auntie Yetta, my father's sister who lived with Bubbe Gelke, walked hand in hand with me to the theater around the corner where we watched movies together.

Auntie Yetta had two children, Donald and his younger sister Liz (Isabel), both older than I.

Donald and Liz

Donald could drive and often borrowed my father's car to take me places like the archery range, where he taught me to shoot a longbow nearly twice my height, or to the pond at the Lincoln Park Zoo Rookery, where we fed the fish in the summer and ducks in the winter as they waddled over the ice.

He felt like the older brother I never had.

Feeding the ducks

I was still quite young when Donald, then a medical student at the University of Illinois, was conscripted into the army and sent to Fort Bragg in North Carolina. It was late on Thanksgiving night when I learned of the tragedy. There had been no turkey dinner that day, though I hadn't understood why at the time. My mother and I were cuddled in bed reading a book when my father entered the bedroom, having just returned from Raleigh. Donald was killed in a car accident, and Dad had to go identify the body. He tried to explain to me what had happened to Donald. When he finished, he handed me a board game that he bought during the trip. The Game of States consoled me, but only a little. Mostly, I felt very sad. I loved Donald and missed him. Auntie Yetta gave me his marksman medal and two bows, arrows, and quiver, which I cherished and brought out every Lag b'Omer. During my last trip to visit Liz in Pasadena, I gave them to Jonathan, Liz's youngest son.

I loved Liz almost as much as I loved Donald. While sitting on her lap at a family gathering, I whispered, "Liz, I'm going to marry you." I was three and she was twelve. She'd laugh and say, "OK, when you get older." But she married a Chicago-area pediatrician, Dr. Burton Green, and moved to California.

Heart-wrenching. I wore my first tux—a white jacket, cummerbund, and black pants—to their wedding.

Down the aisle

Liz's son Donald later digitized the wedding photos and sent them to me. When I wax nostalgic, these days a not uncommon occurrence, I revisit the photos on my phone.

Sadly, I have but few photos of my many neighborhood friends. We all attended Graeme Stewart School, the only elementary school in our district. Mark Mosoff, who lived downstairs on the first floor, just across the landing from Mrs. Glasser, was in all of my classes. Burton Slutsky lived on the third floor. His father, Max, a gruff-looking, kind-hearted fellow, was an Andy Frain usher at Wrigley Field and wore an official-looking uniform and what looked like a train conductor's hat. During the summer, he procured tickets to Cubs games for us. We sat in the lower grandstand, ate peanuts, and cheered for shortstop Ernie Banks.

When not in school, our gang rode bikes up and down the sidewalks and trooped to each other's playrooms. I was the cop or the cowboy, my friends the robbers or Indians. We frequented a plethora of local cinemas, some great palaces such as the Uptown Theatre for double features separated by newsreels and cartoons. *The Creature from the Black Lagoon* or

Vincent Price's *House on Haunted Hill* left me ducking down in the seat and covering my eyes with my hands. I suffered nightmares afterward. In the fall, we congregated in our driveway to watch the coal being delivered. It cascaded down a long chute that extended from the truck into the basement right next to the Ping-Pong table. Dust clouds puffed into the air, and we couldn't hear each other speak. In January, everyone came to the extravagant birthday party my mother hosted for me. She lined up my friends and relatives by height and, under the watchful lens of my dad's movie camera, paraded them through a narrow hallway into the dining room. There, dressed in a new sport coat, I blew out the candles on my cake after making a secret wish.

I'm pretty certain my gang was there the day Uncle Sam, who owned a truck, delivered my mother's baby grand piano to our apartment. It was a Baldwin because she couldn't afford the Steinway she preferred. Uncle Sam, the MD (metal dealer), inched the truck down the driveway, then he and my dad rigged a block and tackle to the roof to lift and swing the piano onto the back porch. The back staircase was much too narrow. Slowly, he and Dad hoisted the dangling padded piano, not an easy task. Up, up went the ebony behemoth. I was stationed on the back porch repeating, "A little bit farther. A little bit farther." Everyone held their breath as the piano, its highly polished veneer sparkling in the sunlight, cleared the porch railing and was guided into its new home.

My mother took private piano lessons from Diana Shanks. Every Friday, we rode the bus to her studio. Afterward, we went down the block to the butcher shop, which had a selection of Shabbat prime cuts and freshly shecht chicken. I always wondered about the sawdust on the floor, though I loved to slide in it from side to side. We concluded our chores next door with a vanilla malted milkshake—my mother's favorite, and soon, mine. My mother never became an accomplished pianist, certainly not compared to my brother, Shelly.

Shelly was born at Mount Sinai Hospital shortly after we moved to Gunnison. Although his birth certificate says Sheldon Corey Bernstein, to this day he insists that his legal name was changed to Shelly.

Me and my shadow

We're almost three and a half years apart in age, but we were always four grades apart in school. I graduated high school when Shelly graduated eighth grade; when he graduated from high school, I graduated from the University of Chicago. I suspect he felt like a runner-up; it seemed that he was always my shadow. Even if he had been the taller of us—he's about five inches shorter—he still would have grown up in my shadow. I was the *bechor*, the firstborn son, who stands in the father's stead, perpetuating his continued memory. According to Jewish law, the bechor is the recipient of privileges and a double portion of the family inheritance, regardless of the number of siblings in his wake. I grew up embraced by the feeling of being privileged and special.

I don't recall Shelly being around much during my youth, a bit of an anomaly since I always felt very close to the rest of my family and have clear memories of them. I don't recall the two of us playing Ping-Pong or constructing elaborate structures together with Tinker Toys, Lincoln Logs, or Erector sets. I do know, however, that if I went swimming, Shelly went swimming. If I went to the zoo, he went to the zoo, though never did he go with Donald and me. In our very early years, my mother dressed us alike. In one photo taken in the concrete backyard of our apartment building, Dad holds one-year-old Shelly and I stand next to them. Shelly and I sport matching short-sleeved white shirts and red vests. In later years, when my mother took us to Marshall Field's, Carson Pirie Scott, or Lytton's, I got to pick out my favorite color shirt; if that was Shelly's favorite color, it didn't matter. My mother chose for him.

Lookalikes

Based on the family photo albums, however, one might assume that Shelly and I spent much time together. In one particular photo, I'm standing with a violin tucked under my chin, bow poised to scratch across the strings. Next to me, Shelly sits on a piano bench looking at sheet music, his hands poised to strike the ivories. We look like we could go on tour—the Bernstein Brothers.

The next photo was a result of my mother encouraging us to perform for company. Two brothers fairly close in age, who lived in the same house, interacted with the same family, yet lived separate lives. If we each had our own 8 mm reels of our childhood, I wonder how many frames would be similar.

Violin and piano repertoire

My mother enrolled me in violin classes at age four, shortly after I discovered the old, funny-shaped violin case under Auntie Shirley's bed. Mom would accompany me on the CTA to Lyon & Healy for group lessons. I gratingly bowed across the four strings, but I was no worse than the rest of our little ensemble. She also enrolled me at Sulie and Pearl Harand children's theater studio, recently opened by two Hollywood starlets. Drama, fencing, voice, and dance lessons were included. I particularly despised the dance classes—I had no talent. My brain was left-dominant. At the end-of-the-year play, I was assigned the role of the family dog, complete with a droopy-eared costume my parents were forced to buy. My entire memorized script consisted of "Yip, yip, yip." I barked through all of my lines.

I also took art classes and rode the bus unaccompanied to the Art Institute of Chicago. Once, while not paying attention, I got off too early at Adams and Wabash in the foreboding Chicago loop under the rumbling train tracks. I was lost, petrified, and in tears until a policeman took my hand and walked me one block further to the mighty lions heralding the entrance to the Art Institute. Chicago's finest were not always to be so accommodating years later. The occurrence didn't frighten me nearly as much as being in Marshall Field's ten minutes before closing. That's when a disarming bell sounded, a warning to customers to make their purchases and prepare to exit. That bell terrified me. I was certain that we would get locked in the store and have to spend the night. Over the years, my cleithrophobia manifested in punctuality for appointments, airports, ball games, and concerts.

While others instructed me in the fine arts, Mother taught me to ride my bicycle. It was not the common American Schwinn, but an English Raleigh with hand brakes, gears, saddlebags, and an air pump. No training wheels for this cyclist. The first time that she let go of the handlebar and my seat, the bike went about five feet, then tipped and sent me sprawling nose-first into the cement. The next day, we attended the now defunct Barnum & Bailey Circus. We went every year, but this year featured the Cisco Kid, my television favorite. Leo Carrillo—Pancho—climbed up a couple of rows where we were sitting. "Who skeened your nose little boy?" he said in his trademark Hispanic accent.

O' Pancho, O' Cisco

At that moment, the skinned nose seemed worth it, but years later, I would need rhinoplasty by Dr. Ira Tresley, a renowned plastic surgeon at Northwestern Medical Center in Chicago, to repair the perforated septum that made sleeping very uncomfortable and to remedy the associated stertorous respirations. As a result, I lost my Jewish nose. Contrast this with my son Josh threatening a nose job to rid himself of his heritage. Hasn't happened yet!

While I attended Graeme Stewart, Mother started as a substitute teacher. She took me to school, but I walked home by myself. During brutal winter months, the seven blocks seemed like seven miles. If it were really inclement, she gave me bus fare. I climbed up the back porch stairway, headed straight to the new RCA black-and-white television, and watched *Garfield Goose* or other local WGN children's shows. Mother returned home an hour or two later.

Every day, she always made sure I had my freshly prepared milchig lunch packed in my Roy Rogers lunch box; milk could be purchased in the lunchroom for two cents. I didn't need a reminder to take my bag of marbles for recess challenges. I had boulders, and with a bit of dexterity, enough to do neurosurgery in later years, I usually increased my collection. That was our schoolyard activity. A few of the older kids were bullies and tormented us by grabbing some of our marbles. It infuriated me, but there was nothing that I could do about it.

Maybe that anger explains the day that I left school during recess, walked to Kresge's Five and Dime, and bought a mousetrap. I guess I was hoping to trap a bully. I must not have made it back to class on time because I recall sitting in the principal's office and my mother coming to get me. She was not a happy mother. I don't remember if I got the strap then, but my father's belt was usually the agent of parental discipline.

Our apartment was always empty when I came home from school, since both parents worked. One afternoon, I came home from school, opened the door, and saw the table with the black rotary dial phone, with its UPtown 8-5719 label, knocked over. All the drawers were disheveled. Clothes were strewn on the floor and on the bed. Scared, I ran across the hall to Mrs. Horwitz, who called the police. I was only six years old and didn't fully appreciate the gravity of what had happened or the possible personal danger until much later.

By 1955, Uptown demographics were beginning to change, and my parents felt it was time to move. They decided to build a custom home in Lincolnwood, a quaint little township just north of Chicago, with a significant Jewish community and an exceptional education system.

I had a battery of IQ tests that allowed me to skip a grade and start fifth grade in Lincolnwood.

We packed our belongings, bid farewell to Uptown, and began a new family chapter on Chase Avenue.

Movin' on up to Lincolnwood

Several years later

2

Tarnished

I last visited Lincolnwood during the summer the Cubs were heading toward a World Series championship, baseballs flying off their bats over the ivy walls. Planning to move to Israel in the fall, I wanted to visit Auntie Ettie, now an octogenarian, and take my cousins Sharon and Gary to a game at the friendly confines of Wrigley Field.

I made arrangements to stay with Rabbi Zimmerman's parents, who lived in Chicago not far from Sharon's condo in Lincolnwood. After a bit of cajoling, Sharon agreed to chauffeur me to the house on Chase Avenue.

"You have to get the robin from the lamppost," she insisted on our way there.

Auntie Ettie at ninety years young

I hadn't thought about that robin in decades. Soon after we moved into our newly built home, Dad and I installed the post in the front yard near the walkway. Above the address plate, a painted robin perched in a nest—an eponym for my mother, my father joked.

Robin in winter

As Sharon and I approached the house, we saw the lamppost standing at attention, but alas, only one rusted feather poked up from the nest. The brick house looked smaller than I remembered. Unmanicured shrubs had replaced the large evergreens by the front windows, and the wooden trim was painted a sickly shade of brown. The curbside view of my past propelled me out of the car. So many of my formative years had been spent within this brick split-level. Sharon declined to join me.

As I strode up the front walk, I thought of the elm trees that had flanked the street. Lincolnwood's first mayor, Henry A. Proesel, commissioned ten thousand to be planted as a work project during the Depression. In the fall, my friends and I raked the orange and red leaves into mountains that invited us to take a plunge. At night, bonfires dotted the street, their pungent smoke rising into the crisp air. When the township banned leaf burning, plastic bags full of the deciduous trash lined the streets awaiting collection. After I moved away, those regal giants, whose branches created a canopy of shade over the street during hot, sticky summer days, succumbed to Dutch elm disease.

I rang the doorbell. No one answered, so I used the door knocker. *Tap, tap, tap.* A hazy memory nudged me. I examined the tarnished brass, then rubbed it with my sleeve. A faint etching of "STEIN" emerged. My goodness! Was this the door knocker I purchased and had engraved for my parents' wedding anniversary? With toolbox at my feet, I was ten years old when I drilled two holes in the wood door, affixing the knocker, and covering the holes with color-match putty.

Bang, bang, bang, I knocked louder. A face popped up behind the glass pane above the knocker. The face looked young and somewhat alarmed.

"Good afternoon!" I shouted. "I'm Dr. Bernstein. I grew up in this house. My parents built it in 1957. I just stopped by to say hello." Poor kid. My long white beard, gesticulating arms, and exuberant voice probably frightened him. "Tell your parents I'll be back," I yelled, thinking of Arnold

Schwarzenegger but not wanting to cause him more discomfort.

I gestured to Sharon that I was going to walk around to the backyard. What a mistake. My euphoria immediately dissipated into disappointment. The split-level patio that Dad and I painstakingly set with multicolored Lopez stones, each chosen to highlight the intricate pattern he had drawn, was now a concrete blob.

The patios

My mother's beds of exotic tea roses were nowhere to be seen. The apple tree by the kitchen window also had disappeared. When my parents took Shelly and me to a nursery to populate our barren backyard, I chose the apple sapling, though its fragrant spring blossoms never bore fruit until I left for college. My parents chose a flowering purple plum tree for Shelly. When Dale was old enough, he chose a weeping willow that was planted near the far border of the backyard. It grew fast and was cut down.

Even the expanse of lawn was usurped by a detached garage built on what once was our outfield. On lazy summer evenings, if the mosquitoes weren't biting, Dad hit baseballs to Shelly and me. Sometimes the grounder rolled past us into the honeysuckle hedge, and we had to crawl among the prickly brambles to retrieve it. Our latest family dog was smart enough not to follow.

Phideaux

Tippy died before we moved from Gunnison, so my parents allowed me to get another dog. The only criteria were that it be intelligent and a purebred. One of my father's clients was Addie Klein. Addie and his wife lived on the Gold Coast in Chicago. I often accompanied Dad when he went to their home, where I played with their two French poodles. One was gray and one was white. I loved those dogs and decided we should have a similar one, so I chose a pedigreed miniature French poodle. His American Kennel Club papers showed his lineage as Pixie of Holly Court.

We named him Phideaux but called him Frisky. He was pitch-black and full of energy but with a gentle demeanor. I'd accompany my mother when she drove him to the salon. He'd exit with blue nails and bows over each ear matching his bejeweled collar and a round ball of fur on the tip of his tail and at the bottom of each leg. I'm sure his coiffing cost more than my mother's hairdresser each month. Phideaux could dance on his hind legs forever. When I raked the leaves, he bounded into the pile, rescattering the leaves over the grass. Every day

I walked him down the alley. This was before pooper-scoopers, and our neighbors, the Meyers, didn't appreciate that Phideaux pooped in their driveway. More than once, they called my mother and complained.

Phideaux wasn't even middle-aged when he developed epilepsy. By the time I got to high school, he was getting progressively sicker. I'll never forget the day I came home from school and he was gone. My parents had taken him to the vet and had him put down. It was another very sad time for me.

Now, the diminished yard looked as if it would barely contain a well-hit Wiffle ball. Logically, I expected some change—modernization and improvements. The Gunnison apartment building had been demolished, a luxury condominium built in its stead.

What was

Morse still stood but had been gentrified, along with the entire neighborhood. The house next door on Chase had been replaced by a massive Mediterranean-style residence. Yet, when change collided with my nostalgia, it sent me into a funk. I trudged back to the car, the first drops of a summer rain falling on my kippah.

I couldn't stop obsessing about the door knocker. The robin was gone; the knocker was my only link to the past. Maybe I could convince the owners to part with it. With a promise of a bag of stadium peanuts, Sharon agreed to schlep me back a few days later. This time, a man and woman answered the door.

"My son told me you had visited," the woman said with a Middle Eastern accent that wasn't Hebrew. She smiled warmly, assuring me that her son wasn't traumatized; he had been instructed never to open the door for strangers. She invited me inside.

With a bit of ambivalence, I stepped into the foyer and into the past. The floor was just as I recalled: black and white Italian marble grouted with terrazzo. When guests commented on it, my mother, always gracious and humble, acknowl-edged the compliment. When I built the unique and elegant, did I exude the same humility? I glanced into the sunken living room to my left and had to suppress my shock. Shiny hardwood floors replaced the plush blue carpeting that had been so cushy underfoot. No longer were there white leather serpentine couches, the fitted clear plastic only removed for company, and blue silk drapes covering the picture windows. The elegance was gone.

"Would you like to see the house?" the woman asked.

I intended to reclaim the door knocker, not take a tour. But I couldn't resist. I glanced at the staircases off the foyer; one set ascended to the bedrooms, another down to the recreation room. "Do you use the fireplace downstairs?" I asked.

She led the way. The Crab Orchard fireplace looked the same, but the cabinets and bookcases were gone, as were the bar and card table and the general hominess the room once held.

Warm winters

The door to the subbasement, with the busy sump pump that frequently punctuated the silence, was closed. That's where we had two train tables, the Ping-Pong table Dad built, a coin-operated pool table, and a forties jukebox with colors that lit up in syncopation with vinyl forty-fives of a bygone era. I opened the door and peered down the stairs. Cheap paneling divided the subbasement into small cells. I quickly shut the door. I couldn't bear it.

Instead, like a docent, I started relating to the couple, and now their curious son, historical minutia: how my mother interviewed a number of renowned artists and commissioned one to hand paint a mural of an old Spanish outdoor market on the kitchen walls and soffits; a famous fountain reflected in the mirror over the sinks and counter in the master bath; a birdcage and robins behind the antique roller desk and chair in the guest bedroom.

Mom had chosen pale pink kitchen appliances and a pink countertop, a pink and white wrought iron table and matching chairs with pink upholstered seats. I didn't know it at the time, but according to Sharon, Auntie Robin's built-in ovens and refrigerator were the envy of many women. My mother had seen the appliances featured at General Electric's trade show before building the house.

Artistry

I didn't bother to enter the dining room. Why risk distorting memories of my bubbes, aunts, uncles, and cousins gathered for lively family meals on Shabbat. The mahogany dining room table my mother designed opened to seat ten, a minyan. Mom requisitioned a separate matching table for children. Being the bechor, I always sat with the adults no matter the occasion. Sharon still teases me about that because she and Shelly, the oldest of the "little children," were responsible for clearing and washing the dishes from that table. Meanwhile, I went downstairs to play cards with the adults.

"Would you like to see the upstairs?" asked the man, whose name I forgot in the midst of such upset. I politely declined.

Before leaving, I took a last look at the living room. The bare walls once boasted rococo-framed artwork. I remember being with my parents at a gallery in Chicago when they purchased a red chalk sketch purportedly done by Michelangelo.

Elegance and fine art

They hung it above the Baldwin piano. I always assumed the sketch was authentic, which Shelly vehemently disputed, just as he did whenever given the opportunity to contradict me. Shelly never admitted that he possessed the sketch. When I visited his beautiful home several times in West Newton, Massachusetts, he didn't offer a tour. I suspect that he didn't want me to know what other treasures of my parents he purloined.

"One thing I would like is the door knocker," I said, handing him a hundred-dollar bill. "You'll have a few holes in the door until you can get a replacement."

He put his hands up and shook his head. "No problem. We will send it to you."

I almost suggested loosening the screws right there and then, but that would've entailed removing the putty and creating a mess. Instead, I asked if they had the teakwood panels that used to sit on the countertop in the foyer, dividing the space from the living room. "They were carved with birds and trees. Really gorgeous," I added.

"Yes, yes," said the woman. "They are in the basement."

I held out the Franklin again, saying that it would pay for shipping of the panels and the door knocker. The man declined the offer but promised to ship the items as soon as possible. I have yet to receive them.

Sometimes the past is only important to those who lived it.

3

I Become a Man

Since Lincolnwood didn't have a Jewish congregation in 1957, my family joined Congregation B'nai Emunah of Lincolnwood in neighboring Skokie, which had the only Hebrew school within driving distance. My parents and I never felt comfortable with their nontraditional services. Fortunately, within the year, Rabbi Joel Lehrfield, a young, energetic rabbi from a rabbinic family founded the Lincolnwood Jewish Congregation. LJC services were held a few blocks from our house in a Touhy Avenue storefront, previously a fish market; Hebrew school classes were held across the street in another storefront. I could now walk to Hebrew school, as well as to Saturday services, which I appreciated since it is forbidden to drive on Shabbat.

Six students and I attended Hebrew school, held three days each week following secular school. Classes focused on Hebrew language and Jewish heritage, holidays, and prayers. My favorite subject was (and still is) history. As I frequently boast, "Jewish history is the history of the world." Rabbi Lehrfield enlisted Rabbis Jerome Klein, Naftali Porush, and Mark Slae. Ah, those long walks after Shabbat services for cholent and study. I kept in touch with each of these teachers, even when they relocated to distant lands. The year preceding my bar mitzvah, a special weekly preparatory session was added with Rabbi Lehrfield, which concentrated on Orthodox rituals, traditions, and commandments in addition to learning to chant the haftorah and Torah readings. Of all the rabbis, he most influenced me, inculcating a sense of moral responsibility and a relationship with Hashem. By age thirteen, I was awakening forty-five minutes early to put on tefillin and recite morning prayers.

When I returned to Chicago years later, I wanted to reconnect with Rabbi Lehrfield, who I heard was back from Israel. I arrived at LJC in great anticipation much before the 6:45 a.m. service but was told that Rabbi Lehrfield probably would not be in. Disappointment overwhelmed me. But who should walk in while I was putting on my tallit and tefillin?

"Yisrael! I will never forget those blue eyes!" Rabbi Lehrfield exclaimed, extending his arms. We hugged and cried. Later, we had a chance to talk and talk and talk. Divine Providence.

My religious and spiritual mentor

Under the direction of Rabbi Lehrfield, LJC began construction of a synagogue while I was in eighth grade. I have a photo of Max Gordon holding a shovel and wearing a hard hat at the groundbreaking ceremony. One year later, at the dedication, I was privileged to give the dvar Torah. Max, one of the oldest members of the congregation, drove a shiny white Chrysler Imperial and parked it in the reserved spot in front of the entrance. His wife, Sophie, was the hostess of the Sunday Minionaires Club. After davening, Dad and I would remove our tefillin and eat lox on bialys with a schmear of cream cheese in the auditorium adjacent to the sanctuary. Occasionally, a prominent guest joined us, such as Henny Youngman. Fiddle in hand, he inevitably asked us to "take my wife, please," as only Henny Youngman could entreat. As the gabbai, Max assigned honors during services and often chose me to open the Ark. What an honor! After my bar mitzvah, he'd call me up to the Torah for an aliyah.

My bar mitzvah remains a cherished memory.

בר מצוה

*We cordially invite you to worship
and rejoice with us on the occasion of
the Bar Mitzvah of our son
Ronald Allen
on Sabbath morning, the twenty-first of January
nineteen hundred and sixty-one
at nine o'clock
Todd Hall
3925 West Lunt Avenue
Lincolnwood, Illinois*

Robin and Maurice Bernstein

*Dinner
Sunday, the twenty-second of January
twelve o'clock noon
Edgewater Beach Hotel
5349 North Sheridan Road*

You're invited

My mother wanted it to be special. My father wanted it to be economical. I wanted it to be exceptional. Two out of three ain't bad. Rabbi Lehrfield helped me with the interpretation of the weekly Torah reading, Bo, about the Exodus and inheritance of the firstborn. My mother helped me with the grammar and syntax of my speech; then, once I had it memorized, she helped me master its delivery. I've always been told that my voice sounds like Alan Alda's or that of a radio announcer;

projection has never been an issue. The synagogue had not yet been completed, so the service was held in the kindergarten auditorium at Mary Todd Hall Elementary School. I read from the Torah and led the congregation during the entire service as chazzan, a great honor and achievement.

My mother outdid herself with an extraordinary Kiddush immediately following the Saturday morning service, then a formal evening party, worthy of a prince's wedding reception, at the Edgewater Beach Hotel Grand Ballroom, commonly referred to as the Pink Hotel. She booked a klezmer orchestra and famous emcee, cantor Murray Linn, ordered exquisite kosher fare, and agonized over the seating charts. I had no choice but to dance. Like singing, dancing is not compatible with my left-dominant brain. Mother made me take dance lessons at Arthur Murray Studios ahead of time with Betty Frazen, who was a year younger and lived across the street. I suspect Betty didn't appreciate the bruises from my missteps.

Pardon my feet

We danced on tables, sat on chairs lifted high, danced the kazatsky—a national Ukrainian dance—as well as the hora 'til the wee hours. After the musicians packed up and the guests left, my parents, Shelly, and I went up to our suite. I sat on the bed and opened gift envelope after gift envelope while my mother recorded the amount of every check and who had gifted it. She teased my dad that it "almost" paid for the gala.

End of day

I recently was reunited with my bar mitzvah photo album. How wonderful to page through it and reminisce on the good memories. There's a photo of my immediate family: me in my first suit, my father, my mother, and Shelly in a plaid sports jacket. Everyone looks happy. In another photo, I stand between my two bubbes, each grasping one of my arms and broadly grinning.

There's a photo of Liz holding the hand of her husband, Buddy, another of Auntie Anne and Auntie Ettie, who continues to remind me of my mother. Burton Slutsky's father is in one photo, wearing a suit and tie instead of his Andy

Frain uniform, and in another photo, Mrs. Glasser and Mrs. Horowitz are seated next to each other at a table. And of course, there is one Rabbi Lehrfield sitting at the head table.

Honored grandmothers

All my family and friends gathered in one place to welcome me into manhood.

L'Chaim—To Life

4

Lord of the Flies

Middle school science fair projects were mandatory. In sixth grade, I constructed a plaster of Paris volcano that erupted. My classmates showed far more interest in the proverbial project than did the science fair judges. Accustomed to having the highest grades, I was disappointed that the volcano only earned me a plebeian participation award. But I learned. By eighth grade, I had become more ingenious and that year applied the scientific method to a simple but creative project involving genetics and the *Drosophila melanogaster*, more commonly known as fruit flies. Though the project lacked the drama of a volcano that spewed smoke and dribbled lava down its side, it garnered a first-place accolade that almost satiated my intense drive to excel. I had yet to go downstate with an outstanding recognition.

During my freshman year at Niles West, one of two township high schools ("East is least, and West is best"), I came up with a killer idea for a science project, one that was certain to astound local, regional, and national judges. I don't recall if the idea emanated from my biology class, from articles I read in *Scientific American* and other magazines to which I subscribed, or both. For this project-of-all-high-school-projects, I planned to irradiate fruit flies and observe their offspring for genetic abnormalities and mutations. I had just learned of Gregor Mendel's research and discoveries in genetics. Pea plants would take too long to grow; thus, the fruit flies.

By this time, I had designed and built a chemistry lab in the subbasement of our house. What science geek doesn't want his own laboratory complete with glassware that would make *Young Frankenstein* proud? An L-shaped set of plywood cabinets ran along two adjoining corner walls. The cabinets had lockable sliding doors, Formica countertops, and drawers that never worked smoothly. (What do you expect from a thirteen-year-old?) I installed a Bunsen burner with its own gas line and valve coming out of the backsplash and a double sink caulked watertight. In order to run hot and cold water, I had to reconfigure and connect ingress and drainpipes. I spent quite a bit of time down there, and much more the following two years, though as it turned out, not by design. Funny, I don't remember my parents saying anything about the lab or even visiting my sanctuary. They implicitly trusted me in my world. No one was ever set afire.

My baby brother, Dale, supplied all the baby food jars I needed for breeding fruit flies. I didn't pay Dale too much attention; I was preoccupied with being thirteen, and he didn't do much more than eat and sleep. My mother's first cousin, Albert Dorfman, a brilliant professor of pediatrics and biology at the University of Chicago and director of one of their associated hospitals, connected me with some fellow professors who supplied me with the fruit flies. He was always kind, gracious, and modest, traits that took me too long to acquire even though I tried to emulate him. He was like an uncle to me.

I filled each baby food jar with a special recipe for culture medium consisting of molasses and agar, a recipe concocted on my mother's stovetop, much to her consternation. Then I added male and female fruit flies and sealed the jar with a cotton plug instead of its metal screw top. The jars went into the plywood cabinets that I locked. I didn't want Shelly or anyone else trespassing. My cousin Sharon remembers going into the basement and swatting at fruit flies. I don't share that recollection.

All I needed was radiation. My dentist owned an X-ray machine with enough rads to affect the fruit flies' genes. Elm leaves still littered the sidewalks when I started my weekly trips to the dentist's office toting a box filled with baby food jars. First, I etherized the tiny insects so that I could separate them with a fine camel-hair brush and count them under a magnifying glass, noting their gender, eye color (red or white), and wing formation. I attached my Nikon SLR camera with micro lens (a bar mitzvah gift) to the tripod and photographed them, then zapped them. I observed whether second, third, fourth, and fifth generations had mutations, which of course they did. The project concluded about the time I had to mow the spring lawn for the first time. At the end of freshman year, the Illinois Junior Academy of Science awarded me the Outstanding Award for the entire state of Illinois.

With that esteemed honor came an invitation to present in Washington, DC, the following spring. I was ecstatic. A year, however, is a long time. I had things to do and life to live.

Most importantly, I needed a summer job.

Outstanding

The pharmacy on Lunt and Sheridan placed a classified ad in the local paper for a boy with a bike to deliver pharmaceuticals. The druggist interviewed me and offered seventy-five cents per hour. I soon discovered tips. The more stairs I had to climb in an apartment building, the larger the tip. When not making a delivery, I helped out behind the counters. The first time someone requested rubbers, I directed them to the galoshes and umbrella section. Sometimes men would ask me to grab a magazine from the high racks behind the counter. I was tall and could reach the most recent issue of *Playboy* and *Hustler*. I tried not to show my embarrassment.

The biweekly checks supported my model train habit, much more so than card games. Darryl Ellis, my next-door neighbor Steven Meyer, and Donny Weil down the block and

I met every Saturday night after Shabbos to play hearts, poker, and occasionally Klabiash, a game taught by my Uncle Sam, until dawn. We rotated venues. No drinking or drugs, just penny-ante gambling. Once a week, I bicycled three or four miles to the hobby shop on Touhy and purchased some item for my HO trains. My father originally bought me the pre–World War II train set, a simple oval of track and five cars, for Chanukah when I was three or four. Each subsequent holiday, he would add cars or accessories.

Just like Dad, who always needed some tool from Walt's, I always needed some track, rolling stock, or accessory.

5

In the Arms of Morpheus

Labor Day weekend stamped the end of summer. As we had done the previous year, Mom and I convened at the kitchen table and chose honors courses that would lead to the Advanced Placement track in junior and senior years. My mother had spent her entire life in Chicago and envisioned me attending an Ivy League university.

Fortunately, I didn't need more German. Knowing that one third of my progenitors perished in the Holocaust had instilled a negative bias against anything German. The only benefit to learning the language was that I could understand my bubbes' Yiddish (though I consider Yiddish a perversion of German) and eavesdrop on my parents clandestine conversations, though I doubt they recognized my deciphering abilities.

I again signed up for orchestra. I still took private violin lessons from David Glass, an older, robust gentleman with thick glasses, thick black hair, and a thick Hungarian accent.

"If only you would practice, Ron," he would say, making me feel guilty.

I did practice, sort of, but homework, Hebrew School, the Jewish youth group Chaverim, and science and math clubs kept me busy. Fortunately, Mr. Glass was kind and understanding; we both knew that I would never be a virtuoso like Yehudi Menuhin, my favorite.

Our high school orchestra met twice a week during the last period of the day. We had enough violinists to comprise two sections: ten or fifteen violins in the first section and probably an equal number in the second section. I began freshman year in the latter, around the middle chair. Being a lowly freshman, I had little chance of starting in the first section, but felt I deserved better. Once a week, we could challenge another student. When I felt confident, I would challenge a leading violinist. With baton in hand, our music director, Mr. Hugh Magee, picked a passage for each student to play. I quickly moved up, and by the end of the year, I was happily ensconced in the first violin section. What an accomplishment—at least that's what Mr. Magee said when he awarded me the large red and white N for my letterman's sweater. No mistaking me for a jock, however.

In the spring of sophomore year, the orchestra was practicing for the school production of *My Fair Lady*, or maybe it was *Brigadoon*. The final dress rehearsal was on a Wednesday after school. My friend Joanne Netzky had a lead part in the show. She was dating one of my close friends, which I disapproved of because I wanted to date her. Her father, Lester

Netzky, started Tom Thumb Players—a children's drama school similar to the Harand studios—which he later franchised in Tucson. Joanne was an all-around talent—acting, singing, dancing—and was sweet and pretty. A few years later, she committed suicide. It was my first time dealing with heartbreaking tragedy; it wouldn't be my last.

For dress rehearsal, I wore the black lightweight wool pants that my mother recently bought me along with a sport coat. Usually, I called Mom from a payphone after rehearsal, and she picked me up. But on this particular Wednesday, another student offered me a ride. Why inconvenience my mother? Six of us walked to the roundabout where the car was waiting. I don't recall much about it except that it had front and back vinyl bench seats. Three people sat up front, including the driver—a senior girl unfamiliar to me—and the rest of us slid across the back seat. The last to climb into the vehicle, I scrunched against the back passenger door, its metal handle protruding into my side. We turned out of the school parking lot and headed for Lincolnwood, everyone talking and laughing, including me.

The next memory remains excruciatingly vivid to this day. I was telling someone who was trying to cut the leg of my pants that they couldn't do that. "These are brand new pants," I said. Then the world went as black as the pants.

Again, I awoke to bright lights and a hazy sense of commotion. "I'm wearing contact lenses. You need to take them out," I said. Then, boom, back into blackness I sank.

The next time I awoke, I was in a quieter room, pain clawing at every inch of me. In and out of consciousness I drifted, riding the waves of heavy doses of morphine. At one point, I heard a stranger tell my parents that if he didn't operate *now*, I was going to die.

Years later, while in medical school, I read the medical reports from the car accident. Continued internal hemorrhaging. Pelvic fractures in four or five places. Retroperitoneal hematoma. Renal contusions. Concussion. The records also indicated that I was clinically dead for a short period of time at the scene. No pulse. No breath.

Rabbi Zimmerman asked me about the experience. Had I seen something, maybe white lights or a tunnel like some folks report seeing?

Approaching Death

I can only answer in the negative; I don't remember any of it. Not the crunch of metal of the other car crashing into the passenger side of the car in which I was riding. Not my head surely thudding against the window or the seat in front of me. Not the sudden silence of shock experienced by all involved. Not the screaming sirens or possible crying and moaning of those injured, but no one as severely as I. Not being resuscitated at the scene. Not the ambulance ride to the hospital.

The instant after impact, I lost consciousness—a blessing.

X

I spent six weeks in the hospital learning that morphine can be a patient's best friend and sponge baths a close second.

Like an addict, I impatiently watched the clock and begged my parents for the next injection. Someone always seemed to be with me—Mom, Dad, an aunt or uncle. I couldn't do anything for myself, not feed myself, not turn from one side to another. Even with help, any movement proved painful. I had polyethylene tubing running into every orifice. When I finally could sit up after a month, propped by pillows, I played double solitaire with petite card decks that Auntie Anne brought. I watched comedian Steve Allen on TV. It hurt to laugh. Rabbis Lehrfield, Slae, Klein, and Porush rotated visitations and arranged for kosher meals at the St. Francis Hospital of Evanston, a very Catholic institution. Then there were the bevy of doctors and nurses who poked, prodded, pricked, and punctured, and the candy stripers in their pink and white uniforms who buoyed my spirits and soothed my wounds with sponge baths.

I exited the hospital in a wheelchair, happy to be leaving the pervasive boredom despite the many visitors. When I finally could ambulate with crutches, Mother threw a big backyard party to celebrate my homecoming. I suspect she was equally relieved to have me out of the wheelchair. At the time, I didn't consider the strain on my parents. When you're a teenager—especially a teenager recovering from a major accident—you're self-absorbed.

That summer, I remained at home, convalescing. I particularly was disappointed to miss the trip to DC to receive the commendation for my science fair project. A few of the candy stripers occasionally stopped by, as did several interns, residents, nurses, and a plethora of Mom's colleagues and students. Dad procured an antique coin-operated pool table and jukebox from one of his clients and had them set up in the subbasement. I'd hobble down to practice my Willie Mosconi trick shots.

Then there was Ilene Rattner. I met her at the backyard homecoming party. When I look at Ilene's yearbook photo now, she reminds me of Annette Funicello, with the same hairstyle and pretty smile. Ilene was younger than I and lived in Lincolnwood a few miles from me. Mom would drive me to the Rattners' house. Ilene and I listened to records—the Beatles, Beach Boys, Rolling Stones—and played Scrabble or gin rummy. I was still on crutches, an excellent excuse not to dance.

Decades later, I still suffer from the physical and emotional residua of the accident. When the weather changes or I'm sitting in a chair, discomfort grips me, especially in the coccyx. For several years, I endured painful follow-up tests with urologists, orthopods, gastroenterologists, and general surgeons; I probably glowed from all the radiation. For the first fifteen years or so, I refused to ride with a female driver other than my mother, and even then I was anxious and usually insisted on driving. When Sharon happened to drive past the site of the accident, I experienced déjà vu.

"*Please* be careful here," I couldn't stop myself from saying. "Particularly as you traverse the overpass. You can't see what's on the other side."

The accident had occurred on the other side of that freeway overpass. As our driver crested the hill, she failed to slow down and went through the stop sign just before an exit ramp. At roughly the same time, a car exited the Edens Expressway. It zoomed up the ramp but never yielded at the top. Two cars racing along, perpendicular to each other. One driven by a high school senior with six other kids crammed in; the other driven by an older woman, her husband in the passenger seat. *BAM!* The car exiting the ramp T-boned the other car on the passenger side where I was wedged.

The other six kids walked away from the accident. The girl driving was so upset she missed her high school graduation. The two people in the other car, both in their eighties, were returning from a party. I'm not sure if they rode in the ambulance with me, but they did spend time in the hospital. Both drivers were cited at fault. The car was demolished. Everyone hired attorneys, and an out-of-court settlement ultimately was reached several years later. For ten years, I "celebrated" May 22, welcoming the Hebrew blessing for one who survives a harrowing experience.

I spent junior year on crutches. About the time I gave them up in May, I graduated from LJC Hebrew High School, class of one. Rabbi Lehrfield suggested that I enroll in the Skokie Hebrew Theological Seminary, the same yeshiva where Rabbi Slae studied. I wanted to continue my studies, but inwardly, I already knew that my desire to conduct research would lead me down a scientific path. I discontinued my studies a year later when I graduated from high school.

As the school year concluded, I knew that working at the pharmacy was out of the question since I couldn't ride a bicycle. I landed a job at a Skokie factory working night shift from 11:00 p.m. to 7:00 a.m. on an assembly line pressing plastic boards, which reminded me of Lucille Ball and Vivian Vance on their chocolate line. I drove my mother's car, returning it in time for her to leave for Chicago Jewish Day School, where she taught English during summer school. Sometimes I chauffeured her so I could use the car. I secretly hoped my reliance on her automobile would pressure my parents into buying me a car. The only thing it did was encourage her to buy herself a new vehicle. I insisted on accompanying her to the dealerships along Western Avenue.

It was a warm midsummer afternoon when we arrived at the Plymouth dealership, having already visited a number of competitors. Tucked among the boxy Belvederes and Furies was a bright yellow Plymouth Barracuda, a sporty fastback coupe with distinctive wraparound back glass. The back seat folded down, creating an expansive trunk that easily fit my crutches. With its black vinyl top and black pinstripes, the car was hot.

"Mom," I implored, "you've got to get this."

She finally capitulated, perhaps due to my entreaties. When she drove that car to Mather High School, she pulled in alongside the students' cars.

Mother's hot wheels

Mrs. Bernstein, parking her sports car, emerging in high heels and a tailored Jackie Kennedy dress. The image conjured is a far cry from the image of Dad teaching her to drive standard transmission.

I may have appreciated the Barracuda even more than my mother did. I now had my license. I drove Ilene to the Rolling Stones concert at the Arie Crown Theater. But it was Joanne Netzsky who I kissed in that car. After Darryl broke up with her, Joanne and I went on a date. It probably took me over an hour, or so it seemed, to get my nerve up to kiss her. Then, within minutes, or so it seemed, a Lincolnwood policeman was knocking at the car window asking what we "kids" were doing. Sigh.

That summer of '64, my parents took me out east to tour colleges and do some sightseeing. We visited Harvard, Yale, Princeton, Brown, MIT—impressive institutions that felt far from Chicago. I could apply through early admissions to one school. I chose Harvard. My mother seemed eager to have me attend. I felt only relief when the letter arrived declining my application. I then applied to all the Ivy League schools, as well as to the University of Chicago, fondly called the Ivy League Grotesques and Gargoyle school of the Midwest. Each of them offered admission. The decision of where to go was simple: I didn't want to leave Chicago. A few of my classmates also decided to attend U of C. We celebrated during graduation, compared notes, and signed each other's yearbooks. I keep my high school yearbook next to my mother's yearbook from her senior year at Marshall High School. *The Spectrum 1965* next to *The Review 1938*. Inscriptions from classmates and teachers fill the pages of both books.

We both graduated at age seventeen, and while I wasn't valedictorian, I did graduate in the top 5 percent of my class.

6

Gargoyles

My parents bought me a Royal typewriter for my high school graduation, a useful gift, as my English professor assigned an essay a week, much to my dismay. The typewriter sat on my desk in the exiguous dorm room to which my roommate and I had been assigned. We lived in New Dorms, the newest of the undergraduate residences and certainly the most modern. It consisted of three two-story structures configured to form three sides of a square. On the fourth side was a building with a cafeteria and commons area. Joseph Weintraub and I lived in Lower Flint House in Woodward Court, room 103. Before school started, I had a chance to meet Joseph, a Jewish fellow from Chicago, who I immediately discerned was the more worldly of us. When he told me his address, I realized that I had delivered his parents' mail a few times as a substitute carrier. By midsemester, it occurred to me that the university either mistook me for a radical post–high school liberal or had an arbitrary matching system, for how else had I been selected to be Joseph's roommate?

Within a few weeks of moving into the cramped dormitory cell, Joseph put his intellect to work, borrowed bricks from a construction site, and built a fireplace. The edifice was ensconced in the five-foot space between our beds, further restricting living space, and abutted the window, which served as the flue. I watched with a mixture of curiosity and discomfort as Joseph roasted marshmallows and hotdogs. I silently hoped that the dorm's resident head would ban the structure, but no, he condoned it and even brought his own roasting stick and marshmallows. Who knows what other ingredients Joseph brought to the cookouts? After all, it was Lucy-in-the Sky 1965. I never inquired what drugs were floating around the dorms, nor did I ever roast a marshmallow. I doubt the latter was kosher, and even if it were, I still would have eschewed as many barbecues as possible. As a result of those savory-unsavory events and the dates with girls, which Joseph frequently hosted in our room, I became well acquainted with the stacks in various campus libraries.

New Dorms was coed, another eye-opening and somewhat uncomfortable experience, at least initially. I had grown up with two brothers, though I had many friends who were of the opposite sex, as confirmed by my address book. After my accident, one of the candy stripers had gifted me a miniature gold box with twenty-six accordioned pages, each page assigned a letter of the alphabet. The candy striper conveniently added her name and phone number. Over the next few years, I filled every page with friends' contact information—only girlfriends. That was the rule. I think my ex-wife glommed onto the case before 3 Gorillas had a chance. Even if I still possessed this cherished repository, my present presbyopia would prevent me from deciphering the tiny ballpoint print. I was even more shocked that condoms were openly sold in the commons. (Later, they were dispensed without charge, purportedly for health reasons.)

There I was, a sheltered, naïve, conservative, Orthodox, seventeen-year-old attending a very liberal university. I felt a world away from the home where I had walked to services on Shabbat, studied with Rabbi Lehrfield, and fraternized with like-minded suburbanite friends. Oxford and Cambridge might not have felt as foreign! Let's just say it was a jolting start. But I acclimated and soon grew a beard and long, mangy hair and bought a secondhand army jacket that I still own. One winter, maybe junior year, I purchased a Polish navy officer peacoat, complete with an inscribed, minimally voweled surname inside, also from a consignment store. It was knee-length, double-breasted with two rows of untarnished brass buttons and a flip-up collar. Decades later, I had it dry cleaned and gave it to my son, Michael, who lusted after it.

During orientation week, incoming first-year students filed into Mandel Hall to take accreditation examinations. My exam results, combined with AP credits, enabled me to start school with a second-year standing. My mother had helped me plan well. I succeeded in placing out of the lower-level math courses and into advanced calculus, which proved challenging. Twice a week, I sat with a graduate TA, who patiently guided me through homework exercises.

One of the two required courses was expository English, a class that I found particularly abhorrent, having little interest in the subject matter. During the first quarter, we were assigned the task of writing a fable. The professor instructed us to create characters, develop a plot, and conclude with a pithy maxim. This was beyond me. I could breed and irradiate fruit flies, but writing fictional anthropomorphized prose? My paper came back with a big red D scrawled at the top. Not only did I sink into abysmal despair at having received my first (and fortunately only) D, I was completely mystified.

"I was wondering if you could elucidate why I received this grade on my paper," I said to the professor during her office hours.

She looked at me suspiciously. "Mr. Bernstein, at this institution, we do not plagiarize existing pieces of literature."

I was nonplussed. Plagiarize? She proceeded to explain that I had taken a well-known fable and changed a few characters, but basically kept it the same. "You were supposed to engage your imagination to construct an authentic story," she said.

To this day, I can't recall what fable I supposedly plagiarized. I rewrote the fable, and while I didn't emulate Aesop, I plodded through the remainder of the class like his famed tortoise. I managed to finish with a passing grade. In this case, I was happy just to be *average* in a class of ten.

Fortunately, I had Dr. Lorna Straus for advanced biology.

Dean of the college

She was an associate professor who became my adviser and later served as dean of students for the undergraduate college.

Later, she would keep me out of harm's way. Lorna, as she was affectionately addressed, was personable and cared about her students, earning her two Quantrell awards honoring excellence in teaching. She personally introduced me to professor Donald Steiner, soon to become chairman of the department of biochemistry, and counseled me as to which advanced courses I should pursue in his program, including organic chemistry, chemical kinetics and dynamics, quantum mechanics, and thermodynamics. Lorna's recommendations culminated in my earning a rare bachelor of science degree with special honors in biochemistry.

College challenged my mind like nothing I previously encountered. I studied and studied and studied and pulled all-nighters before tests. Yet I took advantage of the university's intellectual milieu. The bookstore was stocked with U of C publications—treatises on everything you wanted to know about everything and outstanding books by outstanding preeminent authors. If I wanted to study economics, I could delve into writings by the likes of Gary Becker, Paul Samuelson, and of course my professor, Milton Friedman. I often bought syllabi from other classes, as well as the assigned books; decades later, many of them ended up in the clutches of 3 Gorillas. Could they read them, let alone understand the subtleties of Thomas Mann? Once or twice a week, undergraduate and graduate students amassed in Mandel Hall, one of my favorite buildings with its foyer plaque commemorating William the Conqueror. This ornate auditorium could seat up to 1,066 people. Here, we raptly listened to presentations by Nobel laureates and other esteemed experts. Regardless of lecture topic—politics, music, history, art, economics, science—I made an effort to attend. Even then, I knew that I was experiencing something special, something elite. Intellectual stimulation became my drug of choice. So did bridge.

Two freshman girls, who lived on the floor just above me,

played bridge with another male student. One day the trio was searching for a fourth and asked if I would like to sit in. I could be "dummy," they said. I inferred this was a term specific to the game and that I shouldn't be insulted.

"I've never played," I said, half expecting them to recruit someone conversant with their competitive pastime; instead, they offered to teach me. So while Joseph was in our room communing with Lucy and her diamonds, his feet perched on the edge of the fireplace, I was upstairs playing bridge into the wee hours of the morn. I had found my game.

I also took advantage of living near the Regal Theater. Motown had one hit after another in the 1960s, and many of the artists played at the Regal, about eight blocks west of campus. To get there, my friends and I had to skirt the expansive public park with its looming statues. It was like being in an episode of *Dr. Who*. We never cut through the park because it was a hangout for the Blackstone Rangers, a surly group of renegades none of us were keen on encountering. No one ever bothered our band of six or eight students. It was well worth the anxious trip to attend live performances of Aretha Franklin, Smokey Robinson, and James Brown.

By the time snow covered campus walkways and the collar of my peacoat was flipped up, my apprehension and unease had morphed into a sense of belonging. The gray, gothic architecture of the buildings felt venerable, and the bug-eyed gargoyles atop Cobb entrance gate no longer glared.

At the end of winter quarter, I was rushed by Delta Upsilon fraternity. There were only seven fraternities—no sororities—on campus. I pledged Delta Upsilon because the brothers were mostly Jewish and many played bridge. In keeping with DU tradition, the brothers launched the pledge master, the commodore, into the murky waters of Botany Pond each year. Fortunately, I didn't receive the honor. I spent more time at the house. I'd stop by for lunch and play a few hands of an ongoing bridge game. Weekends were a different story. The fraternity could have been featured in *Animal House*. We even had our own Mortimer Moose hanging on a wall of the wood-paneled meeting room, where monthly compulsory meetings were held for all members. I remember the seniors stealing the anchors from the Northwestern University's quadrangle. Real anchors. Heavy anchors. They ingeniously transported them off campus. The FBI eventually curtailed this annual harmless prank.

Every May, the fraternity held the Rose Dance. The brothers installed trellises adorned with blooming roses throughout the house and into the basement's bar and dance floor. Some of the upperclassmen had become friendly with a group of nurses who worked at South Chicago Community Hospital, located a few miles from campus. I was volunteered to pick up some of these nurses. I schlepped to Lincolnwood for my mother's Barracuda. Seating capacity was limited, but the coupe certainly looked sporty and added to the festive feeling of the evening. One girl sat in the front passenger bucket seat, and three others squeezed into the back. They chattered excitedly. A few of them had attended the dance the previous year.

That evening, I met Andrea Dior LeMontre. She was petite with curly auburn hair, a good sense of humor, and a sharp wit, and like me, she was an observant Jew. I was still not enamored with dancing, but we danced a slow dance and probably several more. Before driving the nurses home, I asked Andi for her phone number. A few days later, I called her for a date. She lived with her parents much farther south of campus in a Jewish neighborhood. I borrowed the Barracuda from my mother again and drove to Andi's house, met her parents, and took her out to dinner. I learned that she had been raised in Chicago and her parents were of French descent. She asked me questions about myself. I briefly recounted my car accident and talked about wanting to pursue a career in academics and research. She was encouraging and easygoing. We didn't wait long to meet again and then again. She was a few years older than I, but that didn't bother either of us or my parents, who liked her the first time I brought her to Lincolnwood for Shabbat.

That July, tragedy struck. A twenty-five-year-old alcoholic with a lengthy rap sheet broke into the nursing dorm associated with South Chicago Community Hospital. Richard Speck held eight nurses hostage, then systematically raped, tortured, and killed each one. A ninth girl hid under the bed and was saved. The news of the mass murder hit Chicago hard but hit the Delta Upsilon house even harder. Two of those young women had ridden in my car on the way to the Rose Dance. Others had attended the dance. Though school was not in session, word spread through the Delta Upsilon community. We were all in shock. Thankfully, Andi was not part of that group. I would have been devastated.

I was in love.

ℳ

Vietnam was devouring America's youth. The draft ushered jeans-clad students out the campus door and into khaki uniforms. Now a sophomore, I was sheltered in the ivory tower of academia. Classes again proved demanding. I moved into an apartment with Steven Henikoff and Joel Weinstein, both a year ahead of me. I was a Shabbat regular at the Hillel House, played a lot of bridge, and saw Andi as much as possible. In the fall, she and I attended U of C football games at Stagg Field. The games were known as "classes" because the team's homework was to practice during the week. The Maroons, however, never regained the stature Monsters of the Midway that they had achieved during the reign of Coach Amos Alonzo Stagg in the early 1900s. I related how the Manhattan Project culminated in the first controlled nuclear reaction under the stands of Stagg Field. We walked down to Promontory Point, part of Burnham Park at the edge of Lake Michigan.

The Point

We talked and laughed and held hands, went to shows and concerts, listened to my records, ate at Maury's deli, visited the Delta Upsilon house where Addie the cook fed us, and often went up to my parents' house for Shabbat. I assumed that Andi would accept my invitation to the next Rose Dance.

The first hint of spring was in the air. The trees on campus and in the surrounding neighborhoods had buds. The five-foot snow drifts of the Great Blizzard of '67 had finally melted.

Snow, snow: go away

The days short on light and long on frigid cold, howling winds, and low hanging gray skies were about to end. I could almost smell the metamorphosis. The gray gloom was finally coming to an end. I looked forward to the upcoming weekends and spending time with Andi. I'm not sure if we were going to see a James Bond movie or one of Clint Eastwood's spaghetti westerns—the cinema on campus in Ida Noyes Hall played old movies—but we were together. Out of the blue, Andi said to me, "I think I'm getting married."

"What did you say?" I asked, thinking I misheard her.

"My boyfriend's back," said Andi. "He's an attorney, and we're getting married, Ron."

Boyfriend? Marriage? Andi?

That year, spring lost its luster. For the first time in my life, I experienced the anguish of heartbreak. I dragged myself to classes, lost myself in the stacks, forced myself to keep up with studies. My friends dragged me to social events and encouraged bridge as a diversion. I tried to smile and dredge up enthusiasm, but it was a chore. A moribund cloud hung over me. The last quarter at the University of Chicago was unbearable. Somehow, I studied for finals and maintained my class standing.

The thought of spending the summer in Chicago felt utterly depressing. I needed to get away. Far away. Israel, I thought; I could go to Israel. The more I contemplated the idea, the more appealing it became. Back in Hebrew high school, Rabbi Lehrfield had encouraged me to visit Israel. The seed had been planted. I wouldn't just visit Israel, I would immigrate there. Certainly the university in Rehovot, the Weizmann Institute of Science, would accept a University of Chicago student. I could complete my degree and launch my research career.

Suddenly, I had a purpose and a plan.

7

Hatikvah: The Hope

I woke up groggy, unsure of my surroundings. Then I recalled dozing off as night filled the sky and the El Al Boeing 707 flew eastward between heaven and earth. I raised the shade covering the small window and peered out. Sunlight glinted off the plane's wing, and blue sky stretched to the horizon. Below, the Mediterranean Sea rolled dark and mysterious. I shifted in my seat to relieve the dull ache at the base of my spine.

"*Boker tov*," said a stewardess through the overhead speakers. She continued her announcement in Hebrew, then repeated it in English. "Good morning. The captain has just informed us that we are about to enter Israeli airspace and will be landing shortly." By the time she finished repeating the statement in French, passengers spontaneously had risen to their feet. In unison, they began singing "Hatikvah," the Israeli national anthem. My heart soared.

Our hope is not yet lost,
The hope two thousand years old,
To be a free nation in our land,
The land of Zion and Jerusalem.

Ever since making dreidels out of clay in the basement of the Agudas Achim Congregation, I heard "Hatikvah" sung at the commencement of Jewish events. I raised my voice in song. Hebrew lyrics filled the cabin. The woman next to me wiped her eyes. The words touched my soul, too.

I had hoped to embark on my Israeli journey a month earlier. Although my mother commiserated about my breakup with Andi and agreed that a change of venue would do me good, she was wary about my traveling to Israel. Political tensions were building. An ominous feeling pervaded conversations among congregants in the Chicago area, not to mention media reports around the countryside. Mom contacted her relatives in Israel, and they assured her that they would take good care of me. While my parents weren't enthusiastic about their nineteen-year-old son venturing alone to a country on the brink of war, they finally acceded to my wishes. I applied for a passport and got the proper vaccinations.

I was packing my bags when war broke out, abruptly halting all commercial travel in and out of the country. On June 5, Israel obliterated the Egyptian air fleet; by June 10, the Israel Defense Forces had chased Syria onto Damascus's doorstep and recaptured the old city of Jerusalem. The war ended after only six days. B'ezrat Hashem, with G–d's help. Israel had sustained casualties, though not nearly as many as

Egypt, Jordan, and Syria. The joy of a victorious Israel, united in thought and pride, was palpable. I booked a flight and by mid-June was Israel bound.

The plane began its gradual descent. I felt a surge of excitement. It had been a long trip from Chicago's O'Hare International Airport. My ears popped as I watched the landscape below turn from sea to desert, then to miniature homes and streets configured in what I assumed were neighborhoods. I had no idea where we were. I only knew that we would land at Israel's sole international airport in Lod. From there, I'd need to find my way to the suburb of Haifa, where my cousin Pepi Solaz and her husband, Itchy, lived.

The only other time I had flown was as a five-year-old tucked in the seat between my parents, Miami-bound. We ran into a lightning storm and severe turbulence over Georgia and were forced to make an emergency landing. I don't know into how many bags I emptied my stomach contents during that flight. Fortunately, this flight, with its calm weather, kosher food, and accommodating stewardesses, had been far less harrowing.

The plane's wheels bounced against the runway, and applause filled the cabin. I was in the homeland! The plane taxied past soldiers and military jeeps to the far end of the tarmac. I patted the passport tucked in my inner sport coat pocket. I had Israeli pounds in my wallet, along with a long list of names and addresses of people to contact: seven families related to my maternal grandmother, former members of the Lincolnwood congregation, and friends of friends who lived in Israel. Meeting everyone on that list would require nearly the entire summer.

Anticipation and curiosity accompanied me as I deplaned and followed the line of passengers being guided by uniformed soldiers toward a long row of temporary structures that looked like outhouses. Passengers were ushered in individually. When

I came to the front of the queue, an IDF soldier with an Uzi slung over her shoulder ordered me to wait. She was about my age, with eyes almost as blue as mine. I was smitten. She said something to me in Hebrew.

"*B'anglit bevakasha*," I said, asking her to please speak in English.

She smiled and said, "How long do you plan to stay?"

I had just discovered the first thing about Israel: the country conscripted some really beautiful soldiers. Back in the states, I had been told that *sabras*—the name for Israeli-born citizens referring to the indigenous cacti that is prickly on the outside but sweet on the inside—did not take kindly to the recent influx of wealthy American Jews retiring to the Holy Land. This soldier was anything but prickly. She escorted me into the standing-room-only unit, drew the curtain, and patted me down. My turn to smile.

My next challenge was to collect my luggage and find a sherut, a service taxi which ran from the airport to Haifa. I gave the driver the Neve Shaanan address for Pepi and Itchy and watched wide-eyed as we passed soldiers and tanks outside of Lod, then wended our way through the crowded streets of Tel Aviv to the coastal road leading to Haifa. Pepi Solaz was the oldest daughter of my great-uncle, Menachem Mendel Kanner. She and Itchy had immigrated to Israel from Bucharest, Romania just after World War II. They arrived along with one third of our family. Another third of the family, including my bubbe, had chosen years before to settle in America. The last third perished in the Holocaust. I had met Pepi and Itchy during their visit to Chicago when I was in grade school. I knew they didn't have children, were retired, and were old, though at nineteen everyone looks old. I wondered if they'd recognize me.

The sherut turned onto a dirt road. We bounced along past small abodes, then stopped in front of a building located halfway up a hill. I paid the driver and grabbed my luggage. The front door opened before I had a chance to knock, and out emerged a distinguished woman, gray hair piled on her head, her arms already extended.

"Ronnie!" Pepi exclaimed, her thick Yiddish accent making a long *o* of my name. She was all hugs. We were both so overcome with the reunion that we ended up in tears. She insisted that she recognized me even with my long hair and beard. Itchy was not far behind. Our greeting was equally ebullient. By the time I stepped into their humble home, I felt completely welcomed and loved.

Pepi and Itchy spoke fluent Hebrew with an Israeli accent and fluent Yiddish with a Transylvanian accent. While I was able to use a few conversational Hebrew phrases and sentences, my German enabled me to converse fairly intelligently with their Yiddish. That first night, I pulled out my Fodor's travel books and showed Pepi places that I wanted to visit. During the weeks I stayed with them, perusing those travel books became an evening ritual. Pretty soon that book was exploding with annotations. I kept it for years.

Every morning before sunrise, Pepi crept out the front door and walked to the marketplace. Every morning, I awoke to a bright world and a fresh Israeli breakfast consisting of flavorful Middle Eastern fare. Later, Pepi might take me sightseeing in Haifa or up the Carmel Mountains to visit Shela (Rachel), the youngest of her three sisters, and Shela's husband, Eli (Eliakim), a policeman, with a lunch stop of pita stuffed with hummus and falafel. I was accustomed to American kosher food like bagels, lox, and cream cheese. That was Jewish food, not Middle Eastern Israeli food. If Pepi and I returned to Haifa late on a Friday afternoon, we walked arm in arm through the marketplace, which closed before sundown and didn't reopen until after Shabbat, and purchased needed items. Couscous, shawarma—my palate was expanding.

Sometimes I traveled alone using the Egged bus system. Pepi wrote down the transfers. Or, extending my travels farther, I tramped (the name for hitchhiking) and stayed in hostels or with relatives. I explored the Galil and the Banyas in the north, the Negev Desert in the south, the Red Sea, the Sea of Galilee, the Dead Sea, and the Great Sea—the Mediterranean. Most importantly, I spent days in Jerusalem.

One of the first solo trips I took was to the Shuk, the Arab market in the Old City of Jerusalem encircled by ancient, crenellated walls. I happened to venture there the day it reopened after the war. For almost twenty years, Israelis had been banned from this area. I navigated narrow alleys with vendors hawking almost everything and anything—rugs, scarves, spices, shoes, books, housewares, vegetables, fruit. The scent of cumin, ginger, Turkish coffee, lamb cooking on spits, and sandalwood incense wafted around me. I was surrounded by a throng of humanity including many uniformed soldiers. I bought a shofar, some Hebrew books with silver filigree covers, and a sheepskin mat. Initially, Arabs' understanding of the Israeli monetary system was limited to pound notes. The next day, the Arabs discovered agorot coins, also called *grush*, and one-pound items were now one pound and fifty agorot.

My days were filled with travel and exploration. I visited the Kotel (the Western Wall) and rode a camel at Be'er Sheva through the desert. Dirty and smelly, these ships of the desert expectorated everywhere. I went on an overnight horseback trip at the Vered Hagalil dude ranch in the Galil, started by Yehuda Avni, a fellow Chicagoan. I saw Shuly Nathan sing "Jerusalem of Gold," the song she made famous in the months just after the Six Day War. Many Israelis mused that this song would replace the national anthem. I kept her autographed album for years. As the weeks flew by, the heritage of the Promised Land osmosed into me, flooding each cell, mitochondria, and DNA strand. It was intoxicating.

With the recent mobilization of reserves, Uzi-carrying soldiers were ubiquitous. My seventeen-year-old cousin Livia had completed her matriculation test and was conscripted. Her boyfriend, Danni, who had just returned from the Suez Canal, happened to be my size.

A Volunteer

I donned one of his uniforms, and he and his army buddies acquiesced to unofficially accompany me toward Suez. I was eager to see the canal. We passed soldiers, tanks, and burned-out military vehicles. I even acquired an Egyptian parchment map of what appeared to be Sinai encampments. We made it as far as Little Bitter Lake, as proceeding to Suez would have been too dangerous, but I did get to wear that uniform and sweat like an Israeli soldier; it was only a costume, but it reinforced my desire to immigrate. Then I learned that if I enlisted, I would lose my US citizenship. While I was unwilling to expatriate myself, I was quite willing to accept Danni's uniform when he bequeathed it to me.

What I desired more than a uniform was a lab coat, one that I could wear while conducting research at the Weizmann Institute. Pepi helped me schedule meetings with professors at Weizmann, then accompanied me to the institute. I still held hopes that I could transfer. But that was not to be. The esteemed professors iterated the same message: research might be possible as a postdoctoral fellow *after* I obtained my degree at the University of Chicago. I could then share my knowledge with Israel rather than expecting Israel to support me. I had played my hand as best I could, but I was being forced to fold and reluctantly return to the United States. I mailed a postcard to Steven Henikoff saying that plans had changed; I'd be moving back to the apartment in January.

The day came to say goodbye. Pepi, Itchy, and I were family, and it was terribly difficult to leave them. The people, the land, the culture—I wanted to remain with all. I promised to return as soon as I graduated. I boarded the plane and waved *lehitraot*—see you later, as they say in Hebrew. Goodbye is too final. As we circled O'Hare, no one sang "The Star-Spangled Banner." One more year, I thought. One more year before I could return.

But then came Nam.

8

The Times, They Are a-Changin'

It was the winter of my discontent when I moved back into the Hyde Park apartment with Steve and Joe. Frigid winds blew off Lake Michigan, and gray skies hung low. Even the gargoyles looked cold. More than four hundred students took over the administration building to protest the firing of Marlene Dixon, a sociology professor with radical Marxist leanings who had stepped out of a stately university procession in honor of U of C's new president to join students chanting opposition to the war. The students' sit-in lasted two weeks. Though I did not participate, the tension and chaos only added to my misery. I missed Israel and still missed Andi. Not having a car, I had to navigate snowy sidewalks, plus take public transportation, not deemed terribly safe, to

Lincolnwood to do laundry, collect care packages, and spend holidays with my parents. It was time to buy my own car. The thought instantly cheered me.

April showers were in downpour mode when I found a classified ad in the Sunday *Sun Times* for a very used Austin Healey, an English car that somewhat resembled an E-Type Jaguar.

Not a Jaguar

Back in high school, a car magazine ad described the Jaguar as "the most extraordinary icon of the motoring world." I agreed. The Jag sizzled with British pizzazz. During homeroom, I doodled drawings of it. At poker games, my friends and I discussed it in detail. Unfortunately, my meager savings could not bankroll one. Hence, I schlepped to the South Side to check out the Austin Healey. The dealership turned out to be co-owned by retired Cubs player Ernie Banks. I recently had switched my Major League Baseball allegiance from the South Side White Sox to the North Side Cubbies, so I didn't mind paying Mr. Cub his asking price of seven hundred dollars in cash.

The car, a four-speed manual transmission repainted British racing green, had floorboards pocked with holes where heat and fumes escaped the exhaust system. Nothing a few floor mats couldn't fix—or at least cover. Plastic sliding side curtains were bolted into the doors. It took a rather Herculean effort to close them, as well as the convertible's top. Of course, closing both trapped the exhaust fumes, inducing drowsiness and nausea. The front seats had been re-covered in vinyl; the back bench might have been, but spring and stuffing innards protruded.

Before driving the car off the lot, I requested that the salesman ride with me and show me how to shift. I still had memories of my father teaching my mother how to drive in the Morse Beach parking lot. Start, stop, grind, jump, stop—a clutch nightmare. I offered five-year-old encouragement from the back seat. The salesman's tutelage proved effective. I managed to drive the car to Lincolnwood without having to restart it. After inspecting my new purchase, my parents did not appear happy. I, on the other hand, felt ecstatic.

They definitely were not happy the day I was arrested while driving the car. The incident occurred about four months before the infamous Chicago riots and mayhem, when left-leaning protesters clashed with the city's police force during the Democratic National Convention. I had taped "Dump the Hump" posters on each door, which were not meant to be menacing. I merely supported Eugene McCarthy. I was driving to my parents' house at dusk on a Friday, intent on arriving before Shabbat candle lighting, and opted to take Lakeshore Drive rather than risk hitting bumper-to-bumper traffic on the Dan Ryan Expressway. Warm, pleasant temperatures had motivated me to wrestle the top down and store the side curtains in the boot. I had just passed through an intersection along the Gold Coast when I noticed a police car behind me, lights flashing. I pulled over.

One of Chicago's finest approached my car. "Did you know your taillight on the driver's side is out?"

"I didn't know it, officer," I said. "I'm on my way to my parents' in Lincolnwood." I thought that the addendum would help. His expression never changed. "Hit the brake," he demanded, walking toward the back of my car. "You don't have a brake light either," he said upon returning. Nor did I have a left directional light.

"Officer, it's probably the same bulb. One of those three-in-one bulbs. I'll replace it first thing tomorrow morning." The suggestion went unrecorded; the three separate moving offenses did not.

"Follow me," he said.

We drove to the police station at 113 W. Chicago Avenue. He ushered me to the sign-in desk, where I immediately was fingerprinted. Was I a criminal? I started to get scared. Maybe I'd be jailed and have to spend time with who knows what kind of riffraff or maybe even one or more members of the notorious Weather Underground. Someone asked me if I wanted to make a phone call. By now it was one o'clock in the morning.

My father answered, and I explained the situation. He said that he and my mother would be there as soon as possible. He didn't sound too thrilled about having to bail out his son from jail. At least I wasn't actually incarcerated, just assigned a seat on the bench by the front desk. The three of us drove home in absolute silence. The next week, after paying an exorbitant storage fee, I was reunited with the Austin Healey.

Driving the car was fine during mild Indian summer days, but not quite as comfortable when chilly autumn rains fell. When it started to snow, I had to retire the car. It barely could plow through an inch of snow, and the snow came up through the floorboards. My parents must have been concerned for my safety because they surprised me one weekend with a brand-new Mercury Cougar. The XR7 model had been out one year, and this was the second improved iteration. A metallic lime green with a white vinyl top, it was a two-door with Sherwood Forest green leather bucket seats, a wood interior and dash, and an extraordinary sound system. In addition, it had hideaway headlights and in the rear, sequential turn signals. The car was gorgeous, and I hated it.

I was miserable and made sure to let my parents know just how miserable. I appreciated my parents buying a car and putting a *for sale* ad in the paper for the Austin Healey. It promptly sold, or more accurately, was almost given away. Their choice of vehicle, however, was not the fast, sexy British Jaguar over which I salivated. I couldn't help myself—at every visit I kvetched and moaned.

"But a Jaguar is expensive," my mother said. "As expensive as Dad's Cadillac."

By that time, my father had traded his way up to a four-door Cadillac Sedan DeVille. He pointed out the Jaguar's impracticality for winter driving. He also felt it would be too audacious parked in front of the house near the Barracuda and Cadillac—that is, until the neighbors bought a Corvette and parked it directly across the street.

Finally my father said, "OK, trade in the Cougar. Get the car you want. We'll take the money from your settlement." That was the first mention of a consummated settlement from my accident. I had died for the Jaguar.

I drove the Cougar to Imperial Motors in Wilmette, one of three Chicagoland Jaguar dealers. As I parked, I could see a gorgeous sable and cinnamon Jaguar Coupe front and center in the showroom. Upon entering, I shook hands with a salesman and boldly proclaimed, "I'm going to buy this car, but before I do, I want to test-drive it." He gave me a skeptical look, then fetched the owner of the dealership, Allen Aron.

Mr. Aron took one look at me and said, "Come back with your parents, little boy."

And so I did. As it turned out, Allen was a retired general

from the 1948 Israeli war. We got along quite well. I exited the dealership driving that Jaguar and circled the Baha'i Temple three times before heading home, the proud owner of the most extraordinary icon of the motoring world.

※

Violence continued to erupt around the country due to civil rights issues and the Vietnam War. The Blackstone Rangers, soon to be renamed the Black P. Stone Nation, had infiltrated the South Side. A University of Chicago student was found shot to death near Promontory Point. I lived on Ingleside in Hyde Park, not far from the university quadrangle and only a short walk to the lake. I know the incident disturbed my fellow students, and it certainly unnerved me. I was frightened to walk back and forth to campus and to the Argonne Cancer Research Hospital lab, where I spent many hours doing research. I often observed groups of teenagers walking along the sidewalks; up until the murder, I never sensed anything sinister. But now, despite the increase in campus police and Chicago patrol cars meandering the streets of Hyde Park, I decided that I needed further protection. I preferred a Deutsch dog to a Deutsch firearm like a Glock.

I looked in the newspaper and located a trainer of attack dogs. The manager at the kennel introduced me to a German shepherd named Baron. He was muscular with menacingly long black hair and big ears that stood at alert. He weighed over one hundred pounds and was trained to kill.

I brought Baron with me almost everywhere except to class. When we walked through the neighborhood, the teenagers and younger kids crossed to the other side of the street. Baron had an air about him. It said, *Don't mess with me, man, or I'll get in your face and do damage*. If I returned to the laboratory at night or on a weekend, Baron accompanied me and, tethered, lay in a remote corner of the entryway. When I took Baron home, my parents tolerated him, though they were somewhat intimidated by his size. My seven-year-old brother, Dale, rolled and wrestled with Baron on the blue plush rug. Dale was half the dog's size but seemed to enjoy the workout.

My protector

When I ran errands, Baron joined me, riding in the front seat, head out the window. When I got out, he jumped into the boot directly behind the seats. That's where he was the day I ran into a thrift store to purchase another jacket. I parked between less desirable cars underneath the elevated train tracks in Woodlawn on 63rd Street. It was dark even though the sun shone brightly. I checked to make sure the rear vent window was open and cracked the driver's window for additional ventilation.

When I returned, a large black man was standing next to my car, holding his arm in a strange posture. He glared ominously at me. I tried not to slow my pace, but I had the explicit feeling that this guy wasn't going to ask me for directions. I was terrified. The guy never took his eyes off me.

"Look what your dog did to me," he growled, a few feet separating us. He unwrapped a black leather jacket from around his arm. Blood oozed from what looked like a divot in his biceps.

Somehow, I managed to keep my composure and appear calm. "How did the dog get to you?" I asked.

"I just opened the door to look inside. I didn't see a dog."

With that, I opened up the door and Baron jumped into the driver's seat. "We can settle this right away with the help of the police," I said.

The guy took one look at Baron and quickly left. He had the chutzpah to wait for me in hopes of extorting me, but Baron wasn't about to let that happen.

I should have taken Baron with me on the drive to Colorado to go skiing with one of my fraternity brothers, whose parents owned a place in Breckenridge. I left all traces of Chicago behind and was enjoying the change in scenery along I-40 when I zoomed past a Cadillac. The driver sped up and passed me. We played this game of leapfrog, passing each other three or four times. Finally, he pulled over with his warning lights flashing and motioned me to stop. I did. He greeted me and said that he wanted to show me something. We walked to the back of his car, and he opened his trunk. A sinister-looking cache of automatic weapons and ammunition greeted me. The Israeli Uzi that I held in the Sinai never gave me such a creepy feeling. I said no thanks, quickly walked back to the car, and took off. I exited the freeway as soon as possible, then parked my car, shaking in fear.

Steven Henikoff and I had some wild adventures, but never anything ominous like running into an arms dealer. Steven's parents had a beautiful home in Miami, which we visited during a few winter and spring breaks. One December, with his parents gone and nothing tying us to Miami, we decided last minute to venture down to Nassau in the Bahamas in order to attend the annual Junkanoo Festival celebrated with a parade and revelry on December 26. We found a cargo plane that could get us there. Being really intelligent PhD candidates and Jewish, we didn't think to make hotel reservations even though we planned to arrive on December 25. The cargo plane didn't have seats, of course, which made our adventure feel even more, well, adventurous. It was cloudy when the plane landed, and the ground was wet from intermittent rains. We rented a motor scooter. Steve, being senior, drove; I sat on what the dealer described as the rear seat.

The pillion

We spent most of the day driving to hotels and hostels trying to find a place to stay. We had no luck. It had to be midnight when, soaked to the bone, cold, and tired, we pulled up to the back of a neighborhood church. It had a thatched roof, and water had puddled onto the pews in the deserted sanctuary, but we didn't care. We needed sleep. Some hours later, a thin beam of light woke us, and a deacon demanded that we leave. He must not have appreciated finding two young white men with thirty-six-hour beards and crumpled sport jackets sound asleep in his church, because he was less than welcoming; in fact, he was downright brutish.

This holiday incident came to mind a few years ago, when Rabbi Zimmerman and I decided to stop at Costco after services. We pulled into the parking lot around noon. Not one car was in sight. Neither of us could figure out why the huge lot was empty. Then we remembered: it was Christmas Day. We still laugh about our faux pas.

$$\text{)K}$$

In the spring, before graduating, Henikoff and Weinstein received their draft notices. Weinstein eluded conscription by crossing the Canadian border, never to be heard from again; Henikoff went to boot camp. The war was edging closer, affecting my closest friends. I would have fought for Israel; as an ardent Zionist, I felt the cause just. My feelings for the war in Vietnam lacked that passion. At least I remained safe for the time being in the hallowed halls of academia. I poured attention into my research at the Argonne Cancer Research Hospital. I relished the challenge of deciphering the complex mechanism of protein synthesis.

I worked under the supervision of research professor Tokumasu Nakamoto. On Friday afternoons, Mas, as he was fondly called, took his graduate students to Jimmy's, where he ordered beer several pitchers at a time. I reluctantly joined his mandatory social gatherings. I slowly slipped from the same stein, while everyone imbibed one beer after another. I'm sure my compatriots knew I wasn't really drinking. Beer and I never have gotten along; it causes tremendous gastritis, probably due to the accident. About the best I can do is kosher Moscato that I buy for the rabbi sometimes for Shabbat. "Just a half a glass, Rabbi," I remind him as he pours me an over-flowing goblet as per Jewish Halacha (law).

Although I didn't drink beer, I did get to know some of my colleagues from Nakamoto's laboratory. Ed Klem was a polite and friendly grad student. Married, with a baby, he was finishing his PhD. In contrast, Benjamin Blumberg was a crusty New York Jew doing postdoctoral research. When I shattered a glass vial into the palm of my hand, he reacted with, "Don't worry, Ron, it'll stop bleeding. It isn't even your dominant hand." The scar extended my lifeline.

Ben moored his sailboat at Belmont Harbor about a half hour north of campus. The three of us would sail out past the breakwater. The only other boat I recalled being aboard had been the *Jungle Queen* in Miami, which chugged through a calm intracoastal waterway. Lake Michigan was usually not so polite. In fact, I almost got concussed as we came about and began tacking back to the harbor.

That summer, the summer of my delight, I spent time with Anne Garber. The daughter of one of my biology professors, she had returned to Chicago for the summer from New York, where she was enrolled at Sarah Lawrence College. We enjoyed listening to records and eating corned beef on rye. She was a strange bohemian with long straight hair. Her summer guest was Lesley Goldstein, who I believe had just graduated from Sarah Lawrence and had tagged along, ready for a Chicago adventure. On first blush, Lesley was a rather plain girl. But I had seen her on *American Bandstand* and other television shows, headlined as Leslie Gore and singing her signature hit

"It's My Party." Lesley had a Jaguar, a green XK-E. We commiserated over the Smith gauges and Lucas electronics, which frequently malfunctioned. Our conversations expanded to many other topics held during outings to Promontory Point, downtown Chicago, and the one kosher deli in the area. When she returned home, I was left with pleasant memories and an autographed photo: *Ronnie, To my second love, Lesley.* I've always wondered who her first love was and secretly hoped it was music.

I received a letter from the Selective Services System regarding mandatory registration at our neighborhood post office. I panicked. I planned to continue work with Professor Nakamoto, complete my PhD, and pursue a life in academics. My doctoral thesis was nearing completion but not yet defended in front of my committee. I scheduled a conference with my adviser, Lorna Straus, who by this time was dean of the college, to discuss my options.

"You have a choice, Ronald," she said. "Either you apply to medical school and matriculate or you go to Nam."

The windmills of my mind whirred. I hadn't filled out an application, much less taken the MCATs. Biochemists were nonessential, but biochemists with MD after their names were indispensable and deferred during their medical training. Though I was not intent on becoming a practicing physician, I was even less intent on becoming a member of the United States Armed Forces, beating down the jungle brush or ending up a rice paddy casualty. Over the years, my mother had hinted more than once that it would be nice to have a son who is a doctor. I thought of Donald's medical instruments stored in a box in my closet.

"Let me make some phone calls for you," Lorna said.

To this day, I don't know how she did it, though I suspect she had some pretty strong connections. She managed to get me accepted into the Medical College of Wisconsin in Milwaukee, known as MCOW. The Hebrew term for "it's not what you know, it's who you know" is protexia, and Lorna Straus knew the right people. Lorna Straus had built some strong protexia. As I later learned, many University of Chicago graduates held prominent chairmanships there.

My plans quickly solidified. Baron and I would move to Milwaukee a few weeks after I graduated so I could begin my first year of medical school. Much to my delight, Lorna also arranged for me to continue research. I breathed a sigh of relief.

Ivy had greened Cobb Gate and algae covered Botany Pond when graduation festivities began. I bartered to get a passel of extra tickets. My parents, Shelly, and Dale attended, as did my dear aunts and uncles. It was a special moment: the firstborn graduating college with special honors.

One more tassel

The ceremony was impressive but chaotic. The students expelled as a result of the January sit-in managed to position themselves in the balcony of the Rockefeller Chapel and shouted nasty expletives as the graduates passed in review. The audience, including my family, was appalled.

Their raucousness fit the times, the times that were a-changin' and changing the course of my life.

9

Abra Cadaver

I was on the road to satisfying my mother's dream of "my son, the doctor," not to mention my desperation to avoid the nightmare of Vietnam's rice paddies and jungles. My classmates must have been determined to do the same, because our class of seventy or so had an unprecedented number of established professionals—engineers, lawyers, PhD graduate students, all presumably eschewing the draft. A few weeks into the semester, we held elections for our governing board. In absentia, I was nominated and elected vice president. Though not keen about the extra work, I accepted.

My most celebrated contribution occurred during the first year. On a whim, I decided that MCOW needed a logo. What better than two cows standing on hind legs as bookends to the school's official coat of arms. My roommate, a graphic artist and cartoonist whose work had appeared in *The New*

Yorker, donated his talent. I had the image printed on clear plastic backing—a perfect bumper sticker. The administration was none too happy with the creative project. Udder nonsense, they said, but it sure eased the doldrums of memorizing human anatomy.

The first laboratory course was gross anatomy. My assigned station included two older graduate students and a young woman, a recent college graduate. As we dissected Abra, our cadaver, the three men, including myself, smoked cigars to overcome the stench of formaldehyde and decaying body parts. Our first dissection was of the mammary glands. The dissection manual described pointers, droopers, and super droopers, terms I found particularly crude. When the time came to study the gross anatomy of the brain, I had the honors of manipulating the autopsy saw and lifting the calvarium. This was my first glimpse of a human brain, though one pickled in formaldehyde. During my career, I would view hundreds of living brains. The organ's astonishing complexity and brilliant design never failed to impart a feeling of awe and reverence, just as I felt as a young boy sitting in the sanctity of Agudas Achim, eyes focused on the Ark.

During study sessions, I started mooching cigarettes. I sensed that fellow students kept me at arm's length. I had a degree from the University of Chicago, drove a fancy car, and was an arrogant bastard, though I'm not sure that I recognized that at the time. In an effort to fit into the crowd, I smoked. During my next ski trip to the Rockies, however, I gasped for air in the peak altitudes. Thus, I ended my fledgling smoking habit and concomitant risk of lung cancer. If only the hazards of frequent exposure to the bright Miami sun had been known back then and Coppertone, the gold standard of sunscreen, had today's protective SPF, I might have avoided skin cancer.

Although I met Jewish professors and their families,

who graciously invited me to their homes for Shabbat, I was dismayed that no services were within walking distance, so I commuted to Lincolnwood every third or fourth weekend. On one particular Friday, by the time I merged onto I-94 in late afternoon, the snow that had steadily fallen all day now whirled in eddies. It was a veritable blizzard. The only plowed lane heading south was the left lane, usually the fast lane. My speedometer hovered below thirty. I gripped the wheel with as much concentration as I would one day use to grasp the crowning head of a baby being delivered. The latter was far more gratifying than squinting through the windscreen into squalling snow. Even the triple wipers struggled.

Suddenly, a deep thud resounded and the Jaguar jolted. I instinctively hit the brake as a daredevil car sped past. The Jag spun one hundred eighty degrees on the slick pavement and stalled just in time for me to notice two headlights bearing down on me. They grew brighter. This time, unlike in high school, I heard the crunch of metal, felt the impact of the crash. For a moment, I heard only the wind howling. I opened the door and, unscathed, calmly exited. That's when I saw the eighteen-wheeler blocking traffic and the seven-foot bonnet of my once seductively sculptured car accordioned against its grill. The Jaguar's heavy cast-iron engine block and accoutrements had absorbed the impact, most likely saving my second life. I don't recall what the Cook County Sheriff and I discussed during the thirty-minute drive to Lincolnwood in his cruiser. My mother appeared unnerved when she greeted me at the front door. Only when the sheriff appeared a few minutes later did she begin to cry. Needless to say, I missed candle lighting.

My parents never fully appreciated the extent of damage and mortal danger until the next week, when they visited the auto yard where the remaining carcass of the Jag had been towed. My mother paled. I arranged for an insurance loaner, a small palliative gesture, for a short time, as I thought this would be an easy claim to settle. Weary of waiting for the insurance company to replace my Jaguar, as they were obligated to do, I headed to Allen Aaron's Jaguar dealership intent on taking charge of the situation, but the nearby Maserati Citroën showroom waylaid me. Through the front window, I could see a gleaming dark blue Maserati Bora with a polished chrome top. Although considered superior in all aspects to my six-cylinder Jaguar, with a cost almost six times as much, I felt the Bora lacked the Jag's glamour and mystique. One plus: the pedals adjusted forward or back to match a fixed driver's seat, emblematic of the gimmicky hydraulics Citroën added after the company purchased Maserati. I bought a used Bora, an eight-cylinder that I drove until the following winter.

My lawyer's investigator finally discovered why the car was not declared a total loss. My insurance agent had been stealing parts from my Jag and giving them to his son, who also owned a Jaguar. I began writing letters to the insurance commissioner and even the attorney general of Illinois. The letter to the insurance company CEO describing the agent's criminality elicited the desired response—the company ordered my new car! I had no idea then that those letters were a prelude to the dozens that I would write over the years to attorneys, insurers, and examining boards for far more serious reasons.

Eventually the new Jaguar, which by this time had morphed into a 5.3-Liter V-12 2+2 Jaguar E-Type fixed head coupe (Series III), arrived from England. Painted British racing green with a suede green leather interior, a very popular European color combination, the car quickly visited the paint and leather shops to revert to its predecessor's sable exterior and cinnamon interior. I owned that car for over forty-five years, though I suspect I replaced every part—electronic, mechanical, frame, engine, interior—at least once. I finally traded it in for a new Ferrari, a simple, reliable old man's car. No clutch pedal, free servicing, everything automatic. Maybe I'll ship it to Israel.

X

Much to my academic delight, I was given permission to engage in independent research. I participated in a seminal statistical study on obesity led by Dr. Alfred Rimm, who allowed me to play in his computer center. During my second year, I was introduced to Roland Pattillo, a brilliant scientist and clinician studying ovarian cancer using BeWo tissue culture cells. He nurtured me through clinical rotations, especially gynecology and obstetrics. Delivering babies was a new, different, and wondrous experience.

A brilliant scientist

I decided to take twelve months off from coursework to pursue research. First, I wrote an NIH grant proposal and was awarded the grant money that supported my research. I then published several papers resulting in an invitation to present at a prestigious medical conference in San Francisco. Dr. Pattillo volunteered to foot the bill and chaperoned. Thanks to my mother's efforts, the local Lincolnwood newspaper printed a flattering article about my involvement in "curing cancer." The conference resulted in my fortuitously meeting Wenda, thanks to Dr. Pattillo and Divine Providence, though at the time, I wasn't cognizant of the latter.

A streetcar named desire

I can still envision Pattillo and me boarding an historic streetcar in downtown San Francisco. From the corner of my eye, I noticed two attractive young ladies. Dr. Pattillo also must have observed them. We hadn't clanged up and down more than a couple of blocks when he started nudging me with his elbow.

"Go introduce yourself, Ron," he said.

I kvetched. Why did I have to be the conductor of the street-car named desire? But I capitulated and stood up to say hello. One of the women was named Wenda. She explained she and her friend had traveled from Houston and were spending the afternoon sightseeing. Pattillo joined in and suggested we all meet later for a drink, which we did. Dr. Pattillo strategically excused himself with a wink. As it turned out, Wenda, whom I called Wendy, was an observant Jew with a sparkly personality, a thick Texan drawl, and vernacular filled with "y'all." The following night, she and I went unchaperoned to dinner and agreed to keep in touch after returning to our respective cities. Over the ensuing months, my long-distance phone bill increased exponentially.

With my research concluded, I now had to choose an elective rotation. How convenient it was that a cardiology elective was available in Houston. Matters of the heart come in many shapes and sizes. I arranged to extern under Dr. John Lancaster, a cardiologist and colleague of world-renowned heart surgeon, Dr. Michael DeBakey. Though surgeries proved interesting, the specialty never whetted my appetite other than the diagnostic procedure of angiography, also used in neurosurgery.

Wendy arranged for me to live with her parents. I drove the new Jag to Houston, an unbearably hot and humid city with cockroaches the size of your fist. She and I saw each other as much as possible. After I returned to Milwaukee three months later, she frequently visited. The two of us enjoyed wonderful weekends eating Serbian food at a local restaurant, watching movies, and even visiting Door County on the state's peninsula to pick cherries. Her presence greatly reduced the tedium of medical classes.

I've come to believe that Hashem brings people into our lives at different times for different reasons. Perhaps my stepping into Wendy's life helped her as much as her presence in my life helped me. I don't recall how we ended our relationship, but we did. The pain of separating probably stung, but it wasn't an excruciating heartache like the breakup with Andi or the devastations that were yet to come.

I was developing a profound interest in neuroanatomy. A third-year medical student, I attended a guest lecture by Dr. Frank Goldstein, an adjunct professor in the neurosurgery department and a full-time private practitioner. Afterward, I approached Dr. Goldstein and introduced myself. Could he help me secure a rotation in neurosurgery? He said that he would try.

Much to my delight, he succeeded. Dr. Goldstein arranged for me to accompany him to the private hospitals in Racine and Kenosha where he practiced and to assist during his surgeries. Sometimes we drove from Milwaukee in his Rolls Royce; other times I drove my Jaguar to the hospital parking lot, our British car cousins parked side by side. In a single morning, he could perform three anterior cervical fusions, known as Cloward procedures, named after Ralph Cloward, MD, a fellow University of Chicago graduate. Each surgery required an iliac crest bone graft, which he showed me how to extract.

Despite his clinical acumen and excellent results, Frank was not well liked. He could appear arrogant and had prickly relationships with university physicians. Maybe they were jealous. To me, he was an influential mentor. Frank passed away tragically several years later. I heard he died while playing tennis during a hospital tournament. Rumors alleged that of the many doctors in the stands, not one tried to resuscitate him. How they reconciled their consciences, I do not know.

As the end of my rotation neared, I began to focus on a residency program. Northwestern University had one of the premier neurosurgery residencies in the country. I interviewed with Dr. Anthony J. Raimondi, the head of the program and a pioneer in pediatric neurosurgery.

He appeared impressed with my curriculum vitae. For ten minutes, we discussed what that program would entail. I requested that I be able to complete my PhD at the University of Chicago, and he agreed. For the remainder of our casual meeting, we talked about exotic cars, particularly his Porsche and my Jaguar. The next week, I received my formal acceptance letter into the program.

The Chief

I had satisfied my mother's dream: she now had a son who was a real doctor—neither a PhD nor an MD (metal dealer) like Uncle Sam, but a bona fide medical doctor. And I was ecstatic, having successfully completed medical school.

I was returning to my beloved Chicago.

10

I'm Fired

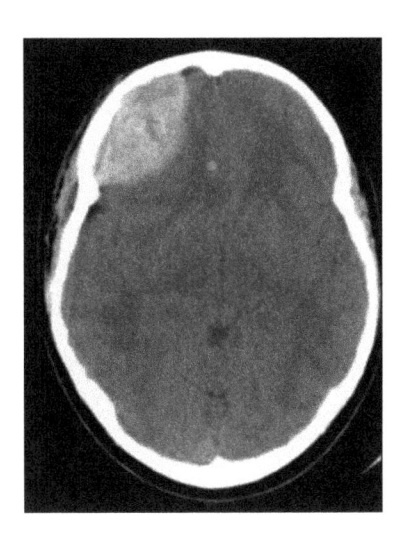

"Go ahead and drape the patient, Ron."

Dr. Joseph Tarkington watched me unfold the teal sheets. Forty-five minutes earlier, I had interrupted his late supper to summon him to the hospital to perform emergency surgery. An unconscious fifteen-year-old boy presented at the Evanston Community Hospital ER. He had been playing tetherball, but with a golf ball attached to the rope instead of the standard soft-touch ball. The golf ball forcibly struck his head. His panicked mother, who'd witnessed the incident, rushed him the few blocks to the hospital. Images from the newly installed CTT scanner, proverbially known as a CAT scan, revealed a large epidural hematoma. The hospital was fortunate to have the cutting-edge scanner coincidentally manufactured in the Milwaukee area in collaboration with MCOW. I was the junior resident on duty and arranged for surgery. Dr. Tarkington advised me to wait for his arrival before going into the OR. Usually the resident will position, prep, and drape the patient, but Dr. Tarkington had not previously operated with me and didn't know my level of competency. I didn't consider myself a neophyte; I had been in the OR with his partner, Dr. Ciric, but didn't know Dr. Tarkington's procedural preferences, so I waited.

Dr. Tarkington readjusted the sheet. "Now, *you* do the craniotomy," he said, peering at me through his wireless glasses. Gray-haired, he had an erudite, reserved demeanor. The index finger on one of his hands was permanently deformed. When I eventually gathered the nerve to inquire why, I learned it was the collateral damage from an accident in his Jaguar.

I proceeded with confidence. Using a manual perforating drill, I bore three holes in the skull and immediately glimpsed the bulging hematoma through the first hole. Relief. Although life-threatening, the blood clot could easily be evacuated. I then used a Gigli saw and guide, making sure to keep the dura intact, cut the bone flap while beveling its edges, and guardedly lifted it up. I gently sucked out the blood, stopped the bleeding, and replaced the bone flap with wire fixation. Tarkington observed, instructing as necessary. I sensed his growing impatience. The entire surgery took ninety minutes.

As we exited the OR, Tarkington grumbled, "The next one you'll do in under an hour."

So that was the source of his annoyance: I had taken too long. Yet, I had exactly followed *Kempe's Operative Neurosurgery, Volume I*, a step-by-step procedure and visual guide that I regularly studied and recently reviewed. Since epidural hematomas did not frequently present in an affluent suburban hospital, versus the hospitals on Chicago's South Side where I would later moonlight, I assumed that it would be weeks, even months, before I had the opportunity to improve my proficiency.

Never assume.

I was still on shift at three o'clock in the morning when another patient with head trauma arrived in the ER. I took one look at the CT scan and saw the subdural hematoma. This can't be happening again, I thought. But it was! This time I woke Dr. Tarkington from a sound sleep. He was not a happy neurosurgeon.

"Prep the patient. I'll meet you in the OR," he said in a gruff voice.

I completed the surgery in under an hour—just barely. Tarkington nodded what I interpreted as "good job" and left for home. I would spend many hours with Dr. Joseph Tarkington in the operating room, as well as a good number of hours at his home enjoying dinners with him and his wife. He would become one of my most influential and dearly beloved mentors. At some point, I learned that he drove a 1950's Jaguar. Normally professorial and taciturn, he talked about Jags like they were neighbors. I don't recall Dr. Tarkington's exact religious denomination, but he was always interested to hear my Old Testament thoughts, honor my Jewish customs, and give me time off for holidays. He reminded me of an elderly Frank Goldstein. I credit my surgical skills to these veterans' tutelage. Over the years, I've received hundreds of letters from patients thanking me for improving—sometimes saving—their lives, including a heartfelt missive from the mother of the boy hit by the tethered golf ball.

Most residents on call stayed at the hospital and slept in

a call room. Fortunately, I eschewed the spartan accommodations. Not because I wasn't on call, but because prior to
starting my residency, I had responded to a classified ad in the
local newspaper for a rental located about a mile from the
hospital. Richard Lundeen, a recently divorced business exec-
utive, owned the sprawling, three-story old Victorian mansion
situated on the corner of Lake and Forest, less than a block
from a private beach on Lake Michigan.

Historic landmark

Urban legend maintained that two sisters and their
husbands had lived in the house. After one of the sisters was
killed in a car accident, the remaining sister, overcome with
inconsolable grief, pined away until she died of a broken
heart. The husbands sold the home to Richard, who moved
into the first floor and rented the third floor to another
divorced fellow, a physicist and contract bridge champion.
Due to Richard's recent divorce and joint custody of his ado-
lescent daughter, he invited me to invest and help defray the
cost of the mortgage. Richard and the physicist agreed to park
on the street, leaving me to use the single-car garage for my
Jaguar. I took to brushing the Old English sheepdog Richard
inherited in the divorce. It was a good trade. I even learned

to play duplicate bridge from the physicist. When I settle in Israel, maybe I'll find some fellow octogenarian bridge players and start bidding grand slams again.

The spacious second floor had a parlor with large bay windows, a living room with an oversize sliding pocket door separating it from the bedroom, and a screened-in, step-down porch off the bedroom. The three of us shared a kitchen, though I had my own fridge because I kept kosher. Before starting my residency, I sanded and varnished the hardwood floors, built a storage closet, and repaired the porch. I purchased a magnificent antique king-size bed frame with carved head- and footboards. Being an enthusiast for state-of-the-art electronics and having such a large living room, I wanted a large-screen TV projector. I regularly went to a bar near the house to play Pac-Man, enjoy a soft drink, and watch Chicago sports on the big screen. When I asked where to buy such a projector and screen, the owner made me a deal I couldn't refuse. I set up the analogue Advent projector and five-foot curved screen in the living room with the projector between two couches and a counterfeit Persian rug covering the highly polished floor.

It was a good thing I had space, because about halfway into that year, I got sick. At first, I thought I had the flu, but my energy continued to dwindle until I could barely walk out of the bedroom. Finally, blood tests led to a diagnosis of non-A, non-B hepatitis, now known as hepatitis C. I traced the cause to an intern who inadvertently stabbed me with a sharp in the OR. The entire team on that floor had to be inoculated. About eight of us gathered, dropped our drawers, and jabbed a needle in the gluteus of the person in front of us. We looked like a bunch of Coppertone kids. Sometimes the practice of medicine is all about efficiency. At the time, I felt too sick to see the humor in it. I went home and cloistered in bed for about two months. The only silver lining was that I missed the general rotations that included procedures in which I had little interest, like proctoscopies and appendectomies.

After I recovered, I resumed my schedule of three or four days of surgical procedures each week with Drs. Tarkington and Ciric, beginning as an assistant and soon becoming the operating surgeon, and making morning and evening rounds. A native of Austria, Dr. Ivan Ciric had lived primarily in Yugoslavia and had a thick accent and a fiery personality to match. One time, I said something to him about the management of a patient, to which he took exception. Right there, Ivan the Terrible fired me. "Go home," he said, pointing a finger at me. I dejectedly did as instructed but returned the next day. I knew that only Dr. Raimondi could fire me. Still, the incident was quite unsettling. Dr. Ciric later apologized and took me out to dinner.

To supplement my meager $9,000-per-year income, I became a *mohel*, the Hebrew term for someone who performs the brith, the circumcision. It was a non-ritual circumcision; I never served wine, nor did I ever receive *semicha* to become an ordained rabbi. Even with the extra income, I didn't have enough money to attend Shelly's upcoming wedding in Israel. He had met Nancy while on the tennis court at the University of Chicago, where he was able to transfer after his second year at Boston University. Shelly was in Cameroon, Africa, doing sickle cell research when they got engaged. My mother called to tell me the news and to inform me that Shelly and Nancy would be getting married in Israel. Would I be able to attend?

I happened to share this concern with Dr. Edir Siqueira, a Brazilian neurosurgeon in private practice who had befriended me. A committed family man, not to mention concert pianist, Dr. Siqueira recommended me for the Sherry Kallick Award. Sherry had been Dr. Siqueira's patient. When she passed, her parents set up a scholarship to be awarded annually to an outstanding resident. I received the award at a formal ceremony attended by the entire medical staff and promptly purchased a ticket to Israel.

Following a long, lonely flight, I met my parents in Jerusalem. If I recall, Rabbi Lehrfield's father officiated the ceremony in his small office. I don't recall much else about the wedding, not like I recall all the vivid details from my visit in 1967. It's amazing how some events fail to make an impression on the temporal lobe.

$$\text{Ж}$$

I appreciated Evanston Hospital—the proximity to my Victorian house, the upscale clientele and neighborhood, the kosher food in the cafeteria—but as the first year of my residency ended, I mentally prepared to be relocated to a completely different venue. I was scheduled to rotate downtown to NMH; this would be quite different in all aspects, not the least of which would be the sleeping rooms at McClurg Court near the medical complex, the long commutes to my Evanston home on nights off, and most certainly different attending physicians; I was apprehensive. I had finally learned the peculiarities of both Drs. Tarkington and Ciric and was no longer in danger of being fired. But could I accommodate to downtown Chicago neurosurgeons? Then, I was handed a gift by Dr. Ciric: though he had fired me much earlier, he had grown to appreciate my surgical skills, bedside manner, critical thinking, and integrity.

"How would you like to stay another year, Ron?" he asked.

It took me all of a second to enthusiastically accede.

About the same time, my mother expressed her concern that I was working too hard and spending too much time at the hospital. Strange, as I think about it now, I made the same arguments to Josh while he was in the thick of completing his JD MBA program. Though he lived within cheering distance of

Wrigley Field, he rarely attended a game or participated in any other social activity. My mother suggested for the umpteenth time that I call Annette Pinhasik and have coffee or take her to the local deli. Annette had been a student in my mother's honors history class. "Just meet her," my mother would say. Each time, I politely declined. I wasn't interested in another relationship, but my mother persisted. She thought Esty, as Annette was called by family and friends, was a perfect match for her son. My stubbornness couldn't withstand my mother's dogged determination, so as not to hear about Esty during every phone conversation, I relented. I called Esty.

My mother proved to be a competent *shadkhan*, a matchmaker. Esty was extremely bright and mature, conversant on myriad topics, Orthodox, and let's not forget beautiful. I believe her parents were Holocaust survivors and were just as delightful as their daughter. One date turned into another and another, and sooner than I would have expected, we were a couple. Esty insisted that I keep strictly kosher at all times. I always kept kosher at home, but while at the hospital or dining out with other doctors, I was not stringently observant, though I never ate treif or mixed milk with meat. As the year progressed and we spent more time together, a chuppah appeared imminent.

11

The Long-Short Road

I didn't get a chance to propose to Esty because she dumped me. I never ascertained if she knew or sensed my intentions and don't recall the litany of reasons, if there had been a litany, for the breakup. I think she felt that we were getting too serious too soon. She had started college and intended to go on to graduate school, perhaps law school. She also felt that I wasn't religious enough for her. Maybe Gino's pizzeria was our undoing. Chicago is renowned for its deep-dish pizza, and Gino's cheese pizza happened to be my absolute favorite. We'd drive downtown, park by the lake, and brave seasonal snow or rain. We carved AP + RB into the wall, alongside other initials. She bristled at the thought that a *mashgiach*, a supervising rabbi, had not blessed the food, and she chastised me every time we ate there or ordered takeout.

Emotional misery weighed me down. Unlike I had after the breakup with Andi, I couldn't flee to Israel. My life was entrenched in Chicago. Ironically, some years later, Esty became my cousin-in-law, though I didn't discover this factoid until the familial relationship was nearly abrogated. My cousin Michael, who is seven years my junior and who used to sit at the children's table during family gatherings in Lincolnwood, had met Esty, fallen in love, and married her. Smart man. I never received an invitation to the wedding. My guess is that someone in the family remembered my previous relationship with Esty and saved us all discomfort and embarrassment. I only learned about the wedding much later, when Michael's sister, Sharon, informed me that her brother was in the midst of a horrendous divorce; his now prestigious, downtown Chicago attorney wife was taking him to the uptown cleaners. When she mentioned the complainant's name, I made the connection. Michael, who I love, was less familiar with Jewish exegesis but by then had become quite observant. I felt sorry for his pain; I have since fully empathized with the devastation that he experienced.

Thankfully, a change in rotations from Evanston Hospital to Northwestern Memorial Hospital distracted me. Several years earlier, Passavant and Wesley hospitals were merged into Northwestern Memorial Hospital. Wesley was known as the Cathedral of Healing because of its vaulted Gothic architecture. When I was on call every other night, I stayed at an apartment in McClurg Court with a magnificent view overlooking the lake. I didn't mind too much except when the call came from the ER in the early predawn hours. I didn't mind being the resident scheduled to perform surgery on ruptured aneurysms or head trauma with intracranial hemorrhage. I was far less enthusiastic, however, when my sleep was disrupted to attend to nonsurgical spine trauma involving long consultations. Northwestern Memorial Hospital was the spinal trauma catchment area for six or seven surrounding states. In the summertime, we'd receive patients who had sustained spinal cord injuries from diving, water skiing, and bicycling accidents; in the winter, from skiing and snowmobiling accidents; and year round, from motorcycle and auto accidents. These traumas too often trapped previously healthy, ambulatory adolescents and young adults in quadriplegic and paraplegic bodies. I would find myself mentally reliving the excruciating months of healing that had followed my high school car accident. The memories always concluded with a surge of gratitude that I had recovered with relatively few trivial restrictions. The pain I witnessed on the faces of patients and their loved ones challenged my professional demeanor. Yes, some of those patients would rise above their challenges, but in those raw, early days of their injuries, the situations were heartbreaking.

Hashem must have looked in my heart and noticed a doleful, lugubrious space that Esty had previously occupied and now was being filled in with the emotions with which doctors learn to contend. The thought occurred to me that a dog might ameliorate my sadness. While in medical school, my bodyguard, Baron, had suffered from cardiomyopathy and diabetes and had to be euthanized, a tremendously sad event. With the start of residency and an uncertain schedule, I had resisted getting another dog. Richard Lundeen's sheepdog was a fine fellow, but he was Richard's and didn't share my heart. The Hebrew word for dog is *kelev*, with *k* meaning *like* and *lev* meaning *heart*. In its totality, kelev means *all heart*. A companion who would give me his whole heart—that's just what this doctor ordered.

I acquired an adult Alaskan malamute. Goodness knows where I got him. I think someone gave him to me, and I called him Wolf. I usually walked Wolf in the alley just like I had walked Phideaux in Lincolnwood. When he crossed his back legs and started pacing by the door, my roommates would let him out in the backyard if I were at the hospital for emergencies. Wolf provided as much companionship for me as he did for the Old English sheepdog that Richard had on weekends when his daughter visited. I don't recall what happened to Wolf. Maybe his purpose in my life was as a temporary Band-Aid; the real cure came shortly afterward.

During my last year at Evanston Hospital, I operated with Dr. Tarkington on a relatively young lady. The day she was discharged, I noticed a gilded frame sitting on the bureau in her private room. It contained a photo of two perfectly groomed, stunning Afghan hounds. Seeing a photo like that stops you in your dog-loving tracks and makes you take a second look. The patient informed me that the smaller, all-black dog was a bitch and the black-masked cream, a male. They were finished show dogs.

"If you ever need to get rid of those dogs, let me know," I said.

Within a few months, the patient called.

"Dr. Bernstein, we're moving from our big ranch outside of Chicago into Water Tower Place and have decided that we can't take the dogs. Are you still interested?"

"I'm on my way," I said, one foot out the door.

When I arrived, she requested that I sit on the couch so each dog could interview me separately. She was more concerned about their comfort level with me than vice versa. The first dog to come through the doorway was the black bitch. She sauntered into the room, sat on her haunches, and stuck her nose up in the air. I called to her. She remained aloof and wanted nothing to do with me. I was looking for a roommate, not a border. The next dog through the door was the handsome black-masked cream. The black tips of his flowing ears matched his face. He pranced right up to me and jumped on my lap. He had fur of silk. I also sensed he had a heart of gold. His name, according to his pedigree and finished world champion papers, was Shazar of Charlot Court, and he was four years old. I later subscribed to *Afghan Magazine*, which featured Shazar at many of the dog shows over which he'd presided. I left with a packet of documents and blue ribbons. Shazar sat in the front seat of my Jaguar, window rolled down, ears flapping in the breeze. I called him Cheezer. We became steadfast friends. A Russian aristocrat among the British gentry, Cheezer never warmed up to the Old English sheepdog.

Blowin' in the wind

At Passavant, I was responsible for following the patients of several attending neurosurgeons, a daily responsibility that included the initial post-op care of crani patients transferred to the general neurosurgical floor. At Wesley, I saw patients in the Neurosurgical Intensive Care Unit. It didn't take long to become acquainted with some of the nursing and ancillary staff who worked in the NICU. One respiratory therapist caught my attention—the one who looked so cute in her white uniform, the one with the name tag "Jeanne."

"It's pronounced 'Jeannie,'" she said, after I greeted her by name.

As the respiratory therapist in charge of the NICU, Jeanne would go from patient to patient and set up ventilators, inhaler masks, nasal cannulas, and all the other crazy paraphernalia. With little memory of my medical school pulmonary physiology, I'd ask her questions, and she'd readily answer. We had a year's worth of medical small talk before I finally asked her out on a date. We went to the Passavant cafeteria for coffee. In addition to her specialized training in respiratory therapy, Jeanne had a graduate art degree. If she had been interested in medicine, I suspect she easily could have gotten into medical school, though in retrospect, she was more interested in a young medical doctor. I recognized her intelligence; unlike me, she had a right-dominant cerebrum and was a talented artist.

We started dating—seriously dating. She was unassuming and easygoing. If I suggested we spend the afternoon at a museum or head to an evening movie, she agreed. We didn't engage in deep philosophical discussions as Esty and I habitually did. Nor did Jeanne assert herself like Andrea. I loved that Jeanne relished Gino's deep-dish pizza as much as I did and that her nose wasn't stuck up in the air like the black bitch or like so many attending physicians whom I daily encountered, whose arrogance preceded them as they walked down the hallowed halls of Northwestern Memorial Hospital.

Over the years, I was accused of hubris, being an arrogant, haughty doctor. If truth be told, I was. But then Harvey W. Cushing, MD, father of neurosurgery, was described as "an egotistical, hard-driving, selfish, mean son-of-a-bitch."[1] I

---

1   J. Michael Bliss, PhD, *Harvey Cushing: A Life in Surgery* (New York: Oxford University Press, 2005).

never considered myself mean! It has required restraint and humility not to present myself as a brain surgeon or chief of staff or member of the board of trustees at several hospitals. I would impulsively blurt these boastful credentials when introduced. It's amazing how tsuris can transform pomposity. I no longer need to be recognized as a neurosurgeon, just a student of Chassidut.

Jeanne's parents had no qualms with their daughter dating a neurosurgeon—to the contrary. They respected my kosher eating habits and holidays. The second of seven children, Jeanne lived in an apartment on the West Side of Chicago near her parents. Her older sister had progressive multiple sclerosis, and I offered my acquiring knowledge of the disease and occasionally free samples of meds. She drove a classic Volkswagen Beetle in which I happily drove her when her MS required a walker. One of Jeanne's younger brothers became a veterinarian, then completed medical school in Washington, D.C., became an obstetrician, and delivered a famous basketball player's illegitimate son at Rush-Presbyterian-St. Luke's Medical Center in Chicago. The family was intelligent and industrious. Her father was in his forties, an outgoing man with a career in sales. I never knew the exact details of what he did, but I did know that he traveled quite a bit. He was in Ohio for work when he suffered a ruptured cerebral aneurysm. He was found dead in bed.

During my years in residency, I saw many patients with similar aneurysms and outcomes. These experiences taught me to savor the time and enjoy the lighter moments that came my way. In my third year of residency, Dr. Jacob Suker, the dean of graduate medical education, offered an opportunity that brightened a few baseball seasons. Dr. Raimondi, who geared his residency program toward academic excellence, encouraged postgraduate education, as well as participation in teaching medical and graduate medical students. I was recommended to be on the graduate medical education staff as an assistant professor but had to officially interview for the position with Dr. Suker. After discussing medicine, our conversation digressed to baseball, not an unusual subject in Chicago since 1908. I relayed my experience about attending White Sox games with my father, then explained how I became a Cubs' bleacher bum during my U of C years with my roommate Steve Henikoff.

"I'm the team physician for the Cubs," said Jake. "I'm looking for an assistant."

By the time I left the interview, I was not only considered a faculty member of Northwestern Medical School, later renamed the Feinberg School of Medicine, but I was an assistant team physician for my beloved baseball team. I sat in the dugout during home games whenever my schedule allowed. Mostly, I saw players for head injuries, allergies, sore throats. If they had a sprain or strain, they'd consult one of the orthopods on staff. I have to admit that in those years, Cubbie games weren't very memorable, except for all the disappointing losses. Jeanne was never a sports enthusiast; she didn't feel neglected when unable to attend.

My second anniversary of being assistant team physician concluded with the Cubs watching the playoffs on television and with me at the research bench. I again resumed my postgraduate fellowship in the department of biochemistry at the University of Chicago. But in fields of science, there are always advancements and new discoveries; I needed to take few courses. To supplement my grant money, with the loss of my meager resident's salary, I spent a couple of nights a week moonlighting in South Side ERs. Dr. Nakamoto was happy to have me back after a ten-year hiatus.

I was less than six months from finishing and was starting to think about concluding my dissertation and then defending it. Maybe it was time to get engaged. I had delayed formally proposing to Jeanne mainly because many of my peers didn't survive their marriage during their oppressive residency. I didn't want to risk an unhappy marriage. After completing my PhD, I'd have one more year of residency; certainly, Jeanne and I could handle that year. Then, I'd graduate and find a full-time academic neurosurgery position. So I proposed, and Jeanne said yes. A chuppah was definitely in my future.

In lieu of an expensive diamond ring, I bought Jeanne an inexpensive car. Her Mustang, an original pony car, looked like it might not endure another Chicago winter. By then, I owned a second car, an eight-cylinder Chevy Monza. Driving the Jaguar on Chicago's heavily salted winter streets had led to a number of expensive replacements of salt-eroded quarter panels. The maxim about Jaguars has always been that you need two because one is always in the shop. I later would embellish upon that dictum with several more Jaguars. Even my Monza turned out to be expensive. Changing the two rear-facing spark plugs required dropping the engine— the engineer's blunder and the owner's nightmare. I did like the Monza, though, and thought it would be a good car for Jeanne. I went to Z (Zolly) Frank Chevy dealership, where I had purchased my Monza. Dudley Derdiger, the manager of the dealership and coincidentally president of Lincolnwood Jewish Congregation, gave me a his-and-her special pricing that fit my budget. I surprised her with a brand new six-cylinder Chevy Monza.

Jeanne and I were in the midst of planning the wedding when an IED bomb exploded in my career path. I had avoided Vietnam and actually was quite pleased with how I had been guided by Divine Destiny. Northwestern's residency program had about thirty residents and foreign fellows in 1974, the year I started. Over the next five years, the program became depleted as fewer residents entered due to cuts in federal funding of specialty medical programs. Too many specialists, decreed the government, and not enough general practitioners. Fellowship money for travel and living expenses was eliminated, so many foreign fellows returned to their homeland. By the end of 1979, attrition took its toll. The remaining ten residents were still needed to cover four hospitals—Evanston, Children's, Lakeside VA, and Northwestern Memorial Hospital. Only Jeff Hirshauer and I remained from our class. Raimondi immediately needed two chief residents. He gave me an ultimatum: be a chief resident at Children's or Northwestern.

I was devastated. There was no way I would have the time to prepare to defend my dissertation. The only way to continue with academics would be to forsake all those years of neurosurgical training—the long nights, the interactions with patients, the tutelage from renowned experts—and pursue research in biochemistry. Or I could abandon the South Side and University of Chicago and return to the North Side and Northwestern University, in which case I would not graduate with an MD, PhD, which had been my intention since entering medical school.

I recovered from hepatitis but never fully recuperated from being unable to defend my dissertation. Would life have gone in a different direction if I had? I've sifted through these questions many times over the years. The choice I made while standing at the fork in the road was to return to Northwestern. The only positive I could fathom at the time was that at least I would have a shorter commute.

12

Soaring High

I have little recollection of the wedding ceremony and even less of the honeymoon, except for parasailing, compliments of Jeanne's cajoling. You never forget soaring close to heaven. I'm not particularly pleased about these scant memories. It's like perusing a photo album with half the snapshots missing, handwritten captions the only reminders of what has been. I don't even have half a wedding photo album, thanks to 3 Gorillas. Jeanne's uncle emailed me photos he still had of that day. There's one of Jeanne and me standing under the chuppah, flanked by our parents.

The bridal chamber

There's another one of the newly wedded Dr. and Mrs. Bernstein walking down the aisle, Jeanne smiling broadly, petite, pretty, glancing at one of her favorite aunts; me looking straight ahead, not grinning, but with a content smile, my beard short, sculpted, and still brown.

Down the aisle again

I wonder if Jeanne has copies, though I doubt it; I think I heard something about a bonfire.

In the photos, family members, friends, and fellow residents fill the sanctuary's seats, the men wearing kippot, the symbol of humility under Hashem. At that time, I didn't wear a kippah every day like I currently do. One of my favorites has a blue *W* embroidered on the back. *W* stands for win, as in "show your W," a Cubs' motto. I ordered it from Israel weeks before the Cubs played the Cleveland Indians in the World Series and picked it up at a Jewish bookstore in Skokie before Josh and I attended our game—Game 4. The Cubbies might not have won Game 4, but they were singing a victory song after Game 7. That was another high-flying experience I'll never forget.

Jeanne and I married on what, in my opinion, is one of the most auspicious days of the year: Israeli Independence Day, Yom Ha'atzmaut, the day that marks the establishment of the modern State of Israel in 1948. This secular holiday happens to fall between the Jewish holidays of Passover and Shavuot, forty-nine days of semi-mourning known as the "counting of Omer." Weddings are prohibited during at least thirty-three days out of this seven-week period; which days are excluded depends on family and communal custom. Rabbi Benzion Kaganoff at Congregation Ezras Israel of West Rogers Park, an Orthodox synagogue where we attended regular services and holiday observances, allowed for Jeanne and me to marry on April 20, during the counting of Omer.

Forty years later, when Rabbi Zimmerman and I discussed the date, he initially took exception to this interpretation. Many Chassidists, which I was not at that time, consider Lag b'Omer to be the *only* day one can marry in this period, while others observe that such occasions can occur on Israeli holidays, like Independence Day, during the semi-mourning period. After further rabbinical consultation, Rabbi Zimmerman mitigated his objections. When you have two rabbis, you get three opinions.

Before the ceremony, Jeanne and I met in Rabbi Kaganoff's study to review the multicolored, graphic ketubah, the wedding contract, especially drawn and prepared for us. It was then read aloud in both Hebrew and English during the ceremony and then signed. Following the chuppah ceremony, a reception with kosher dinner was held at the Lincolnwood Hyatt House, later known as the Purple Hotel, located on Touhy Avenue about a mile from my parents' house.

Historic

Along with the Pink Hotel and the King David Hotel, the Purple Hotel ranks among my favorite accommodations in the world.

I was in high school when it opened. My father celebrated his fiftieth birthday there, surrounded by an ebullient bevy of family and friends. The hotel gained glamour and glitz when international celebrities performed in its five-star dining rooms; it gained notoriety when teamster lawyer Allen Dorfman was gunned down in the parking lot. No relation to my mother, Robin Edna Bernstein, née Dorfman, Allen

Dorfman purportedly had strong ties to the mob. After the hotel closed in 2007, it lapsed into disrepair and finally was demolished six years later. Sharon bought some of the purple bricks auctioned off at a fund-raiser and gifted me one that I could stow in my carry-on and schlep to Tucson. It's basically a piece of cement with a deep purple glaze covering one surface and replete with nostalgia. The Purple Hotel and I share a history of major ups and downs. The difference is that I've managed to extract myself intact from the rubble.

Jeanne, Cheezer, and I lived in a two-story greystone on Touhy, about six miles east of the Purple Hotel but within walking distance of the synagogue and about a mile from where I had lived on Morse Avenue as an infant. Had I come full circle? I moved the mahogany bed from the Evanston house. Jeanne insisted that if we were going to keep a bed from the past, the bed needed a fresh coat of paint. I still can't believe that I covered that exquisite wood with dark blue paint and a faux-grained finish. Oy vey, I must have been in love.

Guest room visitors

I set up a home theater in the basement so that I could watch Chicago sports and hacked a decoder to watch pay-per-view stations. My computer equipment occupied one corner. While living in Evanston, I built my first personal computer, an Altair, and modified the small Bally Arcade system. I joined the Chicago computer club and religiously attended meetings, as long as they weren't on Shabbat. When hard times hit, my aptitude for programming would help save my sanity. Jeanne was as interested in my technical forays as she was in the Cubs, Bulls, Bears, and Blackhawks and thus rarely deigned to visit the man cave.

I also started consulting with Uzi Sharon and Professor Isaac Kaplan of Laser Industries of Tel Aviv, Ltd., who were developing carbon dioxide lasers for innovative applications in neurosurgery. As an incidental benefit of spending hours using a joystick to play video games, I helped them design the micromanipulator microslad, the first robotic medical instrument. Jeanne had no desire to travel to Israel with me. She claimed the journey was fraught with danger. How could Israel be more dangerous than the South Side of Chicago?

During my solo ventures, I usually managed to visit a few relatives and share a meal of shakshuka in the mornings and falafel and hummus pitas later in the day. With each visit, I felt the tug to move there, become a citizen, raise our future children, celebrate Yom Ha'atzmaut every April. I'd board the plane back to Chicago, the dream clasped in one hand, but once back on U.S. terra firma, I immediately reintegrated into the busy life of neurosurgery, research, and extracurricular hobbies, all of which required the use of both hands.

Integrating lasers and computers was a welcome distraction when I rotated to Children's Memorial Hospital. I didn't enjoy pediatric neurosurgery, partially because of the many sad prognoses. I perpetually had to revise ventriculoperitoneal shunts that too many young patients required, often as a result of a birth defect. The shunts, known as the Raimondi unishunt because Dr. Raimondi had developed them, diverted and drained excessive buildup of cerebrospinal fluid from the brain. Some cases proved as traumatic to doctor as to patients and parents.

Probably the most heartbreaking case was Kevin Daley, born with spina bifida. He was the grandson of "Boss" Richard J. Daley, then mayor of Chicago. Kevin had spent almost his entire life on a ventilator, having one life-saving surgery after another, many of which I performed. Dr. David McClone was his attending neurosurgeon, and I was the chief resident. We had been residents together, both opting to pursue our PhDs, but because he graduated several years before in a previous program, he was able to achieve this goal. I did not and always felt a twinge of jealousy. Almost every day, I met with Kevin's parents, Dick and Maggie Daley. The emotional stamina required of us on this journey was brutal. I knew that I could never specialize in pediatric neurosurgery, though I later became certified in both pediatric and adult neurosurgery.

During those last months of Kevin's life, Dave and I sometimes had heated discussions about the moral and theological considerations inherent in removing patients from life support. It wouldn't be the last time that I discussed Jewish ethics, customs, and law (*Halacha*). Decades later, Shelly and I would have similar contentious discussions in the ICU of a Boca Raton Hospital.

※

I had one more rotation before I graduated. It was at Lakeside VA Hospital. In the middle of a January snowstorm,

I received an after-midnight call from the neurosurgery intern at the hospital. He knew everything—or purported to know everything. He was close to hysterical.

"The neurology secretary upstairs was shot in the head. She's just lying there. Should I drill a burr hole to let out evil spirits?"

Now there was a term I'd never encountered in a medical textbook. "Is she breathing?" I asked him, trying to gauge if he were going to start hyperventilating.

"Yeah."

"Does she have fixed dilated pupils?"

"Yeah," he said, still sounding *tsedrait*, Yiddish for crazy and confused. I asked him to describe the scene. Apparently, he had never seen brain oozing out of a gunshot exit wound. Having moonlighted in the ER at three different South Side hospitals, I had seen worse. I suspected the poor woman had already been intubated before my intern even arrived as a consultant.

I didn't want to drive through another blizzard, yet I felt it was my responsibility. My presence was needed. I called Chicago's finest, explaining that I was a neurosurgeon and had an emergency at Lakeside VA. Could they send a patrol car? After all, their motto was "Serve and Protect." The dispatcher said no and remained resolute through my persuasive arguments. It took me almost two hours of creeping down Lakeshore Drive and sundry city streets to get to the hospital. That white-knuckle excursion was more taxing than any potential surgery. Although happy to have the Monza, I would have preferred a snowplow. By the time I arrived, the secretary was pronounced dead. The day before, her husband had returned home to find a lover's tryst. He came up and shot her while she was working.

A few months later, President Ronald Reagan was shot in an attempted assassination. I was privy to his medical status because the chief of neurosurgery at the VA was Nicholas Wetzel, former partner of Loyal Davis, Chicago's first neurosurgeon. Another partner was Dan Ruge, who had been appointed surgeon general by President Reagan. Drs. Wetzel and Ruge communicated via the WATTS line about Reagan's conditions during and after surgery.

Though I only heard their conversations, I would soon have many opportunities to treat gunshot wounds.

13

Academia

Graduation from residency proved a joyous occasion, one warmed by a deep-seated sense of accomplishment. Although grueling, the seven years would serve as the foundation of my career. My only regret was that I could not add *PhD* after *MD*. That omission stung, especially when I would see Shelly's name in print: Shelly C. Bernstein, MD, PhD. His efforts to complete and defend his PhD thesis were not thwarted as were mine. I've come to understand that the wisdom of Divine Providence is far greater than ours and that certain events transpire for reasons we may only discern in retrospect, if at all.

Since a move to Israel remained elusive, I was intent on

finding an academic neurosurgical position in Chicagoland so that Jeanne and I could remain close to family and friends. Research remained my passion, as Dr. Raimondi knew. He introduced me to Oscar Sugar, MD, head of the department of neurosurgery at the Abraham Lincoln School of Medicine, part of the University of Illinois at Chicago Circle campus. A kindly, erudite Jewish man nearing retirement, Dr. Sugar offered me an appointment as associate professor in the department of neurosurgery, an academic position that included tenure, ability to train residents, and research opportunities. Shortly after meeting Dr. Sugar, I met John Oldershaw, MD, the chief of neurosurgery at Cook County Hospital and an ex-naval officer nearing retirement. Dr. Oldershaw welcomed me on board as an associate attending neurosurgeon at Cook County Hospital.

I turned down an appointment at University of Chicago—I had spent enough time in Hyde Park. I would have preferred a staff appointment at Northwestern's Feinberg School of Medicine, but the once-preeminent program was disintegrating. One of the staff physicians was incarcerated for drug misuse, another immigrated to Italy, and yet another career ended in terminal litigation. I had no inkling at the time that someday I would face my own trials and tribulations.

My salary increased substantially, though it was significantly less than that of private-practice neurosurgeons in the area. Per my request, the bank teller cashed my first payroll check in now-extinct thousand-dollar-bill denominations. I singly laid out the legal tender on my parents' living room marble table, then took them out to the Signature Room, informally known as The 95th, the restaurant at the top of the John Hancock Center. I don't recall if Jeanne joined us. I do recall, however, buying her a fourteen-karat solid yellow gold Jules Jurgensen watch, which eventually ended up in the clutches of 3 Gorillas. At least I still have my great grandfather's old-world pocket watch, as well as my grandfather's, cherished keepsakes that someday will pass to Josh and Michael. Unfortunately, my eldest son will never see the Rolex that my father bequeathed him, thanks to my brothers.

Cook County Hospital definitely differed from Evanston and Northwestern Memorial Hospitals. If you've ever seen the movie *The Fugitive* with Harrison Ford, then you can picture the pandemonium: doctors, nurses, EMTs, and police all winding their way up and down corridors filled with patients and visitors. We nicknamed it The Weekend Knife and Gun Club. The unimpressive neurosurgery floor consisted of several semiprivate rooms with five beds, a capacious open ward with around twenty beds, a few closet-size offices, one of which I occupied, and a large office for Ms. Ernestine Daniels, administrative assistant. A black lady of no nonsense, she was the real boss of the division. We got along well.

My daily routine began with a twenty-five-minute meditative drive down Lakeshore Drive, which paralleled the shores of Lake Michigan. I never tired of the expansive water's changing hues of blues, greens, and grays. Once downtown, I descended into lower Wacker Drive, parked, then climbed the stairs to Lou Mitchell's diner, where John Oldershaw and I met for breakfast. One of the best things Oldershaw did was introduce me to this unassuming diner and owner and his famous breakfast entree of donut holes. Unfortunately, I never ate at the renowned restaurant The Greeks, located across from CCH, because it had recently burned down. Afterward, Oldershaw and I drove to the hospital and entered the fray.

I was responsible for the academic teaching and training of about ten residents from the University of Illinois neurosurgery program who rotated through CCH. I quickly discerned that the CCH program was not of the caliber of the Northwestern residency program, though the residents gained some unique experiences, including how to remove a machete embedded in a skull. I sometimes gave them as much grief as Ciric had once given me, though I never fired anyone from the program. I did recommend, however, that one resident pursue an alternate career and another senior resident continue in a neurology program. The latter suffered from narcolepsy. Can you imagine being in the midst of brain surgery and having the surgeon fall asleep while leaning over the operating table?

When I visited Chicago a few years ago, I went to Lincolnwood Jewish Congregation to say goodbye to Rabbi Lehrfield, who was moving to Jerusalem to be with his children. There, I met Rabbi Gordon, the rabbi replacing Rabbi Lehrfield. I introduced myself, and the conversation quickly turned to medicine.

"So, you are a neurosurgeon, Yisrael," Rabbi Gordon said. It was the second time that day he had met a neurosurgeon.

"Who did you see earlier?" I asked.

"Leslie Schaefer."

"He was my chief resident," I said. I wondered if Les would have had anything good to say about me. Sometimes you don't know how the past will be painted in the present.

I often ruminated about my experience with Kevin Daly. Might there be a safer, less damaging alternative to the Raimondi unishunt that Dave McClone and I used on Kevin, as well as hundreds of other children? Our protocol was to surgically insert the shunt tube into the brain cavity containing the excessive fluid. The shunt diverted the egregious fluid to another body cavity, such as the abdomen, for absorption. The unishunt improved upon previous shunts comprised of separate units that occasionally disconnected, requiring an invasive revision. If the physical unishunt could be eliminated altogether, many potential complications would be obviated. But how to accomplish that? I pondered this question more than once while driving along Lakeshore Drive.

When I was chief resident at Northwestern, I used a Sharplan carbon dioxide laser to vaporize brain tumors. The follow-up brain scans revealed a patent pathway created by the laser, meaning that the usual glial scarring had been retarded. I hypothesized that lasers might eliminate the need for silicon shunts. Dr. Sugar's offer included the opportunity to substantiate my hypothesis. Not only did I have access to a lab at the university's Hektoen Institute of Medicine research facility, I also had access to a Rhesus macaque colony.

This research wasn't test tube biochemistry like I had conducted at University of Chicago, as Baron snoozed downstairs. This was clinical research using living specimens. During the first stage of research, I used a laser to create a pathway from the surface of the monkey's brain to the ventricle containing cerebrospinal fluid. None of those monkeys died. None of them suffered infections or other complications. I wrote several proposals and received grants to perpetuate my research. I relished walking from Cook County Hospital to the research facility, donning a surgical gown and mask, and later documenting results. The second stage of research would be to induce hydrocephalus by blocking the egress of cerebral spinal fluid, then perform a laser ventriculotomy as a shunt alternative to correct the condition.

After two years of research and enduring craziness at Cook County Hospital, life's trajectory changed. First, Jeanne became pregnant! With much anticipation, we transformed one of our bedrooms into a nursery and wallpapered the room with brightly colored clowns below wainscoting. We managed to remain married through that exercise. The room was cute. Of course, Elyse was far cuter. Adorable, beautiful, she was both of our parents' first grandchild and was duly doted upon by them.

Our first nursery

I admit to doing my fatherly share of doting too, though I have to admit to never changing her diapers.

A new sense of responsibility settled upon me. Although Jeanne and I lived quite comfortably on our salaries, I began to consider the benefits of private practice. We intended to have more children. Private practice would offer many more opportunities for education, travel, and other family activities. On the other hand, once again I would have to interrupt my research. The uncertainty and doubt that had visited me when I last relinquished research returned.

The deciding factor occurred when Oscar Sugar announced his retirement. After a lengthy search, Robert Crowell from Harvard was appointed chairman of the department of neurosurgery at University of Illinois. By that time, the residency programs at U of I and CCH had amalgamated; he now spent considerable time micromanaging the CCH Division of Neurosurgery, where I was the acting chief. It didn't take long to determine that Robert and I were incompatible. We both had healthy egos, though I would contend that his was inflated, and we often disagreed. Research or not, the time had come to move on.

I began my search for a private practice position to join as a full partner. I approached a local neurosurgeon, a close colleague and friend who was a solo practitioner and observant Jew. After speaking with him, I realized that maintaining my faithful observance would be impossible if he were off during a Jewish holiday and I were on call. Upon further reflection, I concluded that Chicago had too many neurosurgeons and thirty-five Chicago winters were enough for one lifetime; I needed a warmer clime absent snow.

A colleague, Joseph Levine, whom I had met at one of the annual neurosurgical conferences, had a very lucrative solo practice in Fort Walton Beach, on the Gulf Coast of Florida. We talked extensively, and he invited me to stay at his house and further assess the offer to join his practice. The partnership sounded very appealing. Not only would Jeanne, Elyse, and I be living near the water, we also would be reasonably close to my parents, now semiretired in a Pembroke Pines condominium near Miami.

I practically had pen in hand, ready to sign the partnership agreement. I had toured Joseph's office and the local hospital, driven by Gulf homes with docked yachts and backyard infinity-edge pools. What else did I need to see? Joseph's wife, however, suggested a second trip with Jeanne before making such a momentous decision, and I agreed. While touring the area, Jeanne was not as impressed as I and promptly inquired about available shopping. Our hosts ushered us to the best shopping in the vicinity: the Sears mail-order location—no Bloomies, Neimans, or Saks. Thus ended our future on Florida's Panhandle.

Fortunately, when one boutique door closes, another opens. Following that disappointment, Joseph happened to mention my credentials to one of his school chums, a prominent Tucson neurosurgeon, Richard Greenberg, who commiserated about being overworked in his new, solo practice and was seeking a partner. He also was informed of Jeanne's reservations about communities lacking certain amenities. His wife, Elaine, called Jeanne and suggested we fly into Tucson's International Airport. She and Jeanne would spend the day at Scottsdale Fashion Square, the premier mall, only a hop, skip, and ninety-mile drive away. The shopping spree served to offset Jeanne's initial perception of Tucson as a provincial cowboy town.

It was the summer of '83, and our visit occurred during the monsoon and a hundred-year flood. The arroyos roiled with floodwaters that destroyed bridges and homes with a fury equivalent to Lake Michigan in the midst of a squall. In spite of a flood that could float Noah's Ark, we discerned many positives to a life in the Sonoran Desert. Northwest Hospital was about to open, and management was eager to have a neurosurgeon with a strong CV from Chicago; they offered many financial, practice, and academic incentives that allowed for purchase of a large home in the desert in the best school district. When I discussed my Tucson plans with Oscar Sugar, he suggested I meet with two groups of neurosurgeons there that included his former residents. As a courtesy to him, I arranged the meeting. They were well aware that I had trained at Northwestern and was an associate professor at the University of Illinois. I declined the offer to be their scut boy. Their ensuing resentment and animus continued for the remainder of my career. I always disdained the politics of medicine.

At the end of that year, our transition began. Two large moving vans filled with furnishings and cars headed southwest. Jeanne would stay in Chicago with Elyse until the vans arrived in Tucson and were unpacked; Cheezer and I would fly to Tucson, get the house settled as much as possible, and launch my practice. The vans ended up taking different routes. A snowstorm waylaid one in Denver, delaying its arrival by two weeks. At least that issue was influenced by climate rather than by nefarious intentions, as would happen thirty years later with 3 Gorillas' vans.

Cheezer and I boarded the plane. He sat next to me in his own first-class seat and held his head regally as passengers oohed and aahed. We were headed for a new adventure. I had no doubt that our decision to move to Arizona was the right one. Cheezer didn't seem to have any qualms either. A little sedated, he never needed the airsickness bag.

The future seemed as clear and sunny as the sky.

PART II

The Story

Why do you think that happens, that unraveling in life? . . .
The apparent disarray, the unrest in our world, is all the very
   essence of life.
Instead of handing us life on a silver platter . . .
He chooses to unravel the strings and leave them for us to tie
   up.
Yes, the unraveling is for the best.
G-d wants us to appreciate our lives in the deepest and
   sweetest of ways—something we can experience only by
   taking our own steps in this cosmic dance.

—From "Unraveled" by Sara Hecht

14

The New Old Pueblo

No more icy sidewalks, slippery streets, biting winds, mounds of gray snow, or salt stains on my Jaguar. I was ensconced in the sun-drenched Sonoran Desert, the Santa Catalina Mountains' purple majesty rising skyward behind my house. While I missed Lake Michigan's mutable blue-green hues, I reveled in the sunset's symphony of pink and orange. Three hundred fifty days of sunshine wasn't all that bad either. Nor was the swimming pool in the backyard when temperatures hovered over a hundred.

Our home on Calle Los Altos—street of the tall ones—was located in a Foothills community. Richard and Elaine Greenberg's realtor had shown us the house during our pilot visit. They owned a lovely one-of-a-kind home designed by

Tucson's famed architect, Josias Joesler. The unique interior, with its high-beamed great room, piqued my artistic interest, and I suggested to the realtor that we tour the handful of Joeslers on the market. I would have made an offer on actor Lee Marvin's Joesler home had the multiple garages not been detached and the walkway to the house so steep. Instead, we purchased a contemporary residence from a physician, a neuroradiologist. With its three bedrooms, office, and three-car garage, it met our current needs.

By the time Jeanne and Elyse joined me, I was seeing a steady stream of patients. Northwest Hospital was the only southern Arizona hospital that had acquired a Sharplan carbon dioxide laser, and I was the only surgeon using it to vaporize tumors during transsphenoidal and intracranial surgery. I believed it reduced morbidity. A portion of the hospital, along with my adjoining office, remained under construction. Richard Greenberg practiced out of a small office at St. Mary's Hospital, ten miles from Northwest Hospital. We also decided to open and staff offices in Green Valley and Sierra Vista, both south of Tucson. Despite being Jewish, Greenberg had been raised Catholic. During his celebrated holidays, I made rounds and took calls. Richard reciprocated when I had meetings or vacationed and during my Jewish holidays

Growing a private practice required long days and extensive driving between offices. By 6:00 a.m., I was making patient rounds at the hospitals. Morning surgeries followed. Then there were afternoon office hours and evening rounds to check on post-ops. Pulling into the driveway at 8:00 p.m. was considered an early arrival; 10:00 p.m. tended toward the norm. I also served as chief of staff at Northwest Hospital, which required communicating with colleagues while serving as the liaison at board meetings; later, I became a board member.

A Message From The Chief of Staff
Ronald A. Bernstein, M.D.

It was the best of times; it was the worst of times.

This most certainly is an exaggeration of superlatives, but it is an *exciting* time. One only needs to look around the hospital campus to appreciate the logarithmic growth that is occurring in our facilities. The cardiac catheterization lab is a reality as is a first-class cancer center. Soon to be inhabited is the Rehabilitation Hospital. Walls, parking lots and heliports are being levelled to provide additions to a full service health center for the Northwest Community, second to none in quality and scope.

Unfortunately, the regulations, restrictions and governmental involvement in medicine have also expanded logarithmically. Medicine is no longer just the art of healing. It requires business managers, organizational review boards, hospital committees, and numerous advisers versed in the alphabet soup of acronyms just to make it through the daily rounds. This applies to all of us; there is no distinction between the "cognitive" fields and other specialties of our profession. All of us need to heed these new regulations and be cognizant of their ramifications.

Now I'm chief

※

Jeanne and I joined Congregation Anshei Israel, the largest traditional Jewish congregation in Tucson at the time. While attending a High Holiday service, the congregant sitting next to me knew that I was unhappy and suggested that I accompany him for a short walk to the nearby Orthodox congregation, Chofetz Chaim. I felt much more comfortable with the smaller congregation and more traditional services like those at LJC. Jeanne complained. She did not like that men and women sat on separate sides of a partition called a mechitzah. She mistakenly felt this arrangement denigrated women. The reason for the partition is really for nothing to distract attention during the prayer service. The attunement of heart and mind is necessary in attaining unity with G–d.

As my referral base broadened over four neighboring states, my practice grew quite lucrative. My monthly income now surpassed my annual income at Cook County Hospital. Even after contributing money to retirement and investment accounts, we still had substantial discretionary income. I could indulge in home improvements.

Upgrades

We soon had a new, custom-designed entrance with iron gates depicting desert fauna and flora; two Cantera stone sculptured lions, each perched atop a column at the front walkway; stained glass front doors; and the *pièce de résistance,* a year-round sukkah where only the roof covering, sechach, was replaced annually. I worked closely with Richard Greenberg's architect, John Bissell, whose Mexican tile work in the kitchen could have been featured in *Architectural Digest.* While impressive, the upgrades never evoked the same feeling of elegance as the painted scene my mother commissioned for the kitchen.

The wall

Though Jeanne left home design to me, one of the few things she'd insisted on was grass, a rarity in a city preferential to xeriscapes. Not only did she miss the greens of Chicago, she also wanted a place for Elyse to play. The gardeners tended to the yard, keeping it mostly putting-green green even in the winter, when they overseeded the Bermuda grass with winter rye—that is, until I learned of a less expensive option: commercial food coloring. Trucks with long, snaking hoses sprayed dormant grass, and voila! Jeanne had her requisite green turf year-round. She also looked out the kitchen window at the grove of citrus trees in the enclosed backyard. The wall attempted to keep out javelinas, Gila monsters, snakes, and sundry other desert critters that would have antagonized, and possibly agonized, Cheezer. Beyond its periphery stood a phalanx of apple and almond trees, usually netted in spring to discourage bandit birds.

Cheezer loved to race around the grass and water the fruit

trees, much to the gardeners' chagrin. Since Cheezer never showed an inclination to plunge into the pool's chlorinated waters, I didn't worry about him; he was a dog, after all, and dogs naturally know how to paddle. I did insist, however, that all my children take private swimming lessons.

Jeanne seldom appreciated or condoned other allocations of disposable income. But what else is disposable income for if not to be disposed of? She "disposed" of funds at Bloomies and Neiman's at Fashion Square Mall; on facials, coifs, and manicures; and on plane tickets, as she regularly flew back to the Midwest to visit family and friends. Spending money on my passions seemed completely appropriate. And one of my passions remained Chicago sports, which still did not interest Jeanne.

Much to my joy and good fortune, I became acquainted with Foothills physicians with similar backgrounds who would gather in my rudimentary home theater to watch Chicago Bears football games on the Advent screen. I'll never forget the paramount game on October 21, 1985, when The Fridge scored the touchdown to lead the Bears to the NFL championship. You can bet every doctor in the house was a Chicagoan that day. Da Bears went on to trounce my brother's New England Patriots in Super Bowl XX. It was only right.

Not surprisingly, Jeanne declined the opportunity to attend the final game of the Chicago Bulls' first world championship series against the Lakers. But Buddy Green, my cousin Liz's husband, did not. I recently spoke to Liz, now in her eighties. Sadly, Buddy has left this world, but Liz said that he reminisced many times about going to that game at the Fabulous Forum in Los Angeles. How could anyone forget? Michael Jordan was *the* man back then. I thought nothing of spending thousands for first-class airfare, a rental car, valet parking, and courtside seats. Jack Nicholson sat several rows in front of us; Daryl Hannah, a fellow Chicagoan, sat next to me, though I didn't recognize her until someone affirmed her celebrity. She looked like any other young lady in jeans. I'm not sure which team she cheered for.

Then came my decision to purchase a Ferrari. John Medlin, an orthopedic surgeon who partnered with Richard Greenberg and me in the Northwest office, owned one. I coveted that car. Or maybe I coveted its status. After all, I had no reason to buy a Ferrari other than the fact that the car was exotic, unique, and showed that one had reached the pinnacle of success. I figured if an orthopedic surgeon could own one, certainly a neurosurgeon could too. Oh, such narcissism. I hadn't yet learned from Frank Goldstein. I said to Jeanne, "We're going up to Scottsdale. I want to test-drive a Ferrari." She just shook her head and asked to be dropped off at the mall.

The manager of the Ferrari dealership suggested that I wait for the following year's model because it would have a bigger engine and be a four-seat convertible. "It comes in every color if you order it in red," he said, laughing. I didn't want a red Ferrari. That was Enzo Ferrari's color, the Italian who founded the company. I ordered the car in azzurro, a metallic light blue. A year later, I boarded a charter flight to Scottsdale Airpark to pick up my car at the dealership.

Any color but red

The car was a sleek, gorgeous, exotic Quattrovalvole Mondial Cabriolet with a V-8 engine that growled its presence on every street and highway; hand-stitched leather seats melded around me. My mother had fitted plastic coverings made for her silk sofas; I had custom blue sheepskins and monogrammed headrests. Besides the extraordinary electronics, I added special Z-box door speakers, subwoofers, GPS, and VocAlarm, which was a talking alarm system. If anyone came too close to the car, a voice would admonish, "You are too close. Move back or the alarm will sound." Should the intruder hold his ground, the voice counted down from ten to zero, then sounded an alarm and called my cell phone, 911, or whatever number had been programmed, while repeatedly shouting, "I've been violated." The system proved effective the night I attended a concert at the Tucson Convention Center. When I returned to the parking lot, police were milling about because many of the cars had been broken into, but not my talking Ferrari. The Ferrari won first place in a Las Vegas car show, an event memorialized by an aerial-view photo, enlarged to poster size and framed. The license plate was RRRR E, which after a contemplative pause brought a smile to onlookers.

When my parents visited from Florida, my father immediately wanted to ride in the Ferrari. He never liked my little British cars. Their low entry and tight quarters were not built for older accountants. I suggested that he drive, but he declined, so with him nestled in the passenger seat and me behind the wheel, we went cruising. We started down Hacienda del Sol, a curvy Foothills road perfect for acceleration. The top was down. The sun was shining. We were flying. Witness to my exuberant driving was a deputy sheriff. When he pulled me over, he didn't appear to be feeling the same exuberance. My quick-witted father said to the officer, "My son just bought me this car, and I was letting him drive it." The officer asked me for my driver's license but fortunately not the car registration. He took his time, not uttering a word. "Slow down, sir," he finally said, returning the license. I meekly shifted into first and crept down the remainder of the hill.

My practice continued to thrive, which meant our children would have the best education, just as I had, as well as unique family travel opportunities. My parents were healthy and able to visit frequently. I had chosen a career that gave me tremendous satisfaction. I remember driving down Campbell Avenue one morning, the top down, the road winding through desert landscape, three mountain ranges before me, and saying out loud, "Life is good. Really good."

15

Going to the Dogs

Cheezer never got to ride in the blue Ferrari. He had ridden shotgun many times in my Jaguar and flown first-class on a commercial jetliner. He would have loved the wind in his face, his long ears blowing back, his elegant nose pointed in the air. But he did get to spend hours in the backyard, the sun's warmth comforting his twelve-year-old bones, or sitting below an air-conditioning vent during the summer's peak triple-digit temperatures. Although still regal and handsome, after a few years in the desert, he started moving slower and usually had to go out in the middle of the night. Jeanne got up with Elyse; I got up with my dog.

Cheezer's modus operandi was to bump the screen door when he was ready to come back inside. One night, I dozed while waiting for him. A yelp startled me, and I bolted out of bed. Cheezer was floating in the pool facedown. Panicked, I pulled him out and gave him mouth-to-mouth but couldn't revive him. I was so devastated that Jeanne had to make the necessary arrangements to dispose of his body; I couldn't bring myself to do it. We surmised that he was sitting by the side of the pool when he had a heart attack or stroke and tumbled into the water. His unexpected demise shocked me. It took more than five years before I could consider a replacement for Cheezer—the longest period in my life without a dog.

When Elyse started grade school, she wanted a dog. Jeanne searched around Tucson and found a golden retriever puppy. Elyse named him Pumpkin because of his coloring. She adored that dog. Pumpkin was about seven years old when, tragically, a car hit him. The entire family was saddened, though no one more than Elyse. I tried to comfort her, but hugs and reassurances that she could get another dog only eased a fraction of her pain. I shared my own experience as a teenager losing a dog.

Pumpkin on real grass

Jeanne took Elyse to a pet store, where she promptly fell in love with a basset hound. I am not a fan of bassets, but what could I say? The salesperson refused to sell the puppy. We would need to buy his sister, too. Oy vey—just what I wanted. Those naughty dogs peed and pooped everywhere in the house, including on my Persian carpets. After a week, they were gone. Jeanne went ahead and got another golden, and we named him Jordan, after Michael Jordan.

I now realized how much I missed my Afghan and called the patient who had given me Cheezer. She was still living in Water Tower Place and gave me the name of Cheezer's breeder. It took over a year of negotiating and making travel arrangements before I acquired Daisy, a three-year-old bitch who closely resembled Cheezer but was a bit more petite in stature. She wasn't finished as Cheezer had been, so I hired a trainer and groomer. Together they traveled east and west to compete in major dog shows.

A prancing Daisy

To become designated a champion, a dog must win a certain number of points, earned at the competitions. Was it Providence that I was present when she won her last major as Best in Show at the Tucson fairgrounds? I still have the video of the trainer trotting around the ring next to my dog, Daisy's long, silky hair swaying with each step. Reaching the level of champion offers the dog the privilege of attaching the prefix *Ch* to its name. And so she became Ch Buena Vista Just A Dream, her official AKC name, but she still just answered to Daisy.

❫❮

During my first year in Tucson, I met Dr. Richard Silver, a talented Chicago-trained orthopedic surgeon. He had a Great Dane, a gentle soul, that took up an entire couch. In spite of Richie's Porsche, we became fast friends. A few years older, in some ways he felt like a big brother. I attended his grandson's brit; he served as the sandek—the person who holds the baby—at the brit for both of my boys. When Jeanne was expecting our second child and went into labor, we dropped off Elyse with Richie and Margot Silver, who adored her. Richie had a huge orthopedic practice at St. Mary's Hospital, where we often worked as co-surgeons; his expertise was dealing with bone, mine was dealing with nerve tissue. Soon I became recognized for reconstructive spine procedures using instrumentation and bone grafts for failed back patients.

An astute, though somewhat wily businessman, Richie's financial acumen exceeded mine. When Richie invested in land in Colorado Springs, I did, too. In the future, it could be developed into income-producing property. The investments felt reassuring. When it came time to build my mountain estate, I borrowed his builder. Hi had built his grandiose primary residence in the Finisterra community in the Catalina Foothills. He also owned homes in Mexico and Sun Valley, Idaho.

An avid skier, he hosted our family numerous times on ski trips. On one of these vacations, I left a sweater behind in his guest suite. Auntie Anne crocheted it when chocolate cigarettes fell out of fashion. I even wore it back in high school, as documented by the yearbook photo of my classmates and me in the advanced biology lab at Niles High West: Ronald A. Bernstein's amazing technicolor dream sweater. I must have made a dozen phone calls trying to retrieve that sweater. It broke my nostalgic heart to lose it.

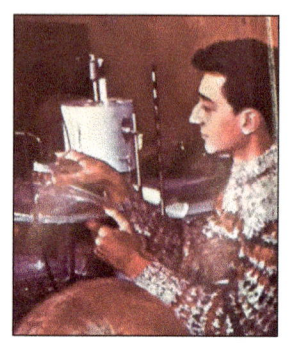

My dream sweater

Jeanne expressed interest in working, but not as a respiratory therapist like she was when we first met. Michael, now a one-year-old, was toddling around, and Elyse had started grade school. We had a nanny, Miss Jenn, a nice Jewish girl who worked part-time as a ring girl at boxing events. She ended up marrying a real estate agent, who two decades later became Michael's business partner. Life certainly has its circular moments.

I suggested to Jeanne that she help in my office. Elaine Greenberg, Richard's wife, was the office manager. Jeanne didn't particularly like Elaine, who tended to rule the office roost with outspoken opinions and a sharp tongue. Jeanne started coming to work sporadically. My maxim was to avoid office politics, so I didn't pay particular attention to how staff members got along. Jeanne and I did not talk about the office at home. Usually, I returned home late, ate dinner in the theater while watching taped Chicago sports, and went to bed.

At that point, Richard and I employed several surgical nurses, a full-time medical transcriptionist, as well as other part-time employees. We needed someone to assist with filing medical claims, so we hired another woman. She didn't get along with Richard's private secretary or my young, attractive secretary, but she got along fabulously with Richard. After months of agonizing, I had enough of their inappropriate office conduct. There were questionable financial matters, including unbundling, where multiple procedure codes were used to create additional charges. Displeased, health-care insurers were not renewing contracts, and we were being disparaged by competition who derisively called us Bernberg and Greenstein. Just as frustrating, Richard had burgeoning malpractice cases, a significant reason to dissociate from him. I asked Richard to leave. He made plans for his family to move back East, but not before taking advantage of me when dividing assets. Divorces are never pleasant and rarely amicable. Still, a part of me felt sad. Richard had been chief of staff when I moved to Tucson and helped me get my practice off to a strong start.

Jeanne stepped in as full-time office manager of the St. Mary's office, a move that I fully supported. To oversee the corporate practice, I hired a full-time independent business administrator named Tom Guard, a tall, amiable fellow whose daughter, living on the East Coast, needed a kidney transplant. A kind man, Tom would tell me about her, his hopes high that a kidney would become available, his fears great that he would not be able to afford it. Our conversations made me think about Elyse and Michael. When you hear of such consequential health issues, how can you not commiserate and think how fortunate your own children are? I thought about

Kevin Daley, too, and the many agonizing conversations I had with his parents. The day Tom announced that a donor kidney was a match for his daughter, I signed a check for fifty thousand dollars to help cover his expenses. It was a loan that would never be repaid, but a loan that I never regretted.

One day Tom asked me if I had been paying five thousand dollars every month to someone in Ireland. His question perplexed me. The only connection I had to Ireland was my brother-in-law, Jeanne's youngest brother, who had married a young Irish lass and settled in Ireland. After investigating, Tom discovered that Jeanne was sending them monthly payments! I was surprised but not angry. I always liked Jeanne's entire family—her parents, grandmother, six siblings, and aunts and uncles. I assumed those checks, which Jeanne put in front of me and I blindly signed, went to cover the mortgage payments on the practice. Jeanne did in fact use them to pay off two mortgages, but she also sent some of them to her brother. I never confronted her about those surreptitious payments. If she had asked me, I would have agreed to send the money to Ireland. I hoped the money helped them.

X

Over the years, disposable income enabled Jeanne and I to indulge in luxuries. I invested in cars, electronics, and art. Occasionally, in a rare moment of unity, we discussed the pros and cons of a purchase and jointly decided. One of the most memorable was the Disklavier, a digital player piano, purchased while we were in San Francisco for a neurosurgical conference.

During my walk from the Fairmont Hotel to the Moscone Convention Center and back, I passed a Steinway piano store. The pianos visible through the front window brought back images of my mother's Baldwin perched on the plush blue carpeting in the Lincolnwood living room. For years, I thought about buying a new piano. As the bechor, I felt that the Baldwin should have been bequeathed to me instead of Shelly, even though he studied the piano and I studied the violin. Now, I had another reason to invest in a piano: Elyse was taking lessons.

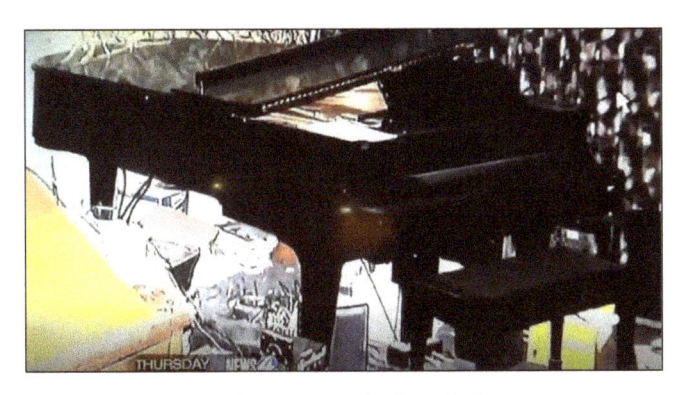

Baldwin replacement behind the parterre

One day on my return trek to the hotel, I stopped at the store. Gleaming Steinways surrounded me. Though they didn't have Baldwins, toward the back were some Yamaha electronic player pianos like those I periodically saw at hotels and restaurants. They played lovely music even without a pianist. I walked past a grouping of uprights with prices hovering around ten thousand dollars. I had no interest in owning an upright. Then, I noticed a baby grand and next to it a stately eleven-foot concert grand with a sale price of thirty-five thousand dollars. No way, I thought. That couldn't possibly be right. Usually those pianos cost over one hundred thousand dollars.

I asked the salesperson if the price was correct.

"Yes, sir," he said.

I couldn't pass up this deal. "I'd like to buy it, but first I want to bring my wife back to see it. In the meantime, I'll give you a check for a deposit." I pulled out my checkbook and wrote out the check right there. I handed it to him. "This is our contract. Don't sell this piano to anyone else."

The salesman agreed.

Jeanne and I returned that night. She had no qualms about investing in the piano and fully concurred that it was a bargain and would help Elyse. The salesman and owner greeted us.

"We made a terrible mistake, Dr. Bernstein," said the owner sheepishly. "The sales ticket was on the wrong piano. The baby grand costs thirty-five thousand. The concert grand costs one hundred twenty-five thousand. That's the one you can put CDs in, connect to your stereo, and print music."

I was not a happy buyer. I reminded him that I had given a deposit that served as an intent to buy. Finally, he agreed to sell for the discounted price if I agreed to pay for shipping, as well as the cost of all the accessories. Even with the extra fifteen thousand dollars, it was one of the best investments that I ever made. Elyse took piano lessons until middle school, when her attention turned to ballet. I programmed it to play my favorite piano concertos. When Jewish friends came to visit, we had Yiddish karaoke night. A guest would choose a song, such as "Belz, Mayn Shtetele Belz," listed on my computer. I then had the MIDI file loaded into the piano through Samantha, the vocal computer interface to almost everything in the home. "Samantha, play 'Belz, Mayn Shtetele Belz.'" The lyrics, previously copied to computer, displayed on the fifteen-foot screen through a ceiling projector. I manually scrolled down lines as necessary. Now, those are memories that never fade!

16

Groundbreaking

It was time to move to a larger home. My practice was continuing to grow and felt more stable without Greenberg. Jeanne and I hoped to have additional children, possibly five, and we wanted more space, as well as space for my parents, who frequently visited. My neurosurgeon's OCD mind cogitated numerous options and finally concluded the best was to design and build our dream home. Our real estate agent mentioned ten acres of mountainside land for sale—un-subdivided Pima County land without covenants, conditions, and restrictions. How ideal. We drove up a dirt switchback to a recessed pad that could not be viewed by curious eyes from below. The view south across the valley was astounding. Only one home had been built higher on the mountain. I instantly knew this was the property on which to build the palatial home I envisioned. A Chicago bank assisted with the financing. Before we even signed the mortgage papers, our first son and our parents' first grandson, Michael Ted Bernstein, entered the world. What joy! What blessings!

Our goal was to pay off the loan before building. For three years, we diligently made payments. At one point, I hired a helicopter and, accompanied by the general contractor and architect, flew over the property. Jeanne begged off. I remember how scary it was to hold the video camera and lean out the open door to film so that we could determine where to place the house, driveways, and pools. Shortly thereafter, we received numerous complaints from residents far below that "Bernstein is building a heliport on the mountain."

The view from Ventana

Just before construction began, Joshua David Bernstein was born. Another healthy baby, and a blessing. I still love the family photo taken on the property by our builder, John Campisano. Jeanne holds infant Josh. I stand next to her wearing the hard hat and holding Michael. Elyse stands in front of us, both hands on a gold shovel. My parents stand on the other side of me. A groundbreaking ceremony like that of Lincolnwood Jewish Congregation, complete with the same hard hat and gold shovel that Max Gordon bequeathed me.

Excitement swelled. Jeanne and I were on the verge of building a spectacular home, one that, G–d willing, would be filled with happy, joyous children and someday grandchildren. John also took videos that day on the mountain: Elyse and Michael jumping around, aware that something momentous was happening; my parents beaming; Jeanne and I hugging; Jeanne kissing me. I opened a bottle of kosher wine to make a shehecheyanu blessing, which is recited in addition to a regular blessing when doing something for the first time. Indeed, our family was embarking on an exciting new adventure.

I intended to make this home unique and elegant, just as my mother had done with our Lincolnwood home and now the Boca Raton, Florida, home in which she and my father lived. I suggested to Jeanne that we explore Europe in order to gather ideas, but she had no interest in such a trip. Although an art major, she didn't share my interest in design, and Josh was too young to travel. I made plans to inspect villas and grand hotels in Spain, Italy, and Israel. Jeanne arranged to take Elyse, Michael, and Josh to her family's summer home in Pentwater, Michigan.

During my overseas jaunt, I took hundreds of photos of Mediterranean architecture. My architects probably never expected me to be so active in their process, but I couldn't help myself. Every day, I dealt with the stresses of life and death. Designing the house was an antidote. Plans for the eight-thousand-square-foot house included a turret foyer, coffered cathedral ceilings, two-story clerestory windows, a second-story spa outside the master bedroom, and a bridge over one-third of the great room.

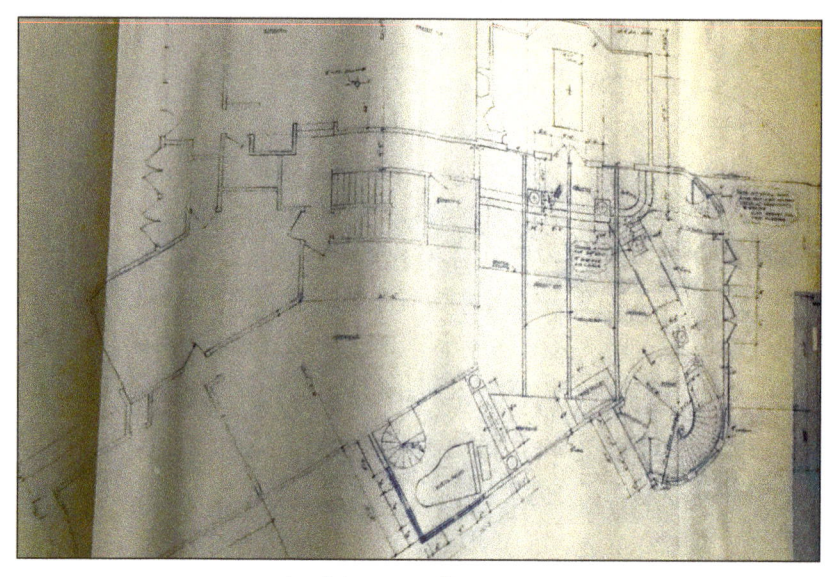

Architectural concept

The kids would have a downstairs dungeon completely carved out of the mountain, allowing any kind of torture to the walls they could imagine. The driveway would pass over a dry moat, which would fill during monsoons, in front of my castle archway. I was concerned about Jeanne and all three children driving up that road, so we transplanted stately saguaros along the edge. Better to get needled than tumble down the mountainside. An indoor/outdoor pool would have a grotto entrance, a waterfall, and a plexiglass negative edge. At night, underwater, you would be able to see a blur of Nogales lights, a feature engineered by the Japanese firm that had designed SeaWorld. As plans took shape and evolved, I became quite proficient at CAD/CAM software and even had some large-scale models constructed.

To excavate the dungeon and pool areas, John Campisano received authorization to blast, removing the caliche, a cemented mineral deposit indigenous to the Sonoran Desert. Kaboom! He unwittingly used too much dynamite. We returned from our annual New Year's trip to SeaWorld and Disneyland to yellow barrier tape cordoning off our land. Pima County claimed that we were no longer in compliance with hillside zoning, so they shut down the project. The owner of the home below had complained, and Pima dutifully sent out inspectors. I filed a lawsuit. My attorney at the time was Jeff Greenberg, who had recently joined the firm that had represented me favorably in the past.

Litigation dragged on for what seemed like forever. Every conference with the county attorneys or the complainant neighbor was excruciating, not to mention a waste of time. It would be a decade before I had a cordial coffee with John. By then, I understood the events and circumstances that I've encountered cannot be blamed on others. The Baal Shem Tov teaches that if someone hurts you, this hurt was meant to happen to you. Thus, why hold a grudge against a human being when that person is merely an emissary of Divine Providence?

When we realized construction would not readily resume, Jeanne and I decided to consider an interim home. She wanted to move to a gated Foothills community. We toured several houses for sale. I wasn't keen on the two-acre lots, but she didn't seem to mind. During winter break, Jeanne took Elyse, Michael, and Josh to Chicago; I remained in Tucson. My frustration with the land litigation grew, and I felt increasingly disgruntled. There were limits to my equanimity.

I returned to the subdivision Jeanne liked and discovered a remote lot on the highest ridge surrounded by desert. A six-thousand-square-foot custom spec home was scheduled to be built. After discussion with the builders about the many modifications I proposed, I purchased it. It was a temporary compromise: I would get to build my house in a community that was Jeanne's choice. It was only five miles from our current home and in the same school district. I thought Jeanne would be pleased, and she was. By the time she returned from Chicago, construction was underway.

It took another eight months for the home to be built. Instead of hardwood flooring, I imported Pietra stone from Italy and hired a stone mason to lay the oversize tiles. The space designated for a four-car garage became the home theater; beyond its sliding glass doors was a full basketball court.

Showtime   *Show's over*

A negative-edge pool with winding water slide was lushly landscaped below. I will never forget the garage. It had nine extra-wide stalls so that I could fully open the door of any car without dinging its neighbor. There was a hydraulic lift capable of raising a Suburban, as well as the smallest of my exotics. The custom floor was fitted with blue and white tiles, the center patterned into the Star of David. Banners of the various marques hung overhead. Each car had its own transmitter paired to a particular door receiver; when a car approached, the correct door opened spontaneously.

Another Showroom   *Enthusiasts gathering*

Over the years, I hosted many garage tours and theater programs. Jeanne did not argue with any of these upgrades. As long as she could decorate the master bedroom and bathroom, she seemed content. She chose white marble, which I disdained, though not overtly.

Finally, we were ready to move. We sold our house to a couple moving from a suburb outside of Boston. At the closing, they commented on the name Bernstein. "Our neighbor's last name is Bernstein," said the gentleman. "Nice couple. Shelly and Nancy Bernstein. They're both doctors. By chance do you know them?"

$$\mathcal{X}$$

Jeanne was still managing my St. Mary's office full-time but now wanted something more fulfilling. I suggested she might want to pursue a master's degree in art. I still had her portfolio and thought her quite talented. She was not enthused with the idea and expressed an interest in returning to school to obtain a degree in nursing. Her plan was to enroll at Pima Community College and become a registered nurse. I suggested she attend the University of Arizona, which has an outstanding nursing program, but no, she preferred the community college. Nothing is wrong with a community college except that I thought she would have no problem matriculating at a top academic program.

RN

"When do you graduate?" I asked Jeanne one day. I wanted to make sure I added the date to my calendar. I kept fastidious track of family events, including all of Elyse's, Michael's, and Josh's activities, and tried to attend as many as possible. While automobiles, attorneys, and architects required attention, my priority was and always has been family.

"I already did," she said. I was shocked. She had graduated at the top of her class, which didn't surprise me, but she'd never told me about the graduation ceremony. This purposeful omission set a very unfortunate pattern.

Jeanne asked me to help her find a part-time job as a surgical nurse. Josh would be starting kindergarten soon, Elyse had just started high school, and Michael was in fifth grade. Part-time sounded reasonable to me. One of my friends in gastroenterology owned a surgery center and needed a nurse. Jeanne started working for him but developed a disdain for the specialty. I empathized with her. During residency, I did not enjoy that rotation with its colonoscopies and proctoscopies. This time, I found her a job with a plastic surgeon, a young fellow. Jeanne seemed quite content with the work, which in turn pleased me.

As always, I had plenty to keep me busy. Driving between three offices afforded me time to think about family, patients, projects, cars, and sports. I was returning to Tucson from my Sierra Vista office when my digital pager scrolled a message to phone the office; my patient from last night had a blood clot and was in extremis. I had a cell phone, but towers had not yet been constructed in that part of the desert, which meant I needed to get to a pay phone. I had a new Ferrari and the road had just been paved, so I hit it. The engine roared as I flew toward the next exit, and the speedometer continued to climb: 110, 120, 130, 140, 150. That's when I saw the gumball in back of me flashing. Of all times, I thought, as I decelerated and pulled over to the shoulder. I readied my driver's license, registration, and insurance.

This was Cochise County. A man resembling Broderick Crawford, the star of *Highway Patrol*, not Johnny Bromfield, the star of the TV series *The Sheriff of Cochise County*, approached the car. Both shows were my '50s favorites. "You know," he said, leaning over to speak to me through the window, "you exceeded my radar, but the spy in the sky clocked you at over two miles per minute."

I handed over my license, registration, and insurance.

After looking through it, he said, "You know, if you're thirty-five miles over the speed limit, we confiscate your car."

"I'm a neurosurgeon, sir," I said. "My patient at Northwest Hospital is dying. I just received a page. Can I use your radio?"

"No," he said, and proceeded to write out a ticket. Right then, another page came through. *Dr. Bernstein, please call us immediately. Your patient is dying.*" I handed the pager to the sheriff. He took a look at it, stopped writing, and handed me my documents, then issued a warning.

"You know, Dr. Bernstein, if you're going fast on this two-lane road and a rabbit or deer jumps out in front of your car, you're going to end up in the emergency room or the county morgue. Now get to your pay phone. But take it easy."

So that's what I did. The patient died, which sadly, was not unexpected. My secretary told me that the sheriff called to confirm my story.

$$\text{)(}$$

But there were many more patients, not all human, and surgeries came in all forms. One day a veterinarian from the Reid Park Zoo called me. Haley, the zoo's prize baboon, had contracted valley fever, not uncommon among the zoo population. Her condition, however, did not improve as it normally would when an animal is given the appropriate medications. A CT scan showed a cerebral abscess. The vet wondered if I would be able to help in any way. Upon reviewing the entire case and examining poor Haley, who was quite forlorn and ill, I felt that craniotomy surgery was indicated to try and evacuate the abscess.

I brought my entire team to the zoo, including anesthesiologist Bob Osborne and my personal scrub nurse. We set up in the examining area, sterilized instruments, and proceeded with surgery. The results were excellent. Within a few days, Haley was scampering in her cage, where many children were thrilled to see her pink bottom as she swung from tree to tree.

Post-op success

The zoo director was quite happy and invited my entire family on a very private tour of the zoo. We boarded several trams and proceeded to various exhibits where Elyse, Michael, and Josh hand-fed the giraffes and the elephants. As we proceeded to the lion exhibit, I mentioned to Jeanne that perhaps she would like to hand-feed the lion. With a chuckle, she demured.

17

My Mother: The Descent

Teacher featured for May '84

by Alan Buchbinder

Mrs. Robin Bernstein, a history and psychology teacher, has been a credit to Mather since 1961. She has been teaching in the Chicago Public School system for over 20 years. She began her teaching career at Wells High School and stayed there for a term of 7 years. After that time she began her teaching career at Mather and has stayed here for almost 23 years.

Mrs. Robin Bernstein (Photo by Frank Galliano).

She is a product of the Chicago Public Schools. She attended Marshall High School and graduated at the top of her class. She received her Bachelor's degree in history from Roosevelt University. After that she attended and received her Master's Degree from the University of Chicago and Northeastern Illinois University. Both these degrees were obtained in the field of social studies. Also, she has a certificate from the Institute of Psychoanalysis.

When asked about her term at Mather she replied, "I've had a love affair with Mather for over 20 years." During her illustrious period she has taught Modern World History, United States History, and some courses in Economics. During the last ten years she has been the Chairperson of the Social Studies department.

When asked about her teaching career, she proudly replied, "I like to feel that I have contributed something to teaching. I, in turn, have been deeply rewarded in my own personal growth. I have seen many changes especially in the ethnic makeup of Mather but the academic ratings have remained very high. I think Mather has the most wonderful students and faculty."

Her hobbies include traveling with her husband Maurice to many parts of the world. They have traveled to Thailand, Africa, Singapore, Egypt, Japan, Israel, and many other places around the world. "My greatest thrill," she says, "is in visiting places that we read about in our school textbooks, such as the Cairo museums." Her other hobbies include gardening, reading, and visiting various museums around the world.

The Bernsteins have three sons who are 36, 33, and 24. The oldest Ronald is a neurosurgeon in Chicago at the University of Illinois and Cook County hospitals. The second son Shelly is a research pediatrician in Boston at the Harvard Medical Center. Their youngest son Dale is in his second year of law school at Coral Gables. Mrs. Bernstein's husband Maurice is a self-employed accountant and they have a beautiful home in Lincolnwood. Also, the Bernsteins have a one year old grand-daughter.

As a teacher, Mrs. Bernstein finds it tremendously gratifying to see former students. When asked about this she replied, "It's extremely satisfying to have students return and tell me the wonderful things they are doing and how happy they are. I have found working with these students challenging, rewarding, and stimulating." With this in mind, it is easy to understand her tremendous love affair with teaching at Mather.

I was at work in Tucson when the call came in from my dad. "Your mother fell and had emergency hip surgery. She's in intensive care," he said, worry and dismay evident in his voice.

My heart plummeted. My parents were visiting Shelly and Nancy, who lived in the Boston area. Even before I hung up, my mind started racing: When was the soonest flight out of Tucson? What would I need to cancel? Where would I stay? Shelly and I were not on the warmest of terms, so it would be better to book a hotel. I landed in Boston that evening and checked into the Copley Plaza Hotel on Massachusetts Avenue, not far from Massachusetts General Hospital, where Shelly was on staff in the department of pediatrics.

I went straight to the ICU, wielding my doctor credentials to enter after normal family hours. I was expecting my mother to be drowsy, but she had not yet regained consciousness following surgery. Alarm gnawed at me. I had assisted Richie Silver and other Tucson orthopods in surgeries and was quite familiar with hip procedures, which required inserting pins and plates, usually fairly simple, allowing patients to get up and begin moving shortly afterward. But complications can arise, including blood clots leading to a heart attack or stroke.

The next day, I met with Shelly, Nancy, and my father at the hospital. Mother remained unconscious. There was the possibility of some post-traumatic brain injury, but more likely, I suspected that she'd had an intraoperative stroke.

"I think we should get a second opinion from a neurologist and order a CT scan," I said to Shelly in the hallway, out of earshot of my father so as not to alarm him.

"I don't think it's necessary," Shelly said, looking like he wasn't going to change his mind. I didn't want to start an argument, so I acquiesced.

My mother remained comatose for several more days. During that terribly tense time, I suggested more than once to Shelly that he order a CT scan. But my brother remained adamant. My frustration festered. I was a board-certified neurosurgeon; I treated adults, some of whom had had strokes. Shelly was a board-certified pediatrician; he treated two-year-olds. Certainly, he could find a neurologist and easily request a CT scan. If my mother had been in Tucson or at home in Florida, we would have had the results of a scan by now. *Just get the test done!* I wanted to scream, but I didn't because the outburst would only further stress my father.

I remained at the hospital most of the following week. Whenever Shelly and I were at the hospital together, the tension in the room skyrocketed. It was extremely uncomfortable interacting with him at any level. Dale, who was around thirty years old, had not flown up from Florida, where he lived. He and I were on good terms at that point, though I don't recall why he wasn't present. When my mother finally awoke, she exhibited signs and symptoms of a stroke. Shelly still refused to order a CT scan. I remained at the hospital most of the following week. The stay proved agonizing. Part of me wanted to speak out, insist that we take the appropriate measures (ones that any neurologist would take!) to gain insight into what had happened to Mother. Yet, I was on Shelly's turf. He was the caregiver in charge. I chose not to intercede. I learned, though not from Shelly, that Mother had tumbled down his basement stairs. Before that fall and subsequent emergency surgery, she'd had no noticeable signs of dementia. I don't blame Shelly for her fall. I do blame him, however, for his rigid thinking, pomposity, and refusal to listen to me and to accept that I had expertise in something he did not. At least he made arrangements for rehab; I wouldn't leave until he promised to do so. Needless to say, it was a soulful return to Tucson.

My mother descended into a world of foggy solitude. It was devastating to watch the cruel, declining mental status steal her independence and identity. My mother was exiled to her own state of galut (diaspora). She had been a distinguished history department chairman at a prestigious Chicago high school, revered by students and faculty. She traveled the world to collect *objets d'art*, played the piano, enjoyed swimming, and constantly read. Jews have long been identified as "People of the Book," and true to her heritage, my mother lived within the realm of books. While teaching, she started acquiring leather-bound first editions of books that I came to love. I remember her reading aloud to me as I sat close, my arm around her shoulder. How many times did we read the *Arabian Nights' Entertainments*? Sinbad, Aladdin, and my favorite, Ali Baba. The strange words "Open, O Simsim!"

opened my mind to adventures in reading. I'm still embarrassed and regretful that I surrendered one of my mother's prized first editions.

It happened when Miss Teitlebaum, a high school teacher at Mather and one of my mother's best friends, came for a visit. Prior to Mather, she'd taught at Graeme Stewart Elementary School and was my third-grade teacher. I had a crush on her. The day she visited our new house in Lincolnwood, I escorted her down to the den. Her attention immediately was drawn to the built-in bookcases featuring my mother's personal library. Miss Teitlebaum scrutinized the spines with great interest and withdrew the *Rubáiyát of Omar Khayyám*. With its elegant illuminations, it was one of my favorites. In my naïveté, I suggested she take it home. I had meant as a loan to read but neglected to mention that detail. Alas, the treasured book never returned. I kept thinking to myself that Mother would never notice the tome missing from the crowded bookshelf. Much later, I realized that she probably knew, but she never said a word about it, nor would she have.

Inevitably, the time came when my father could no longer care for his wife of more than fifty years, even with assistance. He chose to move her to a full-time nursing facility in Boynton Beach, just north of Boca. I flew to Florida to be with my father the day of the transfer, a day that I never could have envisioned happening. The humidity felt particularly heavy and oppressive, even for Florida. Neither Dale nor Shelly joined us. She had been presumptively diagnosed with terminal Alzheimer's with progressive signs of insidious dementia over the years. I knew that my mother demonstrated all the signs and symptoms of progressive hydrocephalus. The only way to determine Alzheimer's, however, was by doing a biopsy. To this day, I believe she was misdiagnosed.

Several years later, my father called just after midnight on January 10, 1998. Only hours before, I had finished celebrating my fiftieth birthday in Tucson. It's strange; I really don't remember how, with whom, or where the celebration occurred. The lines of memory blur. My mother Z"L (honorific for the dead) had passed, he said. Knowing she was declining and anticipating the ultimate outcome seemed irrelevant. The shock and grief that death forces are poignant and painful. She was gone. Yet, we all felt it was a blessing.

We all went to Florida for the funeral—Jeanne, Elyse, Michael, Josh, my brothers, my cousins, my Auntie Ettie. So many people came to pay their last respects to Robin Bernstein. The funeral and burial followed strict Orthodox ritual and law. My father attended to every detail. I don't remember talking to either brother; in fact, I don't even remember much of the ceremony except that it felt funereal. Mother was buried in the Gan Leah (Garden of Leah) Orthodox section of North Lauderdale Star of David Cemetery.

Each year thereafter, I visited the cemetery with my father or Auntie Ettie, who lived in Boca at the time. I placed a small stone at the grave site, a Jewish tradition that honors the deceased and signifies a visitor's presence. Most importantly, the placement of the stone serves as an invitation of sorts for a spark of the departed to descend and rest upon the tombstone for the duration of the visit. That thought comforted me during those mournful visits.

Since my mother's passing, I have worked hard at jettisoning ugly thoughts of anger, blame, and frustration. They've never fully dissipated. After the funeral, my father mailed me my mother's CT scan, performed at my encouragement months before, along with a letter apologizing for not considering my medical expertise. The scan demonstrated large ventricles suggestive of hydrocephalus and consistent with her pathognomonic signs and symptoms. Who better to make the diagnosis than a board-certified neurosurgeon? I keep both the scan and letter with my recovered documents.

I feel guilty that I didn't try harder to encourage my brother to proceed with the VP shunt insertion for presumptive diagnosis of hydrocephalus. I had done hundreds of such procedures. Yet my brother had readily dismissed my expertise and knowledge. He insisted my mother suffered from Alzheimer's. My silence is a regret that has languished all these years, becoming especially intense during Yizkor and Yahrzeit. As a doctor, I did not try to convince a patient or family to proceed with surgery; I explained alternatives, risks, possible complications, and so on. Hydrocephalus is potentially treatable, but Shelly vociferously refuted this fact to my father, and it was easier for Dad to believe Shelly than proceed with surgery, which had always unnerved him, even when I was in high school and needed it to save my life.

For sixty years, I also ruminated about permanently loaning Mother's revered copy of *Rubáiyát of Omar Khayyám*. How it bothered me. In an attempt to assuage the guilt, I searched online and found a similar volume. The replacement cost several months of Social Security income. It sits next to the framed portraits of my parents on my desk. To restore the book posthumously is not the same as being able to share it with my mother. And yet, the slight leather-bound volume is nostalgia, and sometimes nostalgia, be it a book or an apologetic letter, is a salve for the wounded heart.

18

The Beast in the Desert

JaguarSport, a division of Jaguar, intended to manufacture the world's fastest super car. For handling, design, and top speed of two hundred twenty miles per hour, hence their moniker "220," it would be the most sophisticated machine on the road. Only fifty vehicles sporting four-wheel steer, four-wheel drive, and scissor doors were scheduled for production. I salivated over preproduction specs and requested my application form, which now sits atop my Marital Dissolution Agreement. Even with the challenging price tag, I was anxious to sign on the dotted line.

"I'm going to buy a new Jaguar," I nervously asserted to Jeanne. I already had several classic XKEs and just returned from chairing a meeting of the Jaguar Club of Southern

Arizona—arguably the oldest Jaguar club in North America. Returning World War II yanks brought their adorated British cars to Fort Huachuca, Arizona, just south of Tucson, and founded their enthusiast association. Jeanne had never been receptive to the car club and even eschewed annual affairs especially geared to the wives: epicurean dinners with spectacular fashion shows. I intended to trade in the Maserati and two Ferraris, but I still needed a $250,000 deposit.

"How much does this car cost?"

"A million dollars," I replied.

Jeanne looked at me skeptically. We briefly debated my need for such a car but couldn't find any common ground. Was she thinking that this would affect her purchase power at the malls? I bit my lip and refrained from asking.

"You buy this car and I'm gone," she said, walking out of the room.

I went into my office, slumped into my judge's chair, crumpled the application envelope—I would not dare defile the actual contract—and aimed it at the wastebasket. It rebounded off the rim and landed at the toe of my Italian loafer.

The XJ220 beckoned to me, just as my first Jag back in high school had, except this time amplified by a power of several hundred. While the original twelve-cylinder exotic never made production, Jaguar arranged for a few cars to tour the United States as The Fast Masters promotion, nicknamed the Crash Masters because some of those race drivers probably should have been in wheelchairs or ended up in them after the race. Much to my delight, Tucson made the tour. I gathered five-year-old Michael and headed over to Beaudry Motors, where it was showcased. I knew that Jaguar had greatly deviated from the original specs. A twin-turbocharged V-6 engine replaced the V-12 but still produced well over 500 HP; all-wheel drive and steer were now conventional systems, and on and on. These alterations irritated the original investors, who sued Jaguar and lost; the British judge sided with the company, citing that the car attained the equivalent promised speed, the only contractual specification. What difference did it make if rumored features were discarded? As I nestled into the exquisitely bolstered throne of soft Connolly hides and gripped the wheel, I forgave Jaguar.

The XJ220 couldn't be driven on public roads in the United States. Although the car met EPA standards and crash-test requirements, it failed homologation, the certification requirements needed to drive an imported vehicle on U.S. roads. I would not be able to drive my car. The Jaguar would be relegated to a silent life, not uttering one roar, not even a feline purr. These regulations frustrated many an exotic car owner, including Bill Gates. When he drove his Porsche 959 outside his compound, he was stopped by the local police, and his car, which was in violation of homologation, was confiscated. After he threatened to move Microsoft to Canada, the federal government lifted the certification restriction. Owners of limited-edition foreign cars could now drive their vehicles on public roads.

I met Bill years earlier when he came to Tucson to promote Microsoft's nascent operating system. I remember him prancing back and forth on stage, a wireless microphone extending from an oversized headpiece, describing "kilobytes of memory, megabytes of memory, and pretty soon, gigabytes of memory." He pronounced "gigabytes" with a hard *g*. Afterward, I took him aside and said, "You know, Bill, it's 'gigabytes' with a soft *g* because the prefix is Greek, not Latin." He chuckled and we became friends.

Shortly after the Show and Display Law was enacted, Bill called to tell me that it was now legal to bring my car into the United States. I exulted.

Terry Larson, a world-renowned Jaguar enthusiast with an

expansive Mesa, Arizona, garage showroom and workshop arranged for an XJ220 to be transported over to Canada, then down to Mesa under bond so that I could test-drive it. It was one of the last nineteen untitled cars stored in England. The enthusiasm for exotic cars had faded as the market plummeted.

Brimming with anticipation, I met Terry in his garage, built below street level with a steep ramped driveway. I lowered myself into the supple sand leather seat. Terry gave me a quick tour of the binnacle and panoply of gauges and gewgaws.

"Take it for a spin," he said, pointing up the driveway.

I hit the gas, and VAROOM, no turbo lag! I was too scared to glance at the actual speed. All I could see was the fast-approaching single-lane dirt road, a row of giant saguaros, and desert beyond. As the car and I became airborne, all I could think about was avoiding those cacti. The Jag landed, all four tires on the roadway. This car was a beast.

I joined a consortium of twenty North American buyers who vowed that the car would be driven and enjoyed rather than stored as an investment. Jaguar offered the car in five flavors. My dream car was burgundy. The company called it Monza red, but it was a deep, rich burgundy. Only the Sultan of Brunei, who owned five or six of these Jaguars, had his painted special custom colors. I guess you can do that if you're a sultan.

True to her word, Jeanne subsequently filed for divorce. The unraveling had already begun.

My car needed to be returned to Merrie Olde England to comply with emission standards and legal red tape. A year later, I was still waiting, my patience dwindling. To assuage my impatience, I received a video of the car being built at the different factory stations in Bloxham. Princess Di even made a guest appearance on the tape. Jaguar, now owned by Ford but about to be purchased by India's Tata Motors, had shipped the car to a New Jersey Independent Commercial Importer to obtain EPA credentials. They were responsible for replacing the catalytic converters, charcoal canister, and other items to comply with emission standards. No one had any idea how long it would remain there. After another interminable period to palliate me, Jaguar sent a two-foot burgundy model of my car with moving parts. I loved it and displayed it for years in my theater. Sadly, it became a 3 Gorillas casualty.

My XJ220 was shipped by an exclusive enclosed transport service to my home. I had anticipated this day since Michael, then five, accompanied me to Beaudry and sat in the race-prepared prototype. Michael was now almost fourteen. A couple more years, and he would be driving. I arranged to meet the driver at the gatehouse. The two-tier carrier couldn't fit through the gated entrance and parked along the shoulder of the main road. The driver jumped out of the cab, pointing to my car on the top deck; it was shiny, burgundy, and mine. Behind and below were Lambos and Ferraris. He suggested that I flip up the carrier curtains and scale the side girders, squeeze into the car for off-loading.

"Right," I sarcastically answered. The drive down the steep ramp looked harrowing. I suggested that while in the cockpit, he should continue to my house. Our caravan headed out, with me leading in a Ferrari. Halfway there, I looked in the rearview mirror. The Jag had come to a complete stop right in the middle of the winding roadway. I pulled over. The driver got out and headed toward my car.

"Ran out of gas," he snarled.

What could I do but shake my head, go home, and fetch a gallon gas can that happened to be full. With the thirsty bladder only minimally satiated, the car made it safely into my driveway. I paid the driver an appropriate tip and parked in the hallowed space in my garage under the green and red JagSport banner. I dubbed it The Beast; it was the car of a materialistic lifetime.

Excitement grabbed hold of me. It was just past dusk, but I couldn't wait any longer to drive it. I didn't want to take my first spin in absolute darkness. A short drive to the nearest gas station would have to suffice, so I pulled up to the pump and walked around to undo the cap. With its race car machining, it's a work of art—a very expensive museum piece. I carefully placed it on top of the pump and started to fill the car. A gaggle of teenagers pulled up opposite me.

"Hey, cool, you got the new Mustang," one of them cackled. In a friendly way, I set them straight.

Back at home, I parked The Beast. As I walked around the car, thinking of how I would drive it to work in the morning, I noticed a dark hole on the passenger side. Panic surged through me. Then I realized that I left the gas cap on the pump! I raced back to the station. Thank goodness it was still there. I defibrillated and returned home.

At that very moment, all was right with the world!

But not for long.

)(

I drove The Beast to Costco, to the symphony, to the hospital. And I let other Jag lovers drive it if they wanted or dared, or I took them for a ride if they were reluctant or too nervous. One member of the Tucson Jaguar club was Dolores Zimmerman (no relation to Rabbi). She and her husband, Chuck, were great friends and owned the Hummer franchise in Phoenix, but her claim to fame included being a NASCAR race driver. At a Saturday meeting, I handed her the keys. I didn't want to ride with her, as memories of my accident resurfaced.

"Now, take it easy," I said, laughing.

She peeled out of the Tucson parking lot at what sounded to be one hundred twenty miles per hour. I said a special prayer, commonly referred to as *Tefilat Haderech*, for a safe and uneventful trip.

Ten minutes later, she and the car returned unscathed.

"How was Phoenix?" I asked.

"That was hot," she said, looking starstruck.

Indeed, some of my rides were scorching hot, and not just from the desert sun beating down on the glass roof. I owned the car about three weeks when I went to pick up Michael from baseball practice. We weren't far from home when Michael noticed sparks behind the car. I hoped the exhaust system hadn't dropped. My older Jaguars had pulled that stunt many times; they had exhaust pipes anchored to the bottom of the car with rubber doughnuts that slowly disintegrated in desert heat. If the exhaust dragged on the roadway, sparks would fly. Michael looked over his shoulder.

"Dad, your car's on fire!"

Monstrous orange flames licked the glass partition that separated the cockpit from the mid-engine compartment.

"The car's going to explode!" screamed Michael.

I stopped the car and yelled for him to get out, but he couldn't move. He was petrified. I leapt out, raced around to his door, and literally dragged him out. Then, I grabbed the fire extinguisher from the mount on the passenger floor near the center console. Though my older Jaguars were notorious for electrical cables that would smoke as they shorted out—no flames—that accoutrement was not included. Somehow, I opened the latch, aimed the fire extinguisher, and pulled the trigger. Within seconds, dense white powder suffocated the fire. I stepped back, managed my tachycardia, then calmed Michael, repeatedly reassuring him that the car wasn't going to explode. But would it limp home? This was not a movie where everyone dives for cover as the car bursts into a fireball. I peered inside the cockpit. A horrible, smoky stench greeted me. The leather seats and the dash, roof, floor, console, and windows all were covered with white residue. Some engine-compartment high-performance plumbing and cables appeared charred. Michael walked back to the house. An hour later, The Beast and I limped into the garage.

I called Dan Warrener of RM Classic Cars in Blenheim, Ontario, Canada, then Terry Larsen in Mesa, Arizona. They reportedly shipped the singed trophy back to England. The Jaguar repair world isn't fueled by twin turbo engines; it moves at the pace of a Schwinn bicycle. Twelve months later, the XJ220 made it back to my garage. Except for the residual traces of white powder, the car looked beautiful. It still was fast and furious. I installed a new halon fire extinguisher containing a liquid chemical solution that rapidly dissipates, leaving no residue, called each of the other owners, and sent out email "fire drill" instructions. One cohort actually did report a similar fire.

A month later, what happened? Another fire! At least this time, I didn't fear for my life and instead calmly put out the fire. "That's it," I told the voice at the other end of RM Classic Cars, "take the car back. I'm buying a Ferrari." I was angry and disappointed. The Beast was going to sulk back to England, but this time Terry found a special Jaguar mechanic who had taken care of two Phoenix-area 220s. He was only ninety miles away. At least I would have visitation rights.

Those two fires burned a question into me: what had caused them? Being a scientist at heart, I had to know what had gone wrong. After considerable research, my quandary was resolved. The original catalytic converters had been replaced with aftermarket products upon entry into the United States. The glowing cherry-red twin turbos produced temperatures over a thousand degrees Fahrenheit. Platinum, as the catalyst, can't withstand such extreme heat, but the original converters, with palladium and strontium, could. A twenty-thousand-dollar cost-saving measure resulted in repairs costing hundreds of thousands of dollars. Even though the government gave me a waiver to drive without converters, my car still passed emissions testing each year. Subsequently, the correct ones were remanufactured.

A short time later, I picked up Josh from school for a Bruegger's bagel brunch banquet. I parked in the far end of the parking lot, as far away from other cars as possible—a concrete planter next to me on one side and an expanse of empty space to the other. We were halfway through kibbitz and schmear when Josh said, "Dad, that car is getting awfully close to your car."

I looked. The car was not only close, it was in my car! We raced out the door. By the time we got outside, the little old lady had pulled her car out of the passenger side of my now humbled car. The rear fender and side were visibly dented, and I could only imagine the damage to the suspension and engine. This was a horror.

I erupted. "This is a million-dollar car! I just got this car back!"

I'm crying. Josh is crying. She's crying and, through tears, saying, "Now don't you worry. I have insurance. My insurance will pay for this."

She had a $100,000 insurance policy. I settled for her limits, check in hand, rather than enter another lawsuit, and made up the difference of $25,000.

The Jag was transported to a body shop that worked on some of my other exotics. After two engine fires, one learns to explicitly follow the manual: before driving, let the engine warm up. I recited the manual to the owner of the shop, but he didn't follow these directions and drove short distances without letting the engine warm up. Flames shot up, frying hoses and wires. It was a disaster. He didn't know how to open the latch, so he couldn't put out the fire until it was too late. He was lucky the car didn't explode.

By then, I had lawsuits strung up on a clothesline, but back to the attorneys we went and litigated for a couple of years. I drove the car from my driveway to a nearby trailer for transport to Jeff's Resurrections in Texas. Jeff had auspiciously completed service on a friend's 220, sent for parts from the new U.K. Distributor (DonLawRacing), and was to ship it to the United Kingdom when completed. That was in 2011. It remains in England, awaiting our reunion.

19

The Unraveling

I find it difficult to put my finger on the exact point where my life began to unravel. Even hindsight hasn't definitively marked the day, month, or year. While embroiled in the downward spiral of events, I was too consumed dealing with intricate demands to contemplate their possible causes. Only later did I wonder how things might have been different. If I had responded differently here or there, would my wife and I still be experiencing the joie de vivre we had early in our marriage? Would my children still celebrate holidays and simchas with me? Would a corrupt moving company have swindled me? As the Lubavitcher Rebbe of righteous memory said, "There is no journey forward without first a step backward."[2] Or, as in my case, many steps.

Life noticeably shifted directions the day the front doorbell chimed and I happened to be the only one home. When I opened the door, a stranger thrust an envelope at me. My Pavlovian response was to accept it.

"You've been served," the fellow said, turning on his heels and quickly walking away.

Jeanne had filed for divorce. I had absolutely no forewarning. She'd never said a word, and I had missed every clue. For nearly twenty years, I assumed that I was a good husband and father, providing well beyond our needs. I welcomed her as manager of one of my offices and secretly admired her paying off office mortgages. I encouraged and paid for her nursing degree. She could buy almost anything that she wanted, go anywhere she desired. For her birthday, I gave her a ruby and diamond necklace with matching ring, which I helped a jeweler design. I liked being able to do that. Yet, had I ever seen her wear it? Only with encouragement on special occasions. I knew she was disgruntled with my becoming more observant. She never fully embraced Jewish customs, though she did keep kosher at home. After Josh was born, we didn't seem to talk as much. I'd come home, and she would be in a different part of the house. Maybe I had subconsciously ignored her clues of dissatisfaction or pushed them out of sight. I didn't want to deal with discord. We had so many blessings, so many reasons to be joyous.

Jeanne's mood began to change after she started working for the plastic surgeon. That's when the nips and tucks started. A little plastic surgery here, a little there. I didn't say much. The few times I gently suggested the procedures weren't

---

2   From the wisdom of the Lubavitcher Rebbe, of righteous memory; words and condensation by Rabbi Tzvi Freeman, *Wisdom to Heal the Earth*: Meditations and Teachings of the Rebbe, Rabbi Menachem M. Schneerson, Published by Ezra Press and Chabad.org; 11/2/2018

necessary, Jeanne contended that they were an employee perk. My wife was very attractive. She did not need cosmetic surgery. Unfortunately, one of the side effects of too much plastic surgery is acne. When Jeanne's face broke out, she began using heavier makeup, which bothered me, though I remained reticent.

Jeanne became increasingly vocal. No longer was she the demure woman who I had married. At first, I ascribed this seemingly new confidence to her nursing career. I didn't begrudge her becoming more outspoken or self-assured. When she insisted on white marble in the bathroom, I acquiesced. When she wanted a new car, I bought her the newly redesigned Jaguar S-Type sedan in jade green. It was close to black, her preference. I had a black Ferrari, however, and I refused to have two cars the same color. Her response: I hate the green Jag and won't drive it. So I bought her a black Jaguar, which she consented to driving but later traded in for a beige model. Over time, she went from being outspoken to overtly hostile. When irritated, even by small annoyances, she yelled at me, the kids, the dogs. Her behavior grew more and more erratic. Something wasn't right.

I remained baffled until I remembered seeing a bottle of Accutane on the counter in the master bath. Jeanne used it to treat her acne. I researched Accutane's side effects. Personality change was one; irreversible psychosis was another. I called a psychiatrist friend of mine, John Clymer, who confirmed that yes, Jeanne's belligerence could be a result of extended use of Accutane. Under some pretense, I convinced her to see Clymer, and after a lengthy interview and evaluation, he recommmended admission to the hospital, but she refused. Soon after, she filed for divorce.

Devastated and panicked, I hired an attorney. I didn't want to lose my family. I needed to pay a lawyer—and a good lawyer at that. Over the years, I have retained the services of more than thirty lawyers for various reasons, funded who knows how many of their kids' college educations and family vacations. I even funded a new office building for one attorney after our work concluded. Shakespeare was right when he wrote, "The first thing we do, let's kill all the lawyers."[3]

Jeanne and I agreed through our respective attorneys to pursue counseling while continuing to live together. She chose Dr. Sydney Arkowitz, a highly credentialed and well-regarded psychologist who I soon discovered was an observant Jew and almost always aligned with me. Frustrated and feeling betrayed, Jeanne let it be known that she was being maligned. More than once, she stormed out of the session and deliberately remained reclusive for days.

I made a sincere effort to diffuse the tension between us. I could tell that Elyse, now sixteen, was upset, but my daughter only confided in her mother. I was never privy to their conversations so I couldn't run interference and squelch any fabrications. The best I could do was spend more time with the family. I attended as many of Elyse's, Michael's, and Josh's activities as possible, made sure to schedule time for skiing in Telluride and trips to Disneyland and San Diego, and even went to Pentwater, Michigan, for the summer family reunion.

To lighten my workload, I bought a hospital. The purchase was precipitated, to some extent, by Richie Silver's forced decision to stop practicing medicine. He was admitting many poorly insured patients for instrumentation procedures that required St. Mary's to purchase hardware; they were not able to recoup that cost. Sister St. Joan, the disgruntled hospital administrator, summoned him to a meeting with her attorneys. I attended, though I was not in the line of fire of the sister's reprimands. Richie felt pressured to move on for legal reasons and took a very lucrative disability retirement. He returned to

---

3   Henry V1; Part II, Act IV, Scene II, Line 73 –m stated by Dick the Butcher; published in the First Folio of 1623

school, earned an MBA, and continued as an entrepreneur, as well as a consultant to medical companies.

Richie and I discussed purchasing vacant land on the northwest side of Tucson to build a hospital. In the midst of those discussions, an opportunity arose to purchase Tucson General Hospital from the group of osteopaths who owned it and were going bankrupt. The option was far more financially feasible. Richie structured the purchase so that we split ownership fifty-fifty. I came up with the requisite two million dollars, some in cash, most in personal loan notes. Richie projected that when we sold the hospital, we each would net about six million dollars.

Our professional peers and certainly other hospital administrators didn't look kindly on the new ownership. At Northwest, I was no longer the favored doctor; they even removed my hanging portrait as board member from the hallway. The hospital, which we dubbed Tucson Millennium Hospital but which never shed its original moniker, was competition. Their hospitals were losing money; ours was not, thanks to Richie's wise decision to eliminate middle management and my negotiating discounted hardware for surgical procedures. In addition, we incorporated the Spinal Institute of Tucson (SIT) within that hospital complex. We planned to tear down the forty-year-old hospital complex and build upscale homes on the prized Foothills property. It remained a goal until we discovered that demolishing old structures with hazardous asbestos was prohibitively expensive. Richie assured me that we would still make a profit when we sold the hospital.

Owning Tucson General Hospital allowed me to slow down my practice and spend more time with family. I limited surgeries to Monday, Tuesday, and Wednesday. This amended schedule meant that I could be home for the weekends. I was studying Chassidut and becoming more observant. I kept strictly kosher and even hired a kosher chef for the hospital. I could leave home, drive down the hill, and have a kosher omelet waiting for me in the hospital's kosher kitchen. Now shomer Shabbat, I rented an apartment near the synagogue so that I could walk to weekly and holiday services, often with the children. Jeanne had stopped attending services when I joined Young Israel, the Chabad congregation.

Then came another backward step, one that almost toppled me. A colleague came up to me while I was sitting in the doctor's lounge at Tucson General Hospital. He pointed at the side of my head.

"That spot doesn't look good, Ron," he said. "You better get it biopsied." He suggested that I come to his office for the procedure. The biopsy left a small scar.

"A patch of skin cancer, like so many people get. Probably from years of sun exposure during Florida vacations," I told Jeanne and the kids. I also mentioned the cancer to Dale, not seeking sympathy but as a matter of fact. Coppertone hadn't protected us during all those family trips to Florida.

The tissue sample, sent to a reliable lab at Tucson Medical Center, was ominously described as a highly invasive, squamous cell carcinoma. The divorce decree overwhelmed me; the cancer diagnosis devastated me.

I proceeded with definitive surgery. The doctor was certain that after a wide resection, the margins were clear. When I came home from the outpatient surgery donning a bulky head bandage, I minimized the diagnosis and assured everyone that I was going to be fine. I didn't want anyone worrying, including myself, though the thought that the cancer could return occasionally niggled me.

Unknowingly, I again took a stride backward. Shortly after Richie and I purchased TGH, the Physician Self-Referral Law passed. Peter Stark, a California congressman, decided that doctors were crooks and that if they owned a hospital or other medical facility, they would admit patients whether they needed hospitalization or not. It was a crazy assertion. Fortunately, I could maintain my ownership of MRI centers in Chicago, one of the few investments that was profitable over the years, though I did divest myself from Tucson imaging centers.

In order not to violate the law, Richie Silver recruited Mark Yampol, an Israeli who bought and managed nursing homes in Chicago and Tucson, as a majority partner and business manager of our hospital corporation.

Within a few months, Mark started asking me for money—not small sums of money, but large sums: Fifty thousand. One hundred thousand. He always offered a logical explanation for these "short-term loans" needed to pay utility bills or employee salaries until the next month's reimbursements. So I signed personal checks. I thought it was business as usual and never mentioned Mark's requests to Richie.

We scheduled our monthly breakfast board meetings at Ventana Resort. Yampol had been working with us for about eight months when he didn't show up to one. A few days later, Richie came to me with an alarming story. Yampol had absconded to Israel with monies that should have been paid to cover expenses. Our partner was a thief, a gonif. I then related the lamentable story that I had paid Yampol. Not only was I out thousands of dollars, the hospital was in default and ordered closed. A foreclosure sale occurred late in 2000, after which Richie proceeded to politely ask me for the payoff of the balance of my notes signed at the time of purchase. I never imagined the slings and arrows of outrageous fortune could feel so insufferable. I still search for Yampol every time I return to Israel but have never found him.

Fortunately, Jeanne followed her lawyer's advice and

dismissed the divorce. A step in a forward direction, or so I thought. But things are never so bad that they can't get worse. The unraveling was only gaining momentum.

Although I owned my own hospital, I retained surgical privileges at St. Mary's Hospital. Pursuant to this commitment, I was on call every third month. During this obligation, I was summoned to the hospital in consultation to examine a patient who presented with dizziness and loss of hearing. The attending neurologist ordered tests and made the presumptive diagnosis of an acoustic neuroma. Though most tumors located at this cerebellopontine angle turn out to be pathologically benign, they can be deadly because of their proximity to the brainstem. I was trained to do this type of surgery with the patient in a sitting position, head at an angle. Such surgery can be difficult and is associated with venous air emboli, CSF leak, nerve palsies, postoperative hydrocephalus, and even death. I explained these risks and possible complications in great detail to the patient, a large man, and his wife. They decided to proceed with surgery and signed the informed consent.

Robert Osborne, MD, was the anesthesiologist. Bob and I frequently worked together and had become good friends. He knew that many of my patients came seeking amelioration from failed back surgeries. During reoperation, I'd take my time and tediously resect the scar tissue in order to give the patient a brighter prospect of gaining pain relief and mobility. It was meticulous surgery that might last six to eight hours. More than once, Bob commented, "Ron, you really went the extra mile." Hundreds of patients over the years showed their appreciation with handwritten thank-you notes and cards.

A chartered Fellow of the American Society of LASER Medicine and Surgery, I also specialized in LASER resection of intracranial tumors. Rosemary Stubbs, a Southwestern artist renowned for her landscape and skyscape oil paintings, was so grateful for an extended year of quality life following the resection of a highly malignant brain tumor that she presented me with two large works of art that she was able to complete. Similarly, I resected a large glioblastoma from Dr. Stuart Holtzman. Stu was the long-standing medical director of Physical Medicine and Rehabilitation, who returned to golf, ecstatic after hitting a hole-in-one shortly after surgery. I had known him since the introductory dinner when considering Tucson relocation years earlier.

I spent a long time positioning the patient, a particular challenge for this type of surgery and made even more difficult by the patient's large frame. Eventually, I saw the tumor, took a small biopsy, and sent it to pathology. I waited and waited for the report, which concluded that there was "no distinguishing tumor cells." That's odd, I thought. I sent another sample down to pathology and waited. The report was identical. When the third report came back saying the tissue showed no tumor cells, I had Bob look at the tumor through the microscope as verification. I knew what a tumor looked like. And this was one.

Frustrated, I scrubbed out and went down to pathology. It took me less than five minutes to realize that the substitute pathologist, who had just finished her residency, had minimal knowledge of neuropathology. She didn't even know how to make a slide, much less know how to read it! I could not proceed without an accurate pathology report. After meticulous hemostasis was assured, I aborted the surgery. The patient returned to the recovery room, stable and in no worse condition than he had been in pre-op. In the waiting room, I explained the situation to his wife. One course of action was reoperation at a later time.

The next day, I returned to St. Mary's for rounds. I walked

into the patient's room and was aghast at what I saw. The patient lay comatose and on a ventilator. How could this have happened? I scanned his chart and instantly understood. The attending internist had prescribed a blood thinner. Never should a post-op brain surgery patient be given a blood thinner—never. The risk of creating a stroke is exponentially high, as proven by my patient's inability to speak and move. He could still squeeze his wife's hand, but that was about it. He lived two months in that horrible condition. It was such a tragedy.

The patient's wife filed a malpractice lawsuit and also sent a complaint to the Board of Medical Examiners, known as BOMEX, accusing me of killing her husband, which I thought was inane; the internist had that blame resting squarely on his shoulders—the pathologist, too. Up to that point in my career, I had been named as codefendant in two malpractice lawsuits while a resident, as well as several cases over the next twenty years, but all were settled or dismissed. Never had anyone filed a complaint against me with BOMEX. I hired two attorneys: one to litigate the malpractice suit and another to represent me in the BOMEX complaint, the latter of whom suggested that I agree to the committee's stipulation to seek psychiatric treatment for severe clinical depression, because by that time I was indeed depressed, and also refrain from direct patient care.

The malpractice suit included a very confrontational and inaccurate report written by the neurologist, who happened to work for a competitive group of local neurosurgeons. I refused to settle the malpractice suit. I was not guilty. The attorney had several notable board-certified pathologists review the slides, and all agreed: the tissue was tumor, not healthy brain tissue. Jeanne did not appreciate my stance. When I staunchly refused to settle, she took me to court and had me declared mentally incompetent. According to her attorney, if I didn't settle, she could lose everything because we weren't yet divorced and Arizona is a community property state. If I had to pay a settlement beyond what malpractice insurance covered, that payment would be made from our estate. My attorney got the final decision sealed so that it could not be viewed without a court order. Jeanne retained the right to settle the case, which she did. My malpractice insurance paid the claim, and I was removed from the continuing suit against St. Mary's Hospital.

A reporter at the *Arizona Daily Star* learned about the lawsuit and decided to bring it the public's attention. Carla McCain's article appeared in the Sunday newspaper while my boys and I were visiting my father in Florida. I had no idea an article would be published. She was nothing less than vicious, as well as inaccurate. She never mentioned the pathologist or the drug given post-surgery. Carla also claimed I was under criminal investigation. Wrong! That never occurred. By the time we returned home, Elyse and Jeanne—and probably every other Tucsonan—had read the article. Elyse's friends already let her know that her father was the "butcher of Tucson." She was locked in her bedroom in tears. She was devastated. I was devastated. She refused to listen to my side of the story. I'll never know what Jeanne told Elyse about the lawsuit or, over the years, about me.

Some months later, Jeanne refiled for divorce. This time she didn't dismiss it.

20

Rock Bottom

Without a word, Jeanne rented a Foothills home a few miles away, then scheduled movers to pack items she wanted while I was at work. When I returned home that evening, boxes were stacked and strewn throughout the house. Even more shocking were the belongings that had disappeared: my college books, a tapestry, the signed Walter Payton jersey, and other sports memorabilia. Jeanne knew what items I treasured. Fortunately, court orders soon returned the majority of them.

The emails between lawyers left me dizzy and despondent. One string of emails concerned Michael and Josh, who were still minors and spent half their time with Jeanne and half with me. Arranging their schedules proved so arduous, acrimonious, and confusing that our lawyers had to step in to solidify details, most of which Jeanne never followed.

My lawyer, Leonard Karp, recommended a divorce that equally divided all our assets. I was fine with that arrangement as long as it included custody of the boys. Karp advised me that any judge would be reluctant to award custody to a busy neurosurgeon. Jeanne rejected our proposal. She wanted everything—sole custody of the children, as well as full ownership of the residences, including the Telluride condo and both Tucson homes, office buildings, my cars, furniture, artwork, my books, pension and profit-sharing portfolios, investments, and even the Ping-Pong table. She refused to negotiate. It seemed like every week I traveled to the judge's chambers, the mediator's office, or Karp's eastside office. In between, emails continued ad nauseam.

I was irritated but mostly saddened. My first night alone in the house, I walked into the master bathroom, depression nipping at my heels. The white marble glared. I opened the medicine cabinet and much to my surprise found the ruby and diamond necklace and matching ring. Like me, they had been abandoned. I shoved them in the back of a dresser drawer.

I found it increasingly difficult to drag myself out of bed each morning or peruse any newspapers. Daisy padded after me as I forced myself through the morning routine. Soul-searching discussions with my Orthodox rabbi helped, but weren't enough. In accordance with the BOMEX consent agreement, I started seeing a board-approved psychiatrist, John Misiaszek, MD. The stipulation called for a weekly session, but John suggested we meet three times per week. He offered sessions as a professional courtesy, a note he made in the file at our first meeting. The heavy-duty medications he prescribed left me feeling nauseous at first, then dazed. I soon discontinued most of them. John worried about me, as he should have. At one point, I shared that I had been considering stepping in front of a bus as it roared down Campbell Avenue. He insisted I return the next day. Though I never did try to kill myself, I thought about doing so more than once during the two years under John's care—the two lost years, as I now refer to that dreadful time.

I hired another attorney to help me file for disability through my insurance companies. Years before, I had purchased several policies that would pay me if I could no longer practice neurosurgery. I filled out paperwork, requested records, had interviews. I knew the process, having sent a letter supporting Richie Silver's disability claim to his insurance company. He received a large lump sum. My lawyer, Dennis Rosen, passed my case on to a junior associate at his firm, who missed a critical deadline for filing, causing me to lose a substantial lifetime monthly income. If I'd had the energy, I would have yelled and made a commotion. When someone's life is at stake or their quality of life, one becomes especially assiduous. Missing a deadline was inexcusable, though my friend Dennis made excuses for his now-fired associate. The insurance company only would reopen the case if I proceeded with legal action. I paid a new attorney initial consultation fees only to learn that he would charge thousands to litigate. Because the divorce was still being negotiated, I couldn't access savings or investments. The case closed not with bang, but a whimper.

Bob Osborne recommended that I hire Phillip Verrette, a lawyer who specialized in Social Security disability claims. Phil well knew the meaning of disability. At age twenty, an automobile accident left him a quadriplegic, yet he successfully put himself through college and law school. Phil was one of the most competent and effective lawyers I ever hired. After completing many forms, answering emails, and suffering through an excruciating court appearance—it's not pleasant to talk about your mental health issues with strangers—I was awarded monthly disability payments and even qualified for SNAP, the Supplemental Nutrition Assistance Program, which I was forced to use for several months before the first Social Security check arrived. Handing the EBT card to the cashier proved even more humiliating than the court appearance.

Meanwhile, the divorce lawyers continued to volley emails and expensive phone calls. Jeanne refused to budge. After three years of tiresome negotiations, I had enough. I instructed Karp to give Jeanne everything else she wanted except custody of the boys. He tried to dissuade me against doing so, but I held firm. Jeanne started acting erratically; her psychosis, which I attributed to the Accutane, was devastating. Years earlier, I'd installed closed-circuit cameras throughout the house. When I showed Karp the video, he willingly petitioned on my behalf. After the judge viewed the CCTV tape behind closed quarters, he quickly ruled in my favor. The video never resurfaced, which irritated me. Had Jeanne or her attorney disposed of it to prevent further showing? What mattered most, however, was the outcome. Michael and Josh lived with me in the foothills house, the mortgage of which I continued to pay, and Jeanne lived with the material riches that we had accumulated over twenty-three years of marriage. I never stopped believing that I got the better deal.

Shortly after my wife and I divorced, my son Michael planned to drive the silver Jag to his junior prom with his girlfriend, Jenna. Michael was desirous of my silver Jaguar XKE for many years. It was a convertible, and he loved driving it whenever he could. The week before the prom, we cleaned the inside and outside and even polished the chrome wire wheels with a toothbrush. The night of the event, he arrived at my house dressed in a tux and looking handsome as ever. Much to our surprise, the car would not start.

Poor Michael was in tears. He was seventeen years old, and he knew that his mother had put a restraining order on his ability to drive any other of my "fast" cars, including the Ferraris. At that point, I called Jeanne, who absolutely refused to make any accommodations. I then called my attorney, Dennis Rosen, who called the judge and got the order stayed for one night. I gave Michael the keys to the blue Ferrari convertible. He was thrilled.

The next year, the silver Jaguar was up and running. By then, of course, it had a new starter. Prior to Michael's senior prom, I tested the car all week. Michael came again to make sure it was clean and polished. The night of the senior prom, he turned the ignition key, and alas, it wouldn't start! The car had a burnt-out ignition! Michael was not in tears because now he was eighteen years old and did not have a restraining order. So he asked me if he could take one of the other cars. Since he had taken the Ferrari the year before, he asked if he could drive The Beast. I acceded to his wishes. I thought it would be exciting.

Prom chariots

At about 2:00 a.m., my phone rang. It was Michael. There was a problem with the XJ220. He had been driving it with a number of friends who had gone out to dinner. Because it was a two-seater, he'd taken turns with about five or six of his buddies. At the last acceleration, the motor sounded funny. He became quite worried that there was something terribly wrong with the car. His friends, all of them in tuxedos, pushed the car into a parking lot. I assured Michael that it was probably nothing serious and not to worry. I would be right there with my truck.

I quickly donned a bathrobe and left in the Suburban. When I was about halfway there, Michael called me again.

"Dad, please don't let them know that you're my father. Tell them that you're my personal car mechanic," he said.

I didn't quite understand his reasoning at the time but obliged. When I arrived in the parking lot of the very exclusive restaurant, in front of Michael's friends, I announced that as a mechanic, I would take a look at the XJ220. In the meantime, he was welcome to drive the truck for the rest of his evening. When I started the 220, it was apparent that he had blown out one of the vacuum hoses, and thus the head bank of three cylinders was no longer functional. The car could no longer drive at 220 miles per hour; instead, it could only reach about 110 miles per hour. I knew that The Beast and I could limp home.

I waited for Michael and his date, Jenna, to drive off. As Jenna was climbing into the truck, she turned to me, waved, and yelled, "Hi, Dad!" Everyone in Michael's party heard her. Even in the dark, I could see Michael's face turn a bright shade of red.

X

Planning was in full swing for Josh's October bar mitzvah, the last of my children's rites of Jewish adulthood. The service would be held at Congregation Bet Shalom, and the Kiddish would follow with a family celebration at Jeanne's rental house. My father's advanced Parkinson's prevented him from attending. I purchased a large, multicolored, hand-woven Gabrieli talit from Old Jaffa, Israel, for Josh and just before the Jewish High Holidays had him pose, wearing it, in front of my house with a backdrop of full-bloom pink bougainvillea.

Josh becomes a man

Four years earlier, we had celebrated Michael's bar mitzvah. My father attended and looked very proud of his eldest grandson. Neither of my brothers bothered to send a gift or even a card, though they were invited. I knew they wouldn't fly to Tucson for Josh's bar mitzvah. They barely knew him. At least Dale, actually in good spirits as a very proud uncle, had attended Elyse's bat mitzvah.

I still recall that milestone. Jeanne and I shared our excitement, as did my parents, who flew in from Florida. Although I didn't book a band like my mother had for my bar mitzvah, I scheduled the caterer, chose the menu, organized the reception, and scrutinized the guest list. I filled with pride and nachas as my beautiful, talented daughter stood at the congregation's bemah and gave her d'var Torah (a word of Torah) based on the weekly portion in Hebrew and English. Afterward, family and friends gathered in our decorated backyard to celebrate. Some cherished memories never fade, though some bring with them a twinge of sadness.

A few days before Rosh Hashanah, still a month before Josh's bar mitzvah, I received a phone call from my father's caregiver. Dad had fallen and broken a hip. I panicked, thinking of the possible consequences like those my mother suffered. With foreboding déjà vu, I booked an immediate flight to Florida. Much to my great relief, Dad's surgery went well. Shelly flew in for a few days, and we were cordial. Rather than hurrying back to Tucson, I decided to spend the holidays in Florida. My father was scheduled to move to rehab, and I could offer support and encouragement to him. I met with the Chabad rabbi to get a schedule of holiday services. I could attend daily services as well, then fly back to Tucson for Josh's bar mitzvah. It was a good plan, I thought.

As soon as Sukkot ended, I flew to Tucson. Within an hour of landing, I heard the astounding news: Josh's bar mitzvah had already taken place. I had missed it—completely missed it. During the holidays, an esteemed Orthodox rabbi from Israel visited Tucson and offered to officiate Josh's bar mitzvah. Jeanne agreed. No one bothered to inform me.

I've learned that each time devastation hits, it does so with a full-force punch that knocks the wind out of me. I barely could speak. Josh barely could bring himself to speak to me. He was wounded to the core. To this day, he has not been able to forgive me for not being present at one of the most important days in his life. And like Elyse, he is reluctant to hear my side of the story. What he may not realize is that I, too, was deeply wounded. How did it happen that no one called or emailed me about the date? What lies were told? What facts omitted? Or, in my senility, did I confuse the dates, which would be just as devastating? I am resigned to never knowing the truth of what transpired.

University Medical Center proved much more diligent with their communications. Quite unexpectedly, they invoiced me twenty thousand dollars for sessions with Dr. John Misiaszek. John had made it clear from the start that he was granting me professional courtesy, but UMC administrators were businesspeople. What did they care about professional courtesy or any courtesy? In the good ole days, I'd given personal friends, families of friends, lawyers, dentists, pharmacists, and veterinarians similar courtesy, and they'd reciprocated. I met with the attorney for UMC's collection agency, who commiserated and agreed with me. We went to court, and the case was dismissed.

Then another seismic event occurred. One hundred thousand dollars had disappeared from each of the boys' custodial savings accounts. I immediately phoned the banks, my mind tilting with concern. The IRS had levied the funds to partially cover taxes that they insisted had not been paid on assets—property, cars, and pension, profit-sharing, and investment portfolios—that Jeanne starting selling after the divorce. Since I was listed as a co-owner, I was partially responsible for taxes on the capital gains. More phone calls. More interviews. More lawyers. While the IRS conceded their error and agreed that there should be no further harassing letters asserting debt of three to four hundred thousand dollars (depending on penalty and interest), they doubted any reimbursements would be forthcoming. I'm still waiting for a large refund, although I'm not hopeful. Maybe the addendum to Shakespeare's quote should be: "first we kill all the lawyers . . . then the IRS bureaucrats."

The monthly Social Security disability income helped, but it did not cover all my basic needs. I decided to refinance the house and draw upon the equity. I called Dale, who in addition to a legal practice was associated with a mortgage business in Florida. Though I hadn't seen him in quite a while, we occasionally spoke on the phone and enjoyed a comfortable relationship. Dale agreed to arrange a mortgage. Not trusting my mind to deal with details, I asked Michael, a student at the University of Arizona Eller School of Business, to deal with Dale. Bank United of Florida issued a large equity check—financial relief. I promptly discarded the food stamps.

Through all of these challenges, Daisy was by my side, though she was beginning to fail. She used to love climbing the stone steps of the pool slide, then shooting down the curves into the water. Now, she preferred to spend her days under the tangelo tree in the backyard or on the floor of my theater. That's where I found her one morning, lifeless. My companion through the divorce, the depression, and the disability filings had joined Phideaux, Baron, and Cheezer under the Rainbow Bridge.

After I collected myself, I called Michael. I wanted to bury her under the tangelo tree and needed his help. Michael rented a jackhammer to use on the caliche. Sweating profusely, he carved out a grave for Daisy, and we laid her to rest.

I could feel depression closing in but kept busy in an effort to stave it off. I added new features to the Pocket Weather app, continued to communicate with attorneys about sundry issues, and attended Josh's high school basketball games. Jeanne always sat with the away team and never so much as glanced at me if we passed in the hallways. Bob Osborne and I met weekly for breakfast, an outing that helped keep me sane.

One day, Michael said, "Dad, you need a dog." Maybe he was right. Maybe it was time for a new friend. Depression was beginning to suck me in like quicksand. He proceeded to show me photos of German shepherds for sale or adoption. The one that caught my eye was all the way down by the Mexican border. Michael called the owner and inquired whether the dog was friendly and trained and would be a good companion for an older person.

"The owner said the dog would be great for you, Dad. I'm going to drive you down there." There was no negotiating with my son.

The drive took two hours and a few wrong turns, but we finally pulled onto a dirt road. A woman appeared as we were parking. A half dozen chickens scooted about, and a few horses grazed in a corral. The only animal paying us any attention was a very large German shepherd barking excitedly inside a fenced-in pen. He reminded me of Baron. He had to weigh well over a hundred pounds. My first thought: This isn't a dog for an alter kocker. I'm too old for this.

"Can my dad get close to the dog?" Michael asked.

The woman motioned to me. "Oh, sure. Tao won't hurt anyone."

Michael looked at me expectantly. We had driven all the way down here. What else could I do but meet the dog? I followed the woman into the pen. Before she could attach a leash on Tao's collar, the dog was jumping and barking in front of me. He put his dusty paws on my black sport coat and looked me in the eye, but he didn't knock me over. The woman handed me the leash.

"Tao's trained. He'll walk with you." And he did.

Once he calmed down and we had a chance to visit, I could see Tao's gentle side. A handsome fellow with shiny fur, he weighed in at one hundred thirty-five pounds. His papers confirmed that he was pedigree. I still wasn't convinced that he was destined to be my roommate. The woman suggested that I take Tao home with me on a trial basis.

"If things don't work," she said, "bring him back. I just want a good home for him."

She gave me his bowl and toy, and Tao leapt into the back of the Suburban and slept the entire way to Tucson. He was a breed from Nepal and Manchuria, hence the full Chinese name Sherpa Tao, which means "path of virtuous conduct." The owner pronounced his name *tay-oh*. I didn't bother to use the correct pronunciation, as he wouldn't have responded. Tao seemed happy with his name, and I was happy to have Tao, indeed a gentle soul, by my side.

Soon after Tao's arrival, more bright spots appeared to further burn off the gloom of depression. The libel suit against the newspaper concluded. The *Arizona Daily Star* was found guilty. Although I didn't receive one dime from the settlement, I did feel somewhat vindicated. Then, five years after the BOMEX inquisition, Judge Diane Mihalsky recommended that the board dismiss the decree. Even the assistant attorney general, Emma Mamaluy, concurred. I was fully exonerated, at least legally. I didn't get burned at the stake, just deeply singed.

I felt tremendous relief that these two cases concluded. They had consumed much time and energy, fueled my despondent moods, and caused irreparable damage to my professional reputation and career and ultimately to my relationship with my daughter. I prayed Hashem would help bring Elyse back into my life.

21

Journey of the Soul: The Panegyric

"And the dust returns to the ground it came from, and the spirit returns to G–d, Who gave it."[4]

"Earth you are, and to earth you will return"[5]

During the last years of his life, my father had a live-in care-taker named Claudette. A compassionate woman with a lilting Jamaican accent, she took impeccable care of my father, as a daughter would her father. He had arranged for her to live in the spare bedroom. During one of my visits, I inquired if she wanted wall space to hang photos of her own family. Dad had filled the walls with photos, plaques, certificates,

---

4   Kohelet 12:7 (Ecclesiastes)
5   Genesis 3:19

newspaper clippings, and a few paintings. No, she said, she enjoyed seeing Maurice's family and having them around her. She was so sweet and kind and loved the kosher food we shared; I, in turn, enjoyed the conversations about her family and upbringing.

Every week I phoned my father. Years earlier, I had bought him a video phone, but being a technophobe, he never used it. In fact, he used a simple adding machine up until his retirement. As his health deteriorated, Claudette would hold the phone up to his ear, and I'd chat about the weather in Tucson or update him on how the Cubs, Bears, or Bulls were doing, and most importantly, news about his grandchildren. By that time, Parkinson's disease had overtaken his muscles, and he couldn't smile or laugh, much less speak. He lived in a hospital bed in what had been the den next to the screened-in Florida room. In addition to the television that I bought him, he could see the bookcases with his wedding anniversary photos, cards—everything he saved. Two windows offered a view to the expansive yard and, beyond the well-maintained hedges, a glimpse of the golf course. I knew he was comfortable, yet it pained me to think of my father lying in that bed day after day. After I spoke to him, Claudette concluded the conversations with, "Your dad misses you and loves you." It didn't matter if Dad really managed to whisper the message to her or not. When she said it, the words felt true and comforting.

I instructed Claudette to phone me if his condition changed.

"I have your phone number, Doctor, and I know I'm supposed to call you if anything happens to your father, but Shelly insists that I call him."

"That's fine, Claudette," I said. "Go ahead and call Shelly first." What difference did it make?

On the day my father stopped breathing, Claudette did

call Shelly, and hours later, Shelly called me. I never heard from Claudette.

"Dad went into cardiac arrest," said Shelly. "He was resuscitated and taken to the hospital. He's in the ICU on life support."

No! I wanted to yell. No, no, no! The health-care directive that my father and I discussed and posted on the refrigerator succinctly shouted, "DO NOT RESUSCITATE." Jewish law does not forbid withholding life support but does not accept its withdrawal. Father was in his tenth decade of life. He had not died in his fifties as he so often feared but had outlived his father by more than three decades. He was an Orthodox Jew from an observant family and proud of his heritage. My parents' marriage had been the union of two souls; they raised three sons. He was a consummate professional, a numismatist with a coin collection worth more than his IRA, and at one time, an adventurous traveler. He was the man whose hand I held walking to the synagogue so many years ago. My father deserved to have his wishes honored.

I immediately booked a flight to Florida, my heart aching in a way it hadn't since my mother's passing thirteen years earlier. I was angry and disappointed that Dad had been resuscitated, which contradicted his desires. Given his terminal condition, cardiac arrest was probably the kindest outcome. My wish for recovery was as autonomic as my nervous system; however, forty years of medical experience intervened and reminded me such chances were negligible and the quality of life dismal.

I composed several emails to Shelly and Dale elucidating Dad's last wishes and excerpting the Jewish perspective regarding end-of-life issues. Just as Abraham bought a grave for Sarah to be buried alongside him, my father had prearranged everything, including Orthodox funeral and burial services. He and I talked about the eventuality as we went to Shabbat and holiday services. I presumed Shelly would be more inclined to pay attention to the email, but I never heard from either brother before boarding a late-night flight to Fort Lauderdale–Hollywood International Airport, where a car awaited me.

It was a misting March morning when I landed and still pitch-black when I drove the rental car into the hospital parking lot. Though it was well before visiting hours, the staff allowed me into the ICU. Shelly and Nancy hadn't arrived, nor had Dale. My father lay in a bed, his chest rising and falling, synchronous with the ventilator. I had not lost my disdain for the tumult of the ICU. A nurse came in and suggested that I return during formal visiting hours. Lacking sleep, I decided to go to the car and close my eyes for a bit.

The slam of a car door woke me. A young woman walked past and entered the hospital. Though I hadn't seen her in years, I was pretty sure it was my niece Gabby, one of Shelly's daughters. I found her sitting in the waiting room. After I checked on my father, who remained the same, I returned to visit with Gabby. Our conversation calmed the anxiety rumbling around in me. If only the rest of the day's conversations would remain as even-keeled.

When Shelly, Nancy, and their son, Alex, arrived, we all went into the ICU. Everyone remained cordial and focused on Dad.

I turned to Shelly. "You know, Dad didn't want to be on a ventilator."

The same frustration that afflicted me when Shelly and I argued over my mother's health care began to fester. I sensed the family boat was heading into rough seas. Dale soon arrived, and we met him in the waiting area of the ICU. Instead of his two children—Bobby and Samantha Robin, named for my mother—he brought his fiancée, a Haitian woman, and her young son. It took Dale less than five minutes to begin shouting profanities at me. A nurse frowned at us from behind her desk. I ushered him into a quiet stairwell.

"Can't we at least be civil here?" I said, trying my best not to raise my voice. But Dale didn't know the meaning of civility. I walked away, disgusted and dismayed.

I was beginning to feel overwhelmed. I telephoned the Chabad rabbi I knew from previous visits, explaining the stressful circumstances. Could he possibly come to the hospital? I'd welcome his support and input. He consoled me over the phone and agreed to meet me. I found a cup of coffee and a chair and settled in to wait for him. I had no desire to have another encounter with Dale, Shelly, or his wife. Alex meandered over. He was a tall, nice-looking young man, and we had a wonderful conversation, the perfect distraction while waiting for the rabbi. I also had a chance to meet the hospital's Jewish chaplain. Maybe the nurse, hoping to avoid a family feud, had called him.

The two rabbis and I entered the ICU together. Dale glared at us and immediately left. Shelly had admonished me not to call the Chabad rabbi and shot me an irritated look when he saw the black-hatted rabbi walk into the room. The rabbis appreciated my disquietude and began discussing my considerations. With regard to Jewish Halacha, life-saving measures such as nutrition or ventilation should not be withdrawn, but a spontaneous breathing trial, whereby patients attempt to breathe independently without the ventilator, could be performed. Passing this SBT would mean extubation and transfer to a more comfortable environment.

Shelly and Nancy offered their opinions, which reflected a complete disregard for my father's known wishes. Nancy stood next to Shelly, her lips pursed. She would have said anything to oppose me. Rather than further stoke the mounting tensions and blood pressures, I chose to exit the scene. The Chabad rabbi would align my father's interest with Torah law.

The rabbi found me in the waiting room. "Yisrael, Shelly will agree to extubation following a successful breathing trial," he said.

All three sons were present when the doctor extubated my father. I had seen this procedure performed hundreds of times, had sensed the anxiety of the patients' loved ones. Now it was my turn to experience the immense angst. Would his soul soon ascend from a lifeless body? No one in the room uttered a word. Father began breathing on his own. Tears welled in my eyes. My father would get his wish not to be on life support. How long he would be able to continue doing so, none of us, with all our combined doctoral degrees, could say.

"I want him moved to a private room with a window facing east," I said. I knew that he would want to be facing the Kotel, considered the Gateway to Heaven. Thankfully, no one argued.

It didn't take the staff long to make arrangements. They probably were happy to see our bickering clan leave. Shelly, Nancy, Alex, Gabby, and I, along with a hospital aide, wheeled Father down the hall into the elevator, then into a private room. I'm sure we all were watching and listening to his shallow breathing. Dale left with barely a goodbye to anyone. Shelly announced that his family had to catch a flight back to Boston, leaving me with my father. I had nowhere to be but right there. I pulled up a chair next to the bed. I reached out and grasped my father's moribund hand, the same hand I held as a child as we walked to the shul. For almost two full days, I remained by his side, his hand in mine. It is Jewish tradition not to leave a dying person alone—a matter of the greatest respect to watch over a person as he passes from this world to the next.

$$ \text{\textthreequartersemdash} $$

I shifted for the hundredth time in my chair, relieving the pain in my coccyx. It now was late Friday afternoon; Shabbat would soon arrive. A waning light shone through the window. My thoughts meandered back over the years, like they had been wont to do during the last forty-eight hours. So many memories of my father came to mind. Both of my parents were exemplary students, but it was Mother who was the valedictorian of her class. My mother made me independent, made me get on the bus by myself and find my way to art class at the Art Institute of Chicago or to drama class or to my bubbe to visit and make blintzes. But it was my father who took me places: Walt's Workshop. White Sox games. The office where he worked where I embossed faux cheques. The post office where we collected stamps. So many places and experiences. The stream of memories always seemed to end with the image of my father and me, aged five, walking hand in hand to the Agudas Achim North Shore Congregation in Chicago.

I positioned the bed so that my father was facing east. His face was slightly turned away from me, toward his right side. The bed rail was halfway down. As I continued to hold his hand, I was thinking about the magnificent stained glass windows in the sanctuary of the synagogue and their multitude of colors; they flanked the Aron Hakodesh, where the Torah scrolls were kept. Suddenly, I felt slight movement. I looked at Dad. He turned his head toward me, squeezed my hand, and exhaled for the last time.

It was March 11, the seventh of Adar in the Jewish calendar, the date that Moshe Rabbeinu, more commonly known as Moses, ascended Mount Nebo just east of the Jordan River to view the Land of Israel for the last time. The Kabbalists say that a person's destiny is wrapped up in the combination of Hebrew letters that make up his name. My father, whose Hebrew name was Chaim Moshe (life of Moses), entered the world on September 11, 1920. It was the end of his journey on Earth. I was grasping his hand as G–d took his holy soul.

In keeping with Jewish traditions, a shomer, a Jewish person who stays with the deceased until burial, is needed. The soul departs the body and hovers over it while it grieves its loss of the physical form. I made arrangements with the Chabad rabbi to accompany my father's body to the funeral home after Shabbat and spent Shabbat at my father's house. Claudette left to be with her family, leaving me with just my thoughts. I was upset and disappointed that none of my children came for the funeral. Josh was in college, Michael was engrossed with his financial computer models, and Elyse was practicing family law in San Diego. I didn't want to interpret their intentions—they had things to do—but I would've welcomed their support. It made me sad that they didn't feel close enough to their grandfather to abandon their plans.

Shelly drove over on Saturday to pick up Dad's best business suit. "That's what Dad should be buried in," he said.

I vehemently disagreed. Per my father's request, I wanted to ensure a traditional Tahara (washing and purification of the body), Tachrichim (traditional shrouds), a "kosher" casket (a simple wooden casket with holes in the bottom and the Star of David on the top), and the Chevra Kaddisha (Jewish men to see that the body of the deceased is prepared for burial according to Jewish tradition and protected from desecration). But I sensed that Shelly and I were heading toward another major argument, so I deferred. I didn't have the energy to argue over every detail. Still, the fact that my father's wishes were not honored deeply disturbed me.

The funeral was scheduled for Sunday afternoon. Shelly

arrived at my father's house in the morning, shortly after Claudette had returned. He said that he had picked out a casket.

"Did you get something simple?" I asked. Shelly shrugged and said what he chose would be fine.

We reviewed the day's timeline. The funeral was scheduled to begin at 1:00 p.m.

"In that case, you'll have to leave at least an hour and a half early," asserted Shelly.

I handed him a printout of the directions to the funeral home and cemetery. During most of my trips to Florida, I went to the cemetery to visit my mother's grave, sometimes with my father and most recently with Auntie Ettie. I placed a small stone at the grave site. Shelly actually started to argue until Claudette intervened and confirmed the shortest route.

Claudette and I ended up driving together and arrived quite early. After greeting the Chabad rabbi, I entered the funeral parlor. An ornate open casket rested on an elevated stage. I couldn't believe it. Open! Jewish funerals do not have open caskets. Shelly continued to demonstrate his perverted misunderstanding of Torah law. I immediately turned to the rabbi and conveyed my concerns. I was distraught, animated, and loud. Moreover, Shelly had requested that attendees be given a piece of black fabric to pin to their clothing. How egregious! The most striking Jewish expression of grief is the rending of garment by the mourner prior to the funeral service. The tear for a parent must be made with bare hands and attempts to satisfy the emotional need to vent one's anguish. The tear must be over the heart, indicating the broken heart within. What would my father think of all this? It felt like everything was turning ghastly. I informed the rabbi that Shelly and I weren't on the best of terms and asked if he would again speak to Shelly. This was not the time to resolve Shelly's long-standing animosity and contempt toward me.

Although the rabbi commiserated with me, Shelly was quite vehement about wanting an open casket. In fact, Shelly also insisted that a dollar bill be placed in Dad's suit pocket— another disdain of Torah law!

"Why?" I asked Shelly.

"So he can buy what he wants when he gets to heaven."

How utterly absurd, and pagan. Shelly and I engaged in a heated discussion, with the rabbi finally saying privately me, "It's not right, but we shouldn't argue about it here."

I did not concede, however, to Nancy's request that I not speak. I had no intention of speaking in front of an open casket, but I remained adamant about speaking at the grave site. My frustration skyrocketed. Shelly and Nancy's actions were more abhorrent than the CPR that was administered in the face of a living will that instructed otherwise. It seemed as if the fundamental beliefs and traditions that my father cherished and honored throughout his life were not only being abandoned, but contradicted by his own son. I thought for sure that Dad had discussed with Shelly that which he had so intimately deliberated with me.

Was Shelly ever interested in being an observant Jew? Even growing up, I don't recall him continuing with Hebrew school after his bar mitzvah or joining any Jewish groups. Shelly never seemed to have the same spiritual connection to Judaism. Maybe memory doesn't serve me right. I know he never had the opportunity like I did to sit on the knee of his black-hatted Orthodox elter zaide, my great-grandfather, or other relatives who brought Jewish heritage and customs from Latvia and Romania, barely speaking any English. Later, I reflected on Shelly's behavior and surmised that he might never have known what our religion really meant to our father.

Shelly used to say how close he was to our Israeli cousins. Maybe it was the way he said it that bothered me; was he just being arrogantly domineering? To Shelly, I was just a doctor who had forsaken a career in academia and research in order to go into private practice and live a materialistic life. Nancy was not a fan of mine; she always seemed curt and aloof. When she and Shelly trekked all the way from Boston to Phoenix to visit her mother, they would never call or let me know they were only ninety miles away—a mere half hour by air shuttle. Could I have persuaded them to visit? I would have picked them up myself or made flight and lodging arrangements. They never attended my children's birthdays or bat or bar mitzvahs. I would have welcomed them into my world for even a short time. We were family—emphasis on the *were*.

I stood in the back of the funeral parlor while Shelly spoke, but I wasn't listening. One other couple, long-time Chicago friends of my parents now retired nearby, paid their respects. The rest of my parents' friends who shared good times and bad with our family had already passed.

$$\text{X}$$

Shelly and I sat opposite each other in the limousine, silent. When we arrived at the cemetery, we walked with an attitude of somberness some distance behind the coffin. Allowing us to reassess our existence at each stop, the procession paused briefly several times before reaching the grave site. Death teaches us to avoid the life of vanity, to be creative and kind, to repent of evil, to walk in the path of goodness. "Vanity of vanities, all is vanity."[6]

I don't believe there were enough pallbearers from our family; how unconscionable. Where was Dale? Where were the grandchildren? The low-hanging gray clouds looked as if they might shed tears on us at any moment. Folding chairs had been set under a small canopy. I could see my mother's

6 Kohelet 1:2

half-empty headstone on the other side of the excavation, fresh dirt piled beyond.

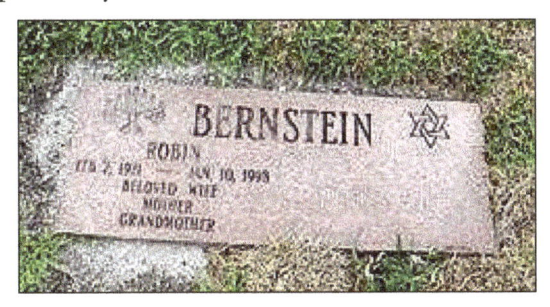

Final words

The rabbi said a few words and a passage from the Talmud in the absence of a minyan. A few raindrops bounced against the canopy, and the humid air held a slight chill. I quickly approached the casket to speak as Nancy was concluding. The clouds scudding overhead still refused to rain. The only thing raining were tears from my eyes. To this day, I can't remember exactly what I said; my tears seemed to have blurred the memory.

The rabbi picked up the spade and poured a bit of earth onto the coffin, then returned the spade to the mound. I made sure to reach the spade next. The custom is for the firstborn son to put three spadefuls of dirt over the coffin. As soon as I replaced the spade, Shelly threw something into the grave—a flower? Once more, I was appalled. Objects used for holy purposes acquire holiness themselves. There are guidelines for disposing of these objects at burial. This was not one of those objects and was probably as inappropriate as having an open casket.

Before the casket was completely covered, Shelly turned to me. "We have a plane to catch," he said. He and Nancy left without further words, tears, goodbyes, hugs, or even hand-shakes.

I remained at the grave site until the last bit of dirt covered the coffin in finality, because that's what an observant Jew does. I recited Tziduk Hadin, a deeply meaningful prayer declaring my acceptance of G-d's decree and prayed to G-d to have mercy upon those who are living. I remained for what seemed like an eternity—not to speak, but just to think and stand guard over the covered earth.

22

See No Evil, Speak No Evil

It was time to move on. The eighteen months following my father's passing had been challenging. Tao and I still lived in the same home where I had happily lived with Jeanne and my children. When I looked out the back window, I could almost see Elyse playing on the painted grass with Pumpkin or a spindly Josh heaving a basketball at the hoop. Every room held a cache of memories. The sweet ones bolstered my spirits; the bitter ones dragged me down, sometimes close to despair. I slumped on the sofa, the supple leather giving way to the weight of my malaise; Tao stretched out on the floor next to me, resigned to inertia for the next four or five hours. I filled time compiling computer code for the PocketWeather and other apps on my smartphone or researching Israeli immigration requirements on the Nefesh B'Nefesh website. More than ever, Israel remained my destination.

"Dad, if you want to move to Israel, you should declare bankruptcy. Get rid of your debts and start over," Michael said.

I told him that if he thought that best, he'd have to help make those arrangements. I had neither the energy nor the mental acumen. He retained a friend of his, a bankruptcy lawyer. The proceedings grew increasingly complex. I finally thought to myself, this isn't what I want to do. I didn't believe—and still don't—in not paying creditors their just due, unless they are ganifs (scoundrels) who unfairly take advantage of a situation. Otherwise, it's my responsibility to repay a debt. For me, it's a moral obligation. If I sold my house, I would have the means to repay my debt. I dismissed the filing.

I asked Michael, a certified realtor, to list the house. Why should someone else collect the commission on the sale? Michael agreed. I would have preferred to leave the house to my children, but none of them were interested. Michael hired a friend of his who appraised the house at three and a quarter million dollars. The proceeds from the sale, less Michael's commission, would be a welcome supplement to my meager Social Security disability payments, my only source of monthly income. I continued to fight the IRS for the two hundred thousand dollars they had falsely levied from my bank accounts.

I was ready to file my Aliyah paperwork in December 2012. I enrolled in the Israeli state-sponsored pilot program that helps new citizens find a place to live and also work, if so desired. After completing the program, I planned to return to the United States one last time to attend Josh's college graduation, dispose of my personal property, visit with relatives in Chicago and Pasadena, and visit my parents' grave site in Florida. I then would move to Israel as a full-fledged Israeli citizen as permitted under the Law of Return, which declares that "every Jew has the right to come to this country [Israel] as an oleh (immigrant)."

When I discovered that my passport expired, I panicked and raced to the passport office. When I explained that I was making arrangements with the head of the Neurosurgical Department at the Hadassah Hospital in Jerusalem for cancer surgery, the clerk moved me to the head of the queue. After five minor surgical procedures, a bone resection (craniotomy) was now indicated under a general anesthetic. She listened to my predicament, then patiently guided me through the convoluted forms. As soon as my property was moved to storage and inventoried, I could leave, hopefully by the end of January.

My brothers knew that I was considering relocating to Israel. I did not intend to visit them before embarking. My relationship with Shelly had never been particularly brimming with brotherly love, and for almost a year, Dale had been sending me scathing, nonsensical emails. Our relationship suffered a rift when I expressed my irritation about the mortgage Dale had arranged, a predatory mortgage. In addition to inherent costs and fees, there was a $65,000 profit. This is *not* how a Jew deals with another Jew, especially one who is family! He didn't appreciate my comments about the mortgage and certainly not about him never visiting my parents. Dale lived in Florida; he could easily have driven or flown to honor his father. As the fifth commandment states, "Honor your father and mother, so that your days may be long upon the land which the Lord your G-d gives you."[7] I didn't interact much with Dale while he was growing up. After all, he was thirteen years younger. In high school, he started hanging out with kids who did drugs. My parents shared their concerns about him with me. They were thrilled when Dale was accepted at University of Florida and went on

7   Exodus 20:12

to earn a law degree from the University of Miami. I attended both graduations and remember his first home abutting the swamp and the alligator that occasionally paid a visit. We exchanged birthday and Chanukah presents. Unlike Shelly and his wife, Dale attended Elyse's bat mitzvah. Michael, Josh, and I visited him in New Port Richey, where he lived with his family. He was a generous host, encouraging me to drive his new Escalade with the kids to Busch Gardens in Tampa Bay. At an anniversary of my mother's passing, he wrote about the round of robins gathered on his back lawn. A beautiful photo accompanied his letter. His daughter's middle name is Robin, in memory of my mother. Dale confided in me about the tenuous relationship he had with Shelly, and I worked to bring the two together and repair their differences. Prior to starting his real estate company, Dale was chief counsel for investment banking firms and senior general counsel for G. Gordon Liddy.

After confidential discussions with me, my father decided to appoint Dale as the personal representative of his estate. I had some qualms with the arrangement. At thirty years old, Dale was still immature, had a criminal arrest record, and spoke of unscrupulous dealings. He boasted about importing endangered birds from Costa Rica, as well as other shady foreign dealings. When I visited his office, he flashed a gun at me. I didn't think he would be able to truthfully oversee my parents' estate. Dad confided that Dale never seemed to have the same opportunities that his older brothers shared. Perhaps it was in part due to the aging of my parents. My critical maturing years occurred with parents in their thirties; Dale's occurred while they were in their fifties. Having children late in life can lead to socio-emotional problems. Maybe this responsibility would help Dale's ego. Dad was seventy-two and beginning to show early signs of Parkinson's. I didn't want to refute his wishes.

After the mourning period following our father's passing, I emailed Dale inquiring when I might come to Florida to retrieve some of the items Dad left me. According to the irrevocable family trust, 50 percent of the estate, which included life insurance proceeds and pension funds, would go to me, the eldest son and bechor, and Dale and Shelly would each receive 25 percent. I told my brothers that an equitable division would be acceptable, though there were specific items described in the codicil, such as the Rolex to Michael, the firstborn grandson, and fur coat to Elyse, the first grandchild. Obviously, my personal belongings—violin, fire hats, bound PhD thesis, and other documents—should be returned. I was far more concerned, however, about retrieving precious Jewish objects like my father's tefillin and tallit, as well as all the 8 mm film reels and photos that Dad had taken over the years, going back to my brit milah in Chicago and even before. Dale and Shelly had never met the relatives who were in those early photos. Why would they care about these items? Yet I offered to make digital copies for them.

Dale responded with obscene emails and phone calls that left me flabbergasted. He accused me of stealing hundreds of thousands of dollars of my parents' assets that remain missing. He called me pond scum, a-hole—horrible names—and told me that I didn't exist and that he would piss on my grave. When his threats grew more violent and he sent numerous defamatory letters to relatives and various people, I filed a complaint with the Florida Bar Association alleging misconduct and advising that Dale cease and desist his communications and allow me to pick up my belongings. Dale retorted with a letter accusing me of stealing Dad's coin collection, among many other valuables.

When my father returned home from the hospital after breaking his hip, he had a new caregiver. Not knowing that person, he asked Shelly to take his coin collection to Auntie

Ettie for safekeeping. During my next visit to Florida, a nervous Auntie Ettie called me. She didn't know why she still had Maishe's coins. They were so valuable. Could I come get them? Dale had told me the collection was worth over one hundred thousand dollars. The single binder that Auntie Ettie handed me, however, did not contain enough coins to be worth half that amount. I had never seen an appraisal for the coins, but I had seen more than one binder in Dad's chest. I wrote to Dale and Shelly asking where the rest of the coins were. Shelly never responded; Dale accused me of stealing them.

Communications with my brothers became increasingly strained. The day after my father's funeral, I photographed all the documents in a filing cabinet full of meticulously titled folders. I found "Sheldon's" original birth certificate. I also found a manila folder marked "Confidential: Do Not Let Ronald See." Inside was a letter written on University of Chicago stationary and signed by two of my biology professors. It was addressed to Shelly. I no longer have the original, which ended up in the clutches of 3 Gorillas, but I'll never forget what it said. I had been very proud of Shelly when he received the MacArthur Fellowship "Genius Grant" and boasted about his achievement to family, friends, and colleagues. The discovery that I should have been nominated knocked the wind out of me. If I had received that award while working on my PhD, would I have chosen to remain in academia when Raimondi had given me the ultimatum between a career in research and a career in medicine? Would I have moved to Israel to work at the Weizmann Institute in Rehovot? Would Jeanne have moved with me? Would we have married in Jerusalem? Perhaps. But that's not where Divine Providence guided me. I never told Shelly that I found the file.

I continued to ask both brothers for a copy of Father's will and irrevocable trust documents. Losing patience with their silence, I hired attorneys who, following years of costly legal proceedings, secured copies. We never did receive the hand-written codicil, which, in addition to the trust document, was never filed. Michael never received his grandfather's Rolex, Elyse, her grandmother's fur coat, and me, even one cent.

Recently, a court ordered Dale to allow me to go to his moldy shed across from his Gulf Coast home, where some items were stored. Because Dale had threatened physical harm, an officer of the court agreed to accompany me. Rats had chewed through boxes and littered the floor with droppings. Dale's representative showed the thirteen boxes earmarked for me. I opened one and was reunited with my bar mitzvah photo album. I shipped the boxes, filled with old photos and film, to Tucson—all thirteen of them. Out of my parents' entire lifetime of amazing worldly collections, artwork, coin collections, books, and more—thirteen boxes made up my inheritance.

I rarely communicate with my brothers. I no longer email birthday or holiday greetings, though I have had limited success in contacting nieces and nephews. Dale remains bitter and vindictive; Shelly remains silent. I'm thankful that my mother and father never had to witness such acrimony and simmering discord. Parents should not be witness to the anger and indifference that festers between sons.

23

Plans Amok

Michael agreed to make all the moving and storage arrangements but then reneged, much to my consternation.

"I'm too busy, Dad," he said. "You research the moving companies, give me the info, and I'll sign the contract and pay for the move."

I wasn't eager to take on the task. Fatigue, the inability to concentrate, and short-term memory loss continued to afflict me. I had created a daily reminder file on my smartphone and continuously referred to it—that is, if I could find my iPhone. I relied on Michael, even though he wasn't as detail-oriented as I. He was astute with financial, real estate, and business dealings, but my challenges were not always his priority. He was twenty-four years old.

I called three moving companies. The first was unavailable

on the requested dates. The second, E-Z Movers, was owned by Israelis. A representative from E-Z Movers came to the house and followed up with a bid. They were my preference, in spite of the fact that I'd had poor prior dealings with Israelis and other Jewish professionals. Mark Yampol had absconded to Israel with money from my hospital, forcing bankruptcy. Corporate attorney Dennis Rosen had handed off my private disability insurance negotiation to a junior assistant who missed a deadline, preventing me from collecting a significant lifetime income. And the list went on.

The third company, 3 Gorillas Moving and Storage, was owned by Troy Emerson. The references and five-star reviews posted on the company website engendered confidence. Arthur Back, an affable fellow in his early thirties with a "Sales Manager/Support Specialist" title on his business card, met me at my house. We toured my house, noting items that needed special attention: the Peloponnesian urn that was thirty-five hundred years old, a priceless museum piece; the dozen or so commissioned Jean Richardson abstract horse oil paintings hanging throughout the house; the two pieces from Rosemary Stubbs, who'd given them to me after I successfully operated on her glioblastoma multiforme brain tumor; the concert grand player piano; my stamp collection; and most important to me, my Judaica. I shared details about everything, including estimated values, and sought details of their insurance coverages and reassurance that 3 Gorillas would take extra care handling these irreplaceable treasures.

"What about the cars?" I asked Arthur. "Can you move those?"

I still had four exotic cars in the garages. The Beast was in England, where it would be serviced before shuttling through the Chunnel to France, then driven over autostrada through Italy and subsequently shipped to Ashdod, Israel. I also had the old soccer-dad Suburban that I drove when I needed extra cargo space. Arthur said it was no problem at all; 3 Gorillas had a flatbed and could transport multiple vehicles.

When I showed Arthur the three bookcases of Judaica in the theater, which I intended to ship separately to Israel, Arthur's interest piqued. He started asking questions about Israel and Judaism, two topics he claimed always interested him. We talked about the Old Testament and what it meant being Orthodox compared to being Chassidic. I enjoyed our chat and suggested we meet at Bruegger's one morning. He readily accepted the breakfast invitation.

Arthur then outlined the moving process. Eight to ten movers would pack the house in a day or two. On the third day, several large moving vans would begin to transport my belongings to an appointed destination and unload. The entire process might take between four and five days. The only pending complication seemed to be the tree limbs overhanging the circular driveway. Arthur said that 3 Gorillas would hire an arborist to trim them so the huge moving vans could park in front of the house, rather than on the road, thus following HOA rules. I always loved the tunnel of green created by the mesquite and Chilean palo verde trees. Being impatient, I wanted an instant canopy over my drive, reminiscent of the elms in Lincolnwood, and had paid a premium for mature boxed trees. I felt a brief stab of melancholy at the thought of those branches being pruned. Before he left, Arthur said that he would prepare an estimate and contract and send it to Michael. I felt confident 3 Gorillas would handle the move professionally and efficiently. We shook hands.

Next, I turned my attention to securing storage space. The conundrum was where to store eight thousand square feet of belongings. Inspiration struck: perhaps renting a private airplane hangar was a more economical solution than individual storage units. My friends Doug and Diane Taylor owned an airplane. During the dark years surrounding my divorce, cancer surgeries, and other temporary setbacks, the Taylors had invited me over almost every weekend for a home-cooked meal and emotional and spiritual support. While they weren't Jewish, they went out of their way to accommodate my dietary laws. Doug's available hangars at Ryan Airfield certainly were large enough, but the prohibitive prerequisite was owning an airplane; plus I didn't think Michael and Josh would appreciate the two-hour round trip. La Cholla Airpark on the Northwest side of Tucson, however, had no such requirement. The airpark manager referred me to John Gutierrez, who was looking to rent his hangar to a new tenant.

Michael, John, and I met at the hangar located at the end of Tailwinds Drive and surrounded by undeveloped desert. It had two stories of storage area totaling about nine thousand square feet and a small office, including a half bath with commode, sink, and utility closet, none of which I anticipated needing. The hangar wouldn't be available until Tuesday, January 15, 2013. Arthur assured me that was not a problem. The movers would pack everything at the house on Sunday and Monday, then load the vans and transport the cargo to the hangar beginning on Tuesday. Perfect, I thought; I will be moved out of the house by Shabbat and in Israel with Josh by month's end. After negotiating with John, Michael prepared an intricate lease agreement and paid the deposit along with several months' rent.

Michael then contracted with 3 Gorillas, which had submitted the lowest estimate. For a deposit, Michael gave Arthur a check for one thousand dollars, as well as one thousand dollars in cash. Unbeknownst to me, he never signed a contract, though he did purchase extra insurance to cover the property value of almost four and a half million dollars. To relieve Michael of further busy work, I called the HOA and the guard house and explained that movers were coming early Sunday morning—no vans, in accordance with HOA rules, just cars.

$$ \text{)(} $$

I hadn't slept well. It's a strange thing moving out of a home that you've lived in for almost twenty years. Memories besiege you. Throughout the night, they pounded against me like waves against Promontory Point, rife with a range of emotions. It was still dark when I finally abandoned any attempt at restful sleep and brewed a cup of hazelnut coffee.

The digital outdoor thermometer displayed a temperature of twenty-nine degrees. The record-breaking low had plunged Tucson into a deep frost. At seven thirty, I called Arthur, whose crew was already a half hour late. He said he was en route and would be there soon. Another thirty minutes passed before the guard at the service entrance gatehouse phoned.

"Dr. Bernstein, your movers are here," he said. He was not the regular friendly guard who opened the gate and waved as I applied ingenious techniques to traverse the speed bumps in my Ferrari. "They have two large moving vans," he said, sounding annoyed.

What? Vans? That wasn't right. He admonished me that no trucks of any kind were allowed in the subdivision on Sundays.

"I know that!" I said. "These guys are a day early. I don't know what's going on." I hung up, irritated. Had the lines of communication already been mangled? I called Arthur again.

"Dr. Bernstein, I'm not sure why those vans are here today," said Arthur, "but as long as they are, why not have them come up to the house? We could start loading some boxes."

"Absolutely not," I said. We went back and forth, with Arthur eventually saying that he would send only the cars with the packing materials to the house, as previously agreed upon.

Still perturbed, I called Michael next, but he didn't answer, so I left a voice message. Soon, several cars pulled into the driveway. Six burly fellows met me at the parking area near the theater. I ushered them inside, hoping Michael would show up soon. I was considering options to the dilemma of what to do with the vans at the guardhouse when a Pima County Sheriff appeared at the front door

"I understand we have a problem," he said.

"I know!" I said, stepping outside to speak with him privately. My breath puffed as I explained the plan that had somehow run amok. Another sheriff's car drove up. I tried to maintain a calm that I wasn't feeling. I think one deputy may have recognized me and was very polite. Over the years, I had volunteered with the county's Emergency Medical Services and knew many of the personnel. Finally, one of them said, "We'll see what we can do, Dr. Bernstein."

An hour later, the sheriff reported that the HOA president would allow two trucks through the gate. "They'll need to park in your driveway, and they'll need to leave before the end of the day," he said. I could live with those caveats.

I was not terribly pleased with how events were unfolding. The moving company had failed to schedule the arborists, so the vans couldn't pull into the drive; they had to park on the shoulder of the main road. Something was rotten in the state of Arizona. There hadn't been this much tumult at the house since family and friends celebrated Michael's bar mitzvah or the exotic car owners descended to tour my garage when the British Car Club showcased it. Back then, I relished gatherings and camaraderie, but not now. It was only midmorning, but I was too exhausted to think about anything besides stretching out on a bed to decompress. There were six bedrooms with movers plowing through five of them, leaving me one queen bed of solace. Rest, however, proved hard to come by, what with strangers handling priceless items. I roamed from room to room, pointing out what pieces needed to be handled and packed with absolute, meticulous care.

"Mark this box 'Judaica,'" I said to the fellow in my study. "It needs to go directly to Israel."

He looked at me. "How do you spell that?

Late afternoon, I scooped up a huge pile of clothes, some of which would go to the dry cleaners and the rest of which would accompany me to the Comfort Suites at Tucson Mall that Michael managed; he had arranged for me to stay there during the move. A few trips to the Suburban left me drenched in sweat and feeling irritable and once again fatigued. I pulled the Suburban out of the garage at the movers' request—it was in their way—drove up the steeply graded asphalt driveway, past the rows of mushroom lights, and parked it near the front entranceway guarded by the Cantera stone lions. One of the movers then instructed the others to help me continue loading the Suburban. Movers inconsiderately placed custom Italian suits, my mother's fox jacket willed to Elyse, and other expensive clothing into heavy wardrobe boxes and schlepped them to my truck.

Then the foreman appeared, a squat fellow with a gruff voice. He demanded my signature on a legal-looking form. He also demanded money. I refused to give him either. "My son is handling it," I kept saying. We started arguing, our voices colliding loud enough for the nearest neighbors several acres away to hear. He pressed up against me, fists raised. I thought he was going to kill me. He used derogatory language about Jews and their money. One of the other movers, a gargantuan fellow, convinced the foreman to retreat. When the vehicle was crammed full, I locked the doors, which set the automatic alarm.

In the late afternoon, I heard the alarm's staccato blasts and rushed down to the garage. In my senility, I'd forgotten that I had parked in the front circle. By the time I reached the truck, the alarm had ceased. When at long last I was ready to head to Michael's hotel, I tried to start the truck. It was dead. I called roadside service believing it needed a battery jump, not even thinking at that time of the earlier alarm, which was set to cut off the ignition in the event of a break-in. That's why I couldn't start the truck. Then I realized that the wardrobes had disappeared. The movers had emptied the truck of all the valuables.

New alarm bells were beginning to toll.

24

The Debacle

I awoke with a start. It was two in the morning. I reached for Tao, but he wasn't next to me. Then I remembered. He was in the enclosed backyard at the house. Concerned, I checked my weather app. It was twenty-nine degrees, too cold for any dog to be outside all night. With all the commotion over the Suburban not starting, I had forgotten to bring him inside. Guilt and worry prodded me out of bed.

Thirty minutes later, I pulled into the circular drive and parked near the theater entrance. The cold air stung as I walked toward the gate. I shoved my hands deep into the pockets of my leather jacket. The next thing I remember, my foot hit something smooth and launched me backward. The world went black.

I have no idea how long I lay on the ground before

regaining consciousness. At least I wasn't in the emergency room demanding the nurse not to cut my pant leg. An incredible pain pounded the back of my neck below a large hematoma. I quickly realized the cause of my fall: black ice. In the light of dawn, I could see water streaming from the outdoor faucet bib; 3 Gorillas must have disconnected the hose, which was nowhere to be seen, but left the tap on. I carefully righted myself and turned off the water. As I opened the gate, a shivering Tao greeted me. We tried to warm up in the house, which proved difficult because the furnace had been turned off. I considered going to Urgent Care, but ever since my high school accident, I had been averse to visiting hospitals. Doctors are the worst patients. Instead, I called Bob Osborne and asked if he would examine me. A little reassurance that I wasn't going to need a craniotomy sounded good. Before leaving, I texted Arthur that the movers could go inside through the unlocked patio door.

Bob found no reason to be alarmed. Over a quick cup of coffee, he commiserated about the move, which I was beginning to view as a debacle.

When I returned home, the same two vans were again parked on the street. I assumed that they contained the boxes that "accidentally" had been removed the previous day. I found the crew hard at work. I asked the foreman to return the items his associates removed from the Suburban. He became belligerent, swearing at me and denying that 3 Gorillas had them.

Furious, I called Michael. "You've got to come here. They're stealing my stuff!"

When Michael arrived, he demanded the foreman contact Troy. The two of them stood outside the theater. I watched them through sliding glass doors. The foreman looked irritated. He took Michael's phone, said something into it, handed it back to Michael, and stormed off. Michael paced, his voice growing loud enough to hear through the closed door as he insisted that he speak to Troy. I suspected he was speaking to Deborah Hall, the office manager. Michael waved his free arm, his brow furrowed. When I asked Michael what Troy had said, my son's only response was, "It's being taken care of, Dad."

I believed him. What other option did I have? The ongoing commotion of movers packing boxes, my belongings missing, and difficult communications with Troy Emerson completely overwhelmed me. I needed Michael to deal with the details. Maybe I was asking too much of a twenty-five-year-old.

By the third day, as scheduled, the movers had finished packing and were loading the last boxes in the vans, after which they would head over to the hangar and unload. The flatbed Arthur arranged arrived at the house, and I attentively watched as the driver loaded the Ferrari. We agreed to meet at the hangar. He would then return to the house to load other items, including the Maserati, a fifteen-foot satellite dish for my Chicago sports, and over fifty planters that held large date palms, multi-limbed saguaros, and other exotic plants. At one time, I envisioned the date palms in the great room of the big house with the thirty-two-foot-high ceilings and clerestory windows.

Plans unrealized

Now they were destined for storage in an airport hangar. I pushed away the sad thought. I confirmed that all three drivers had directions to the hangar, then climbed into the Suburban, anxious for the move to be completed.

The hangar office was empty except for a small desk and a dilapidated desk chair. I took a seat and texted Michael that I was awaiting the two vans' and the Ferrari's arrival. For the next hour, I read my emails and answered sundry texts, none of which were from Michael or 3 Gorillas. Hearing a vehicle, I expectantly looked out the dusty window only to see a pickup drive by. Where was that driver and flatbed? Where were the vans? I walked outside and gazed up the road, ignoring the growing feeling that something was wrong. I called Arthur. I called Deborah. No one answered. I climbed into the truck and headed back to my house. Something must have happened; I just had no idea what.

Pulling up to the garage, the first thing I noticed was that the Maserati was gone. This perplexed me. Had another flatbed taken that car? Had the drivers stopped for coffee? Did one have engine trouble? And what about the vans? Was everyone lost? I called Michael.

"Dad, we'll get it figured out," he said. "I'll talk to Jeff and get back to you. He'll take care of it." Jeff Greenberg was Michael's corporate attorney, the consiglieri.

Jeff Greenberg

Michael reassured me that I could stay in the hotel for the rest of the week, and the following week, if needed, he would put me up in one of his eastside apartments. I was exhausted, frantic, frustrated, and incredulous. A week ago, I had an eight-thousand-square-foot house filled with a lifetime of belongings. At the moment, I couldn't even locate an alternate pair of shoes.

I didn't get much sleep for the remainder of the week. I could barely function. I didn't return to the house until Thursday. Josh brought over sandwiches for lunch, I supplied the Dr. Pepper, and we sat in the empty theater and ate. I had told the movers not to move the U-shaped desk, but they hadn't listened and had unbolted the sections and loaded them into the vans. I looked at the gaping hole in the floor. What had been there? Oh yes, a credenza. But what was below it in the hole? Then I remembered. The floor safe containing Jeanne's diamond and ruby necklace and ring and my Aliyah papers. I immediately phoned Deborah Hall.

"Don't worry, Dr. Bernstein," she sang over the phone. "We have the safe right here."

When I asked to speak to Troy, she said that she would have him call me. My messages must be piling up on his desk or, more likely, the receptacle next to the desk. I was so disoriented and dysfunctional that it would be months before I remembered that the safe also contained a very large sum of cash.

By Friday, I'd had enough. I had not heard from Arthur, Troy, Jeff Greenberg, or anyone who could tell me what had happened to four vehicles and all my belongings. I called Michael and told him that I was going to call the attorney general, the newspapers, and the television networks.

"Dad, Jeff is on it. Don't make those calls. Not yet," Michael insisted. "I'm on the verge of closing multimillion-dollar deals, and I don't want the notoriety."

In spite of my frustration and stress, I agreed.

Shabbat preoccupied me, but only for a short time. I felt certain something underhanded had occurred, but I didn't know what and couldn't do anything. As the fourth commandment states, "Remember the Sabbath Day, to keep it holy. Six days you shall labor and do all your work; but the seventh day . . . you shall not do any manner of work." [8] On Sunday, I moved out of the hotel and drove to the house to pick up Tao. I wandered through the rooms. Trash littered the floor. Some boxes sat empty. A few others were filled with broken pieces of china and other knickknacks. Disgusted, I left a message on 3 Gorillas' answering machine demanding that they return on Monday and clean up the premises. I loaded Tao in the Suburban and headed to the one place that was available: the hangar. On the way, I broke my vow and ventured to Walmart. That night, Tao and I slept on the blow-up air mattress.

The next day, I canceled my trip to Israel. I needed to solve the mystery of what had happened.

𝓧

Josh agreed to accompany me on a reconnaissance mission to the 3 Gorillas main warehouse located on the east side of town in a small industrial park. He picked me up after school. Forty-five minutes later, we circled the property, which was surrounded by a chain-link fence topped with razor wire.

We glimpsed the edge of what looked to be an open storage area adjacent to the office. I could see a red late-model Honda and, next to it, my Maserati and a stack of wooden crates with the word "Bernstein" scrawled on the sides. I started snapping photos on my smartphone. Josh pulled alongside the main gated driveway. Two Dobermans barked viciously, rattling the

---

8 Exodus 20:8-10

fence as they lunged at our parked car. We had no intention of going inside to confront Deborah or Troy; better to be safe and return with law enforcement later.

The enclave

Josh drove to the Arby's parking lot, adjacent to 3 Gorillas' fortified enclave. What caught my attention next were the movers maneuvering a forklift and loading crates onto a flatbed.

In advance of SWAT

Instinctively, I knew those crates were mine. But where were they going? And where was the Ferrari? Remaining out of sight, I videotaped the ominous proceedings on my phone. It was time to call the authorities.

Michael stopped by the hangar to show me the invoice from 3 Gorillas. Instead of the original estimated fee of $8,000, which included the $2,000 deposit that Michael paid, the amount was for $31,000. I almost fell off my desk chair. I couldn't even begin to wrap my head around where they'd gotten that figure. They'd inflated the three-day move into six and invented charges. I called the Pima County Sheriff's Department and described the criminal activity. The department sent Deputy Deborah Hogate to the hangar. She appeared very sympathetic and patiently listened to my story. I gave her a thumb drive of documents, photos, and videos. I also called the Arizona Attorney General and completed the extensive complaint form. Many lengthy visits downtown for interviews with fraud and other departments, as well as FBI representatives, would be required. Michael was not privy to any of these actions. He kept reiterating that Jeff would take care of everything.

Jeff, however, did nothing. I couldn't tolerate his inaction so instead sought advice from Scott Baker, who had successfully litigated my case with Formula One after the negligent Jaguar fire. Scott promptly drafted the necessary court documents and forwarded them to Jeff. I would have preferred to work with Scott, but unfortunately Michael had paid Jeff a retainer, and it wasn't ethical to fire Jeff. In addition, it would have insulted Michael, which I didn't want to do. Scott also referred me to Randy Downer, Jr., a preeminent criminal investigator who I then hired to research 3 Gorillas, Troy Emerson, and Arthur Back.

Randy Downer Jr.

When I wasn't on the phone or answering emails and texts, I slumped on the air mattress, Tao next to me, my energy consumed by thoughts of everything I owned being held hostage. My neighbors across the taxiway, Ron and Cheryl Wiener, were alarmed by my predicament. When I discussed why I was living in an empty hangar, they were incredulous and urged me to contact the local media and authorities. *In deference to Michael, however, I held off on doing so.*

I was frequently invited to dinner; they were always considerate of my kashrut habits. At first, I felt self-conscious explaining what eating kosher entails, but they insisted on knowing the details, saying that Ron most likely had a Jewish familial background. They even offered the use of the shower in their hangar. I forever will remain grateful for their kindness.

For exercise and diversion, I walked Tao around the airpark. I was wearing my kippah the day I heard a rifle blast that sounded like it was directed right at me. An elderly man wielding a rifle walked out of the desert brush and started toward us. In a thick German accent, he asked if I was Jewish. He launched into a story about how his Nazi relatives shot Jews during World War II. I was shocked and appalled. Still frightened, I was somewhat relieved to learn that his weapon was an air rifle used to scare jackrabbits away from his neighboring house. His name was Hubert. During our stay in the airpark, Tao and I listened to many of Hubert's endless stories about his childhood in Germany. Hubert and I even developed a friendship of sorts, perhaps out of mutual loneliness, and took bicycle treks around the airpark on chilly mornings.

Near the end of February, I received an email from a Mr. Rob Francis informing me that he purchased my piano listed on eBay. He found my email address in the piano bench documents and claimed the "wagon"—the computer part of the Disklavier—was missing. When he contacted 3 Gorillas asking them what happened to the wagon, they accused me of having it. What chutzpah! Their scruples, if they ever had any, must have shriveled in some dry wash. I emailed Rob Francis that we should meet at Applebee's Neighborhood Grill + Bar.

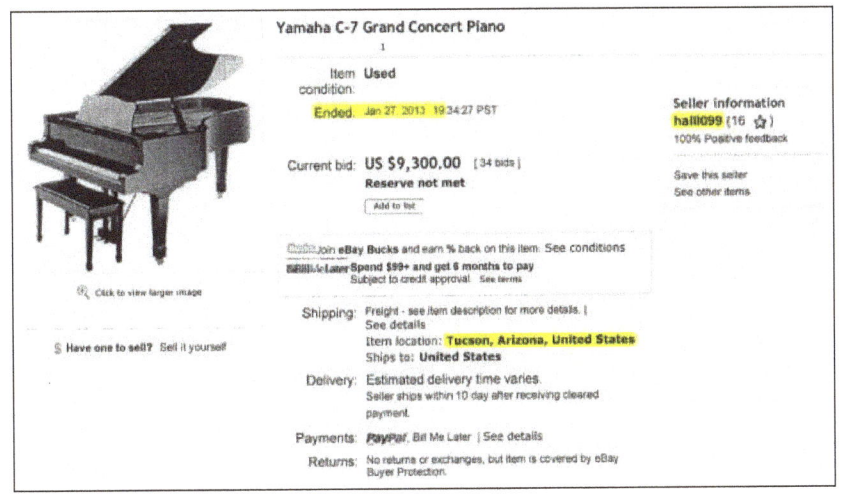

A bargain

Rob turned out to be a professional pianist and a true gentleman. I explained that 3 Gorillas had taken the piano and posted it on eBay without my permission. For years, I intended to have it shipped to my daughter, the family pianist, in San Diego where she now lived. Like Deputy Hogate, Rob empathized with my predicament, but he had purchased the piano from Deborah Hall for $15,000. He talked to a local Yamaha dealer, who was willing to sell Rob a smaller grand piano, listed at almost $100,000, without digital accessories for $60,000. He realized the sentimental value of my original concert grand, and would trailer it gratis to Elyse on his next West Coast trip in exchange. Under the present circumstances, I couldn't afford to replace his piano. It would have to wait.

As the end of February approached, I was forced to concede that I wasn't any closer to reclaiming my possessions, my comfort, my life. Frustration was as constant a companion as Tao, its claws ready to puncture my energy and challenge my hope. Added to my vexations were memories that welled every January, the month my dear mother passed. Then each March came the birthday of my firstborn, Elyse, followed a week later by the passing of my dear father. As the dates of each event approached, my sadness deepened.

25

Visiting Elyse

hadn't spoken with Elyse in almost nine years. The last face-to-face conversation we had occurred the day that I helped her move into a new apartment at Arizona State University. She was a sophomore and had decided to move out of the third-floor dormitory room, where, the year before, I had schlepped furniture. She chose to live with her sorority sisters—friends who'd influenced her original decision to turn down matriculation at the University of Chicago ("Dad, that's your nerdy alma mater") and Northwestern University ("Dad, it's so cold in Chicago"). Of course, at the time, I had no idea it would be the last time that I would sit across from her at a table or hug her goodbye. After that weekend, she stopped responding to my texts and phone calls.

At first, I told myself she was busy with her studies and

friends, but when my voice messages went unanswered, I eventually was forced to acknowledge that she simply didn't want to communicate with me, a fact confirmed when her college graduation announcement arrived a month after the ceremony took place. Those claws mauled me hard. She graduated summa cum laude. She knew that I would have attended. I had attended every major graduation since nursery school and many less momentous activities when I could reschedule my neurosurgical calendar. For her past nine birthdays, I left her a voice message and sent an email complete with graphics of birthday cake and candles. It's something I continue to do.

Do I believe that I will never speak to her again? I've only recently faced that possibility. When I think about it, of course, the emotions are not singular, but complex. Sometimes they come crashing in against my chest like Lake Michigan waves pounding against Promontory Point in Hyde Park. Other times, the hurt, the mystery, the unanswered questions drift slowly through me. During Elyse's freshman year, I attempted to explain to her about the divorce, the medical lawsuit, the loss of the hospital, the cancer, but she didn't want to hear any of it. She halted the conversations before I could share my thoughts. I knew these events bothered her. Maybe whatever Jeanne told her, or was telling her, swayed Elyse's opinions. I attributed much of Elyse's behavior to her age and immaturity.

Maybe it was my masochism that made me decide to fly to San Diego in order to try to see her on her thirtieth birthday—a special birthday. Maybe I finally realized she was not my little girl anymore, but a grown woman with a career and life of her own. Maybe I was desperate for a hangar hiatus, an escape from a life that had plummeted so unexpectedly into an abyss. Or maybe I just wanted to reconnect with my daughter, my "Leechie Nut," as I used to call her.

Most likely, I could find Elyse at her law firm in downtown San Diego. After graduating from law school, another graduation for which I did not receive an announcement, she had worked her way up from a law clerk, to associate, to law firm partner, and now was the director of the family law and divorce division. I didn't believe my visit would please her, but I did hold a modicum of hope that she would at least speak to me. I had just enough money to fly out there and stay in a hotel (at least that's what they called the cubicle with a cot) for a few nights. I consulted Michael and Josh individually before I left. Both thought my trip a frivolous waste of time and money. Maybe if they become fathers, they will understand. I had so much to discuss with Elyse. I wanted to tell her about my plans for Aliyah and make arrangements to give her the concert grand piano. I would be leaving the United States, perhaps for the last time, within the year. This would be an opportunity to say hello—and goodbye.

I decided not to bring a present. Over the years, I had given my daughter many birthday gifts, including diamond stud earrings for a childhood birthday. I was not happy about her matching nose stud much later. I gave her a car for her sixteenth birthday. She'd wanted a yuppie car, one that she could park between the Range Rovers and BMWs that her friends drove to school. She was a leader in the pom-pom line (her poise and gymnastic skills learned from a decade of ballet lessons), a coeditor of the student newspaper, and a participant in student council. She was a very smart young girl who diligently applied herself to academics and extracurricular activities. Of course, I was so proud of her. What father wouldn't be? So a car didn't seem out of the question, particularly in unincorporated Tucson, which still had remnants of a cowboy town in the desert with little public transportation and widely spaced neighborhoods. She worked hard and deserved it. However, I wasn't about to buy the German-made BMW that she wanted—or any German car, for that matter.

As it happened, shortly before her birthday, Norm

Waxman, one of my friends who had been a renowned radio show announcer, had a disabling stroke. I don't recall how I met Norm. I may have operated on one of his relatives, and perhaps that's how we became friends. He and I frequently talked, so he knew that Elyse would soon be celebrating her sweet sixteen. A well-to-do guy, he was in his late seventies and recently had purchased a Mercedes.

"Ron, take the car," he said in his dysarthric phonation to me one day. "Give it to Elyse. I can't drive anymore."

I couldn't just *take* it, so I paid Norm a nominal fee. The Mercedes was a four-door sedan, a recent model. Though it was a German, it also was Providence. The best thing about it was that the front seats would not recline completely, a feature Norm and I joked about; the worst thing was the color—mustard yellow.

I bought a big red ribbon and put it on the car. When Elyse returned from school, I told her that I had a present for her. Though she was a teenager, I could still see the excited little girl in her. I insisted she put on a blindfold. She held onto the railing and onto my hand and giggled her way down the stairs into the garage.

I untied the blindfold. "Surprise!" I yelled.

"Dad, a new Mercedes!" She was so happy that she didn't even comment on the color. Her brothers, however, quickly nicknamed the car the Crap Mobile.

A year later, now a senior in high school and on the brink of her seventeenth birthday, Elyse said, "Dad, I can't drive the Mercedes anymore." I expected her to say that she had gotten into an accident or a tire went flat. Instead she said, "I can't drive it because it's that ugly yellow." So for her birthday that year, I had the car painted metallic midnight blue. "And [she] saw, and it was good."

Although the car always remained in my name, it

disappeared with her after college graduation. I learned of its fate several years later, when I received notice of its abandonment and subsequent towage and storage bill. After paying, I gave the car away but kept the contents that were inadvertently left in the trunk: a tutu and ballet shoes. Elyse took dance lessons at Creative Dance Arts from age three through high school, when she was became a ballet instructor. Though her best friend and neighbor, Cassie, always starred as Clara in the annual *Nutcracker* production, Elyse relished just being in the ensemble. Just as my parents instilled a love of the arts in me, I wanted to do the same with Elyse.

My Ballerina

Though I constantly worried about money and barely had enough to pay for the hangar rent and sundry other necessities like food for me and my dog, utilities, gas, and charity, I felt compelled to make the trip to San Diego. Among the frustrations and fears that kept me tossing and turning at night was the thought of not seeing Elyse on her thirtieth birthday. I tallied my funds, then booked a round-trip ticket to San Diego. Maybe my daughter would be willing to meet me at least for a cup of coffee.

The sun was my ally the day I landed. To conserve money, I walked the few miles from the airport to the accommodation that I had booked near Elyse's office. The fresh ocean air and the proximity of possibility buoyed my spirits. I checked into the hotel, donned my Walmart sport jacket, and walked to Elyse's impressive downtown office building.

I wondered if she chose to specialize in family law to spite me or as a way of resolving the mental conflict of her parents' divorce. I could only surmise. I knew she had a boyfriend, whom I had never met. From what Michael and Josh told me, I suspected that this young man and Elyse soon would get engaged, if they already hadn't done so. As I walked, I thought back to thirty years earlier, when I had been acting chief of the department of neurosurgery at Cook County Hospital, an academician conducting research as well as teaching residents surgical procedures I had learned from exceptional mentors including Goldstein, Tarkington, Ciric, and others. What would life have been like if I'd stayed in academics? Would Elyse be partnered at an eminent downtown Chicago law firm? Would Jeanne and I still be married? Would I still be battling subzero winds whipping down Michigan Avenue in February? Would laser shunts now be used? Would my family be together?

I pressed the up arrow next to the bank of elevators in the glistening marble portico. I was reminded of the white marble Jeanne loved so much in the master bedroom and bath suite and which I hated. I made my way to Elyse's office. The receptionist wished me good afternoon and looked at me expectantly. She had no reason to know who I was. I had texted Elyse and left a voice message saying that I would love to see her for her birthday. She never responded.

"Is Elyse Bernstein in?" I asked. My heart seemed to fibrillate.

"No, I'm sorry," she said. "She's out right now. May I leave her a message?"

"No. I'll give her a call. I was just in the area," I said. Without delay, I turned and walked back to the elevator. I believed the receptionist, who had resumed typing away on her keyboard. When the elevator doors opened, I silently hoped Elyse would exit in front of me, but she didn't.

I headed back into the salty air, keeping one eye open for a beautiful, professionally dressed thirty-year-old who looked like my daughter. No such daughter to be seen. I could have planted myself near the entrance and watched for her to come out, just for a glimpse of her. But what good would that do me? I had a large canvas photo of her on my wall, a photo of her on my computer wallpaper, and a photo on my phone home screen. What I wanted was an exchange of words, a real conversation. I wanted to hug my daughter and tell her that I was proud of her and that I loved her.

Midmorning the next day, I found myself in front of the same receptionist. This time, she asked me my name. She picked up the phone, repeated my name, and hung up. I could feel my pulse quicken.

"I'm sorry, Dr. Bernstein. Elyse is in conference." She kept a straight face, this woman caught between a stranger and employer, a father and daughter.

"Tell her that her daddy says hi and happy birthday," I said. I hadn't used that familial term in ages.

Outside, disappointment and hurt propelled me up and down sidewalks and finally into a coffee emporium. A heavy weariness settled upon me. I sipped the hazelnut-flavored coffee. It tasted bland. Maybe the hot, caffeinated liquid would melt the weariness, but no, it too failed me. I blinked hard and often as I sat there drinking that coffee. Hashem was testing me again. This one was a brutal test.

Not too long after my trip to San Diego, Elyse and her boyfriend-turned-fiancé were married. I didn't find out about the wedding until I saw some photos on Facebook. There was one of a smiling Michael and a puckering Josh on either side of a grinning Elyse. When I first saw the photo, I had no idea where it had been taken, so I asked Michael where they were. Elyse's rehearsal dinner, he said. For the next few weeks, I checked the mail, half expecting an invitation to arrive, but one never did. Though I didn't ask for details, I couldn't help but wonder who walked her down the aisle. Was the ceremony under a chuppah? Was she happy? Did she think of me, even for a second, that day?

My little girl

I still leave messages for my daughter on her birthday. I've told her that she's my favorite pianist and that I can still see her practicing on the hallway floor, patting the paper keys the teacher laid out for her. I have the piano back, not the pianist. Not the one 3 Gorillas stole from me and sold on eBay, but a replacement concert grand player piano that I bought. It's Elyse's when she wants to claim it.

26

Eretz Yisrael: Reprised

Shortly after I returned from San Diego, Josh began complaining of a stomach ailment.

"I don't feel good, Dad," moaned Josh.

For the past two days, he had been anorexic and vomiting. At first, I thought it might be a miserable twenty-four-hour stomach flu, but based on his worsening symptoms and signs, including a tense abdomen, I suspected a more sinister malady like appendicitis. Jeanne concurred. She had witnessed numerous cases during her stint in the gastroenterology surgical center. Josh and I were scheduled to leave for Israel in two days. Instead of heading overseas, he might be heading for surgery. The thought riddled me with indecision.

I phoned a surgeon friend and the hospital and made preliminary arrangements for diagnostic tests and possible appendectomy.

Michael and Elyse both spent time in Europe during their high school years; Josh forfeited his trip to Europe through neglect. Yet, he wasn't that excited about going to Israel. Jeanne always dissuaded the kids from traveling there, claiming the trip was too long, the Middle East was too dangerous. Any of them could have attended an extensive tour and education program, all expenses paid by the Israeli government, but they never showed enthusiasm for the venture.

Finally, Josh said, "I'll go with you, Dad."

I was thrilled. I had set aside money from Scott Baker's successful litigation against Formula One. I instructed the travel agent to book five-star hotels, a white-water rafting trip down the headwaters of the Jordan, a camel ride in Be'er sheva, a gondola trip up Rosh Hanikra, an overnight camping expedition in the Negev, and finally, a recuperative week in Eilat, the Miami Beach of Israel, where we could snorkel in the Red Sea. In each place, I planned to see my Israeli family. I made sure that Josh had cousins his age on leave from ZAHAL who could take him to the nightclubs in Tel Aviv—the city that never sleeps. I wanted him to experience Israel. Maybe he would fall in love with it like I had at his age. The one thing I selfishly did was book a hotel in Milan, Italy, so that my travel guide and I could have a day to tour the Ferrari factory. My printed itinerary now exceeded two inches thick.

I was in a quandary. Should I stay in Tucson with my son, who might need surgery, or fly to Israel and again modify the itinerary that I had tweaked for the hundredth time just the day before? After considerable rumination, I decided that I needed to take this trip. If my carcinoma progressed and somehow left me disabled, I would forever regret not doing so. I called the travel agent and informed her that Josh would not be joining me.

"I add travel insurance to all my trips," she told me. "You'll receive a full refund on your son's portion." She added that she would file the claim while I was away.

The day before leaving, I dropped off Tao at the Royaile Kennel, the doggie hotel located near the hangar. We had visited this establishment earlier for an overnight trial. When I retrieved him, he seemed quite content, so I booked him for a two-month vacation. I reminded Tao that I would return, and if I didn't, I would pay for a ticket for him to join me. Being a young dog and in apparent good health, I already had inquired about how he, too, could make Aliyah. It would not be difficult to arrange.

Divine Providence made plans through a different travel agency. Josh wouldn't be with me. Last-minute arrangements for hired docents to assist me at various junctures were made. I didn't fully trust myself to check in at foreign airports, wend through customs and security, transfer planes in Rome, and collect baggage in Tel Aviv. I had purchased bright orange, recognizable suitcases, though while standing at the baggage carousels, I sorely discovered other travelers had done likewise.

At long last, I boarded the airplane sans Josh. After settling in my seat, I pulled out the list of relatives and their contact information from my shirt pocket. It was the same paper that I had carried almost fifty years earlier as a college student. Somehow it had remained intact and out of the clutches of 3 Gorillas. Although Peppy and Itchy had long since passed, I looked forward to seeing other cousins, meeting their children and even grandchildren.

$$\text{\Large X}$$

Shoshana Greenberg was scheduled to meet me at the Hilton in Tel Aviv. She would be my tour guide for most of the trip. I was waiting outside, looking for her Mercedes. When I saw the car, I flagged her down. A woman with short reddish hair and glasses emerged. "Call me Shoshi," she said, and thus began my Israeli adventure.

My room at the Hilton faced the beach. Every day I watched young bodies clad in wet suits hoist themselves on boards, trying to catch the waves. They weren't large waves like in Waikiki, where during a neurosurgical convention, my daughter tried to persuade me to accompany her. If Josh were with me, he might have tried surfing on the Mediterranean.

Surf's up!

During the first week in Tel Aviv, I called Josh daily. He seemed to be recuperating. His window of interest, however, had closed, and he decided to spend the summer in Tucson. I expected that to happen. I also spoke to Michael, who said he would be in Beijing on business; he could return through Tel Aviv, but probably after my scheduled cancer surgery.

Days began with breakfasts at the hotel's kosher seaside buffet. Shoshi then whisked me away for biblical tours and sightseeing. After a few exciting days, I began to think that scheduling my surgery during this trip was imprudent. I informed Shoshi that upon arrival in Jerusalem, we needed to go to the Hadassah Medical Center.

"Are you sick, Yisrael?" she said, sounding concerned.

"No, I just have to cancel my tentative surgery." She gave me a strange look but the following week accompanied me to the neurosurgery department and Professor Yigal Shoshann's office. I'd met him many years earlier at a conference and at one time even discussed the possibilities of joining staff at his department.

Canceling my surgery freed me. Worry no longer thrummed in the background. Nor did anxiety over 3 Gorillas or IRS issues or lawsuits. Unencumbered, I anticipated every family reunion and could now absorb the beauty and historical significance of every adventure that Israel offered me, and the homeland offered plenty. During college, I enviously passed the King David Hotel in Jerusalem, that grand piece of architecture built out of quarried pink limestone, which I couldn't afford. My suite on the new top floor with all amenities was recently renovated but overlooked the New City of Jerusalem. I asked to be moved to older rooms with Old City views, where dignitaries, royalty, and prime ministers such as Ben-Gurion, the primary founder and first prime minister of the State of Israel, may have stayed. I asked so many questions about the hotel's history that the concierge finally arranged a private tour. Each morning, I ate breakfast in an extensive dining hall. Most days I asked Shoshi to join me.

"Boker Tov, good morning, Professor Bernstein," said the maître d' the first morning.

I smiled. I was not usually recognized by that academic rank. "It's Doctor Bernstein. I really labored to get that medical degree," I teased.

The next morning, he greeted me with "Boker Tov, good morning, Professor Doctor Bernstein." I laughed. And so it went each day.

I had never been to the Temple Mount in Jerusalem and was very keen on visiting, though I heard of halachic reservations and timing considerations. A major problem soon became apparent. Shoshi and I arrived in Jerusalem the day before the start of Ramadan, the month of Muslim Holy Days during which no "infidel" is allowed onto Temple Mount grounds. Ramadan is a lunar holiday, much like those of the Hebrew calendar, and not a set Gregorian date. If the first sliver of the new moon isn't visible at dusk, the start of Ramadan is delayed.

Fortunately for me, the clouds cloaked the moon on that very evening, causing a twenty-four-hour delay to the start of the holiday. I seized the opportunity to visit the sacred grounds that, in 1967, had been so filled with rubble from the war that not even soldiers could easily reach it. After necessary preparations, Shoshi and I ascended the Temple Mount with her special governmental pass through a private gate. It was a singular experience: at the Kotel, one feels the nearness to one's Creator, but here, it is almost as if the hand of Hashem rested upon my shoulder—again.

When I later shared my visit with the rabbi, he expressed displeasure. Observant Jews don't go up to the Temple Mount because of the Shechinah, the presence of Hashem, he asserted. Most agree that we are not to go up there until Moshiach comes and the third temple is built, as prophesied. At the time of my visit, however, that decree was beyond my ken of Chassidut. I later realized that I never neared the most sacred area, which had been cordoned off. When I shared this detail with the rabbi, he softened his admonition.

My visit to another holy site proved less controversial. Outside of Jerusalem is the Mount of Olives, where, according to the Bible, David ascended as he fled Absalom. It's also the most ancient and most important cemetery in Jerusalem. I had never visited this sacred ground.

"We need to pick up a bottle of wine and two glasses before we go," said Shoshi.

Her comment perplexed me. She explained that a first visit to the Mount of Olives required a special blessing, thus, the wine. In fact, she said, the blessing is appropriate for firsts of all sorts, even the first time a fruit tree blooms. After making our purchase, Shoshi drove into the valley, then up the Mount, and parked near a ledge. We walked out onto it, poured the red wine, and said the blessing. Sunlight refracted in the over-filled glasses. It was one of those moments when the breeze blows mystically and you can feel the centuries layered over the city below.

During our visit to Tzfat, one of the Four Holy Cities, Shoshi located a talented artist who did microcalligraphy, an art form in which each image is comprised of a multitude of micro-size Hebrew letters. I commissioned a painting of the entire second book of Moses showing the parting of the Red Sea. Included were the Hebrew letters in Bo, the haftorah portion I recited during my bar mitzvah more than fifty years earlier. Not coincidentally, that portion based on my Hebrew birth date discusses the law of the bechor, as well as the exodus from Egypt. In Kabbalah, that exodus represents a departure from physical to spiritual. When I was thirteen, I never would I have guessed how meaningful that passage would become five decades later.

At the Shuk in Jerusalem, I marveled at the fine Persian rugs I could no longer afford. I felt fortunate to be on this first-class trip, even dressed in the Walmart suits I had packed in the orange suitcases. I purchased religious items that I no longer had in the hangar: tefillin, silver mezuzah and Kiddush cup, and books. I modeled several tallitot of various sizes for Shoshi, who gave me her opinions. Then there was the huge silver-plated kudu shofar that I carefully carried on board the return airplanes.

Before we left Jerusalem and headed north to Haifa, Shoshi reminded me that I had planned to plant a tree in my father's name. Back in Hebrew school, I would fill my little pushka every few months. It was a charity box sponsored by Karen Ami, a Jewish agency that used the donations to purchase and plant trees. Over sixty years, my family and I "planted" many trees in the Nachshon Planting Center on the outskirts of Jerusalem. I wanted to plant one more tree in the Bernstein forest in my father's memory. With tools and sapling in tow, I went to the edge of the forest with the prearranged forester, got down on my hands and knees, and planted the tree into the ground. I was touching as much of Israel as I could, and in return, it was touching me.

In memory of my Father

Four things have the potential to bliss me out, as my medical school classmates used to say in the seventies: nostalgia, history, knowledge, and tradition. Shoshi proved to be a wealth of historical, biblical, archeological, and political knowledge wherever we ventured. She declined to ice-skate in the Galil, though she watched and was surprised at my ability to hockey stop. I told Shoshi how Elyse was so embarrassed at the thought of her ancient father lacing up his ancient ice skates in front of her birthday party friends. I skated forward, turned backward, and sprayed Elyse with ice dust as I came to a stop. My daughter was wide-eyed. I reminded her that I grew up in Chicago

I suggested Shoshi take Josh's place on the scheduled rafting trip down the Jordan River. Again, she declined. I almost did too when I overheard some very fit young men, possibly soldiers, talking about waterfalls. Did I really want to do this? One of the guides said, "I'll go with you, Doctor. But let's take a large raft instead of a kayak." He assured me this would be less wild. *Wild* is a relative term. It was far less scary doing brain surgery than sitting in a rotating raft going over what seemed to be fifty-foot drops, but were probably only a few feet if I had opened my eyes, into roiling white waters.

Shoshi chose not to accompany me into Jordan for a tour of the lost city of Petra, one of the Seven Wonders of the Modern World. She thought it best for me to be with Arab guides who knew the area better. The meticulously preserved expanse of towering rock walls and intricate architecture was breathtaking. On the way there, I rode a horse through narrow canyons, then rode a camel on the return trip. I hadn't been on a camel since 1967.

These messy, smelly ships of the desert spit at their riders, but I was game for the ride. The young Arab guide in the lead proceeded to tell me about all of his girlfriend conquests in very uncouth terms. It was an interesting return to the more modern world. He later gave me his kafia. I kept it and wore it for Purim the next year when I dressed up as Yasser Arafat. (How shameful!)

Another Desert Beast

Shoshi was a scholar and taught me so much, but there was one thing I believe I taught her. We stopped at the new Ferrari dealership in Tel Aviv. She probably learned more about engines and interiors than she ever wanted to know. We also stopped at Laser Industries, where I had collaborated with Israeli scientists and physicians to develop robotic laser surgeries. Sadly, I learned that the last founder had passed away the previous year.

It was time to leave Israel. I visited cousins, ate a sumptuous dinner at the Dan Carmel in Haifa, walked backward into the Dead Sea, and revisited Masada. I needed to get back to the States, back to my children, back to the 3 Gorilla debacle. While in Israel, I received drafts of the lawsuit and planned to read through the newest changes during the flight home. But I had one more place to visit: Maranello, Italy. Any ferrarista has Maranello, home of Ferrari's headquarters, on their bucket list. I bade a fond farewell to my favorite tour guide and boarded a plane to Milan, Italy, where I would meet my driver.

Carol, an Israeli fellow who had married an Italian woman and started a travel business, was more than a tour guide. Once he knew that I kept kosher, he suggested canceling my reservation at the five-star hotel in Milan and moving to a two-star hotel that offered kosher meals. Alas, it was too late to make the change, so Carol made sure to take me to restaurants and sandwich shops with kosher fare. In turn, I introduced him to Ferrari. He knew about the factory but had never been there.

Cavallino Ramparte

When we arrived, I was told that only Ferrari owners could tour. I had to place a few calls to the United States before I connected with a Ferrari dealer, a friend in Oregon, who could vouch that I indeed owned Ferraris. Carol and I then embarked on a private tour of the factory. Pleasant memories of my cars popped in my mind as we walked through the spotless, well-organized complex. Carol took a photo of me standing next to a wax figure of the founder, Enzo Ferrari.

With that excursion crossed off my bucket list, I was ready to head back to the United States. It had been a trip of a lifetime. Israel renewed my spirit. Italy allowed me to reminisce. I felt ready to contend with the future, whatever that future might hold.

27

Swooping Down on the Whoop

Jeff Greenberg finally filed in August what should have been filed the previous January: a formal lawsuit against 3 Gorillas LLC and four defendants, including Troy Emerson and Arthur Back, containing six counts, including breach of contract, elder abuse, consumer fraud, negligent misrepresentation, and conversion (theft of property). After back-and-forth communiqués between Jeff and the judge, Jeff informed me that if I posted a $12,500 bond, I could reclaim non-appreciable items—at last, a step forward. I immediately instructed Michael to wire funds from the custodial account. The court set an August date for us to visit the 3 Gorillas' warehouses.

"How do we know we're going to get these things back?" I asked Jeff. I had submitted a list of forty-six items that I hoped to recover: my children's awards and report cards, personal letters, framed photos, my birth certificate, warranties; and Aliyah, inheritance, legal, and IRS documents.

"They'll get all the stuff in boxes and make them available to us. And I'll have a truck with movers to load that stuff to take home." I anticipated having more boxes than would fit in the back of my Suburban. Could I trust him to follow through? I doubted it. If the boxes weren't ready to go and I didn't receive these items, Troy and his attorney would be in contempt of court. So, I expected to walk in and have boxes sitting there, though I thought some of the boxes might be at the other warehouses.

I asked Jeff if we were in danger. Would we need to have protection from the sheriff's office? Jeff said no. Even so, I invited Deputy Hogate to join us, though I didn't mention this to Jeff. I feared bodily harm without law enforcement present. Jeff suggested we arrive at the warehouse at three o'clock.

"No, I said, "we need to do this early in the morning. There are three warehouses." I had done the research and knew where they were located; I'd even printed out maps.

On the appointed day, Randy drove me to the Arby's parking lot, where six months earlier, Josh and I had recorded video of the removal of my crated property. The memory brought back flatbed-induced dyspepsia that even Tums couldn't ameliorate. We waited in the car for Jeff and a law enforcement officer. Jeff finally arrived, twenty minutes late. Neither Jeff's moving truck nor movers appeared. He informed us that the three of us were perfectly capable of handling the execution of the judge's order and could fit the boxes in our cars. I brushed aside my irritation. The day was too significant to let his ineptness interfere. We headed on foot toward the 3 Gorilla compound, my anticipation rising along with the desert heat.

When we turned the corner, much to my delight and relief, Deputy Hogate greeted us. Jeff looked quite surprised. Hogate must have taken the horrific details of my story to heart, because a SWAT vehicle and four SWAT members dressed in full tactical gear and toting assault rifles accompanied her.

Reinforcements

The SWAT team led the way up the path and ushered us into a small reception area. The overpowering bass of rock music emanated from a back room. Troy, wearing a company T-shirt and jeans, cordially shook hands with everyone. He quickly apologized to Detective Hogate for Deborah Hall's previous insolence.

"Deborah's been fired," he said. Without skipping a beat, he turned to me. "Doc, I found a box out back I think you want." He then reminded me that everything was protected and safe since his crew did a professional packing job.

I couldn't respond. All I could see in my mind was the trash and mess his movers had left in the house after "professionally" packing everything.

Our entourage followed him toward the back of the building. The music grew louder, and then I saw where it was coming from.

"Hey, that's my home theater sound system!" I yelled as we entered a lounge. I pointed to my equipment sitting in plain sight. A SWAT member frowned and shook his head. Troy was busy interacting with Jeff in the front room and didn't hear me. Could Troy even conceive how much that professional equipment was worth? Randy's camera started clicking. Troy caught up with us. His insouciant attitude prevailed as we walked outside to an uncovered area. He pushed a box toward me with his foot.

I opened the water-damaged carton thinking it might be filled with some of the items on my list. Instead, I was reunited with albums, cherished classics like Jefferson Airplane, Beatles, The Supremes, as well as classic violin concertos. I looked around. My collection of antique planters were now filled with withered palms and bamboo. My Maserati still occupied the same space as when Josh and I had seen it six months ago. The driver's door was ajar and the sunroof partially open. The sight sickened me. Randy took multiple photographs. Without an apology or vestige of guilt, Troy handed Randy a box. I opened it. It contained my father's Siddur and tzitzit, cut off at the funeral. Tears welled in my eyes.

Last links to the earthly world

Half a dozen moving van trailers sat in the sun, their back doors padlocked. Detective Hogate ordered Troy to open them. Our entourage gathered around as he unlocked the doors to the first van and swung them open. The items inside looked like they had been haphazardly shoved together. Antique leather chairs leaned against tables, some covered with padded blankets, some not. Boxes were stacked unevenly. A monkey could have done a better job of packing the van. I picked up a box near the door. It felt unusually light. I opened it and discovered only wadded paper. I asked Troy to open the other boxes. All were empty.

Gone

When I asked what had happened to the contents, Troy shrugged. The judge had ordered the items on my list to be sorted, inventoried, and ready for my perusal. Three hours later, Randy and I determined it could take days to find the items on my list. I felt the tears return. Randy put a hand on my shoulder.

We decided to visit Troy's second warehouse several blocks away and inspect some additional vans. Maybe we would find the Ferrari. Several golf carts paraded to the warehouse. Randy and I were in one, law enforcement in the second, and Jeff and one of the movers in the third. Unfortunately, we had no such luck. I felt dusty, defeated, and dejected as we drove back to the main warehouse. The shadows were lengthening when Jeff dismissed Detective Hogate and the SWAT team. Our "raid" came to a halt. Jeff left with a red accordion file thick with papers tucked under his arm. I grabbed the box of my father's Judaica. Randy offered to carry it, but I clung to it as if it were a lifeline to the past.

Evidence

Jeff, Randy, and I returned to Arby's and went inside for a cold drink. Even though I had retrieved some cherished items, I was frustrated with the day's outcome and strongly suggested that we drive to 3 Gorillas' warehouse in Vail. Randy agreed; Jeff refused. When Jeff mentioned the option of filing a replevin bond, Randy became particularly irritated. A replevin bond would have enabled me to take possession of my property before it started to disappear. Jeff should have filed for one back in January. We decided to reconvene our heated discussion in Jeff's office.

Upon entering the office, Jeff told Randy and me to take a seat at the conference table. He left with the accordion file and returned with bottles of water. I was still upset from the proceedings of the day and neglected to ask what was in the file. We discussed the details of securing a replevin bond, as well as scheduling a new moving company that would act as receiver of the goods and a timeline for how long all of this might take. Randy and I left the office frustrated and wondering if Jeff would take any of these necessary steps.

)(

I entered the Jewish High Holidays determined to divorce myself from any thoughts of 3 Gorillas. The holidays were too important to be bogged down by such negativity. I chose to attend Rosh Hashanah services at the inaugurated Chabad of Oro Valley, a few miles from my hangar. This was the same venue where, thirty years earlier, I initially met physicians with whom I would be associated.

Rabbi Ephraim Zimmerman led the service. Recently appointed as the official Shaliach responsible for promulgating Jewishness and Hasidism, he was new to Northwest Tucson, having moved from Chicago, a point of commonality. He was twenty-six, but looked much older with his long Hasidic beard, was married, and had two young daughters. After the services, I introduced myself.

Rabbi Ephraim Zimmerman

"What happened to you?" he asked, pointing at the side of my forehead. I told him about the cancer, then relayed that I lived nearby in La Cholla airpark. He invited me to attend the following week's Yom Kippur service. Showing off my limited conversational Hebrew, I replied, "*Tov me'od*," very good, and "*L'Shana Tova*."

After the holiday reprieve from the 3 Gorillas craziness, I faced a new challenge. Tao could no longer jump onto the air mattress, even though it was less than a foot off the floor. His belly was distended, and I suspected ascites, a result of liver disease involving fluid buildup in the abdomen. I brought him to an emergency vet, who drained the fluid, but it soon reoccurred. Previous tests suggested Tao had cancer. The vet suggested exploratory surgery. I opted to give my companion the chance to survive. I called Michael and asked him to please transfer funds so that I could proceed with the surgery. He agreed but was very upset with me for reasons I couldn't quite discern. He now lived in La Jolla and seemed to be having business troubles. I suspected he was projecting his frustrations onto me, rather than dealing with them himself.

I convinced the vet to let me attend the surgery. I hoped for the best but suspected the news wouldn't be good. The pathology report confirmed that Tao had metastatic liver cancer. I agreed with the vet not to reverse the anesthesia. I drove back to the hangar with a heavy heart and without my roommate, Sherpa Tao, who true to his name provided support for this mountain climber trekking foreign lands.

I lasted two weeks before a stifling loneliness filled the hangar. So as not to lapse into craziness, I drove up to Saving Paws Rescue Arizona in Phoenix. There, I met a shepherd who would have taken down any intruder regardless of size. He reminded me of Baron. The woman running the shelter suggested that I look at a more docile pet that would be comfortable with my hangar visitors. She introduced me to Max, who had been rescued from an abusive owner. Though he didn't jump on my lap as Cheezer had done so many years ago, he pushed his head affectionately against my hand when I petted him. His right ear flopped from broken cartilage, all his teeth had been ground down, and he had suffered fractures that left him with a slight limp. I could never know what he'd experienced, nor could he know what I'd endured. Maybe we empathized with each other in that unspoken language between dog and owner. I returned to Tucson with my new roommate and friend now answering to Maxi, riding shotgun in the Suburban.

I anticipated a trial date would be set for the fall of 2014, almost a year away. In the meantime, I continually nudged Jeff to post the replevin bond so that my belongings could be returned. He was a most aggravating attorney, but I didn't want to start over with a new attorney.

Fortunately, I happened to read an article in *The Jewish Post* about Matthew Schwartz. A veteran investigative reporter, Matt, a New Jersey native, recently had accepted a position with KVOA, Tucson's NBC affiliate. He had a passion for uncovering fraud and corruption. After reading the article with great interest, I called him, though I didn't mention this to Michael. Matt was intrigued enough to come out to the hangar to meet with me. He had heard stories of moving companies ripping off customers but never had reported on one. The horrific details of what had transpired with 3 Gorillas quickly captured his attention. He asked me to notify him each time something new transpired with the case.

In December, I called Matthew Schwartz and told him that Jeff had finally posted the replevin bond and the court had ordered 3 Gorillas to inventory and return all items—progress at last! Matt assured me that he and a videographer would be at the hangar on the appointed day and time. I had spent the week before chalking outlines of the various rooms and their labels on the hangar floor, hoping to facilitate where each carton, piece of furniture, and miscellany would be positioned and stacked.

A bright sun reflected off the moving van as it rumbled down the runway toward the hangar. It had taken eleven months to arrive. Two husky men jumped out of the cab and directed the driver as he backed the long trailer up to the hangar.

Partial return

Museum pieces

I filmed every movement, as did the NBC cameraman. Matt stood next to me, and next to him were the two law enforcement personnel whom I had requested. I didn't trust 3 Gorillas for even a second. One of the movers pulled out the ramp, and the unloading commenced. Box after box was wheeled into the hangar. Some boxes showed minor signs of rain damage. Others looked as if they might disintegrate in the mover's hands. I directed as much as possible. I just wanted them to finish. The next day, they returned with two smaller trucks, and the third day, again with two small trucks. The officers did not return. The videographer and I felt safe enough with Maxi nearby. Troy Emerson did not appear on the scene. As I expected, 3 Gorillas had not inventoried any of the items. In fact, they delivered boxes that were not mine. After six days, all that remained of my property was in the hangar. It was less than one third of the original inventory.

The tedious process of unpacking each and every item began. More than once, the onerous task left me in tears. A porcelain Lladro head turned up in one box, its decapitated body in another box. A Catholic baptismal candle with the name Barbera on it covered my Jewish holy books. All fifty-plus plants were returned dead. Many of the boxes weren't even mine. Someone else's last name had been written in thick black marker on the outside of the carton. The blatant carelessness of the 3 Gorillas never ceased.

Matt arranged for his videographer to film every minute of the inventorying. Not including the lunch breaks when I took him out for pizza, we worked six to eight hours per day for two weeks, thoroughly examining, photographing, and describing every item in detail. The videographer probably left with a very sore back and shoulders. I downloaded the audio files of my comments to my computer and annotated them. I created a separate inventory for missing items. That proved the longer of the two inventories. Only one third of my property had been returned, and of that, many items were in need of repair or absolute replacement.

Inventory   *Remains*

I did attempt—and in a few cases I even succeeded—to find the grateful owners of orphaned items. Everyone I spoke to told the same story: they hired 3 Gorillas, and somewhere in the process of moving from one location to another, property went missing. It became apparent that 3 Gorillas wasn't a band of gorillas, a whoop; it was a band of thieves.

A set of nursing books now in my care had a phone

number in them. I located the registered nurse in Phoenix who was eager to reclaim them. One of the boxes had the name Barbera and a phone number written on the outside of it. Karen Barbera lived only a few miles away. I invited her for a casual meeting and coffee and to see the fiasco for herself. Karen was in the process of filing a claim with her insurance company. I made a mental note to tell Michael to do the same. Neither Michael nor I had thought to do so at the time of the theft. Matt had advised me to keep her baptismal candle so that he could use it in his report. It also would be used as a court exhibit.

No one with whom I spoke had a story of such extensive loss and damage. The invoice that 3 Gorillas sent me was for the hefty sum of $31,000, more than triple the $8,000 fee in the original contract. The invoice included fees for packing and moving 823 boxes and for six days of work. The company delivered 209 boxes. Sixty-six of those boxes were not mine. The most the crew worked was four days. And the delivery was eleven months late.

My rendezvous with Troy Emerson and Arthur Back at Tucson's Superior Courthouse couldn't come soon enough.

28

The Trial

The trial was set for October 7, 2014, and was expected to last four days. Another dozen deadlines, from conference calls to filings, needed to be met between January and October. I posted all dates on my calendar and emailed Jeff reminders as each approached. Even with this badgering, Jeff continued to miss deadlines, resulting in the court rescheduling the trial for January 2015. Not only did this require a costly change in my Israel plans, but the huge letdown sickened me.

Between uncomfortable meetings and communiqués with Jeff, I kept busy. I purchased superglue at Walmart and with the steady hands of a neurosurgeon glued the head back on the Lladro. A three-foot-high regal ceramic Jaguar, once a sentinel in my garage, had lost large chunks from his torso during his encounter with the gorillas. He came through surgery well and was reassigned to guarding rows and rows of packing boxes in the hangar. Hubert and I continued to ride bicycles through the airpark, and Ron and Cheryl Wiener invited me to dinner once or twice a week.

During the first year in the hangar, I befriended John Gutierrez, who lived in the large house next door to the hangar. After his divorce, he rented the house and moved to a trailer, where he often invited me for barbecues. When I first met John during the initial visit to the hangar with Michael, I assumed he owned the property. Actually, his mother Josie owned it. An elderly, very sharp, devout Catholic, she often visited John and would always say a warm hello to me and Tao. We became good friends. I took her to Tucson's only kosher deli, and she raved about the corned beef and matzah ball soup. I fixed her irrigation system and cleaned up the weeds in her yard. She shared my grief when Tao passed and readily accepted Maxi. To this day, Josie calls me every few weeks from Oregon, where she now lives. Most recently, she called to wish me a very "Merry Christmas, happy holidays, healthy life, and happiness." I will let her know when I go to Israel because she wants "to keep track of" me, which makes me wonder if much differs between the loving hearts of Jewish and Catholic mothers.

Most significantly, I spent more time with Rabbi Zimmerman. He continued to be my main support, this man who felt like a son at times and a father at other times. Our frequent discussions ranged from Jewish history, customs, practices, and services to studying Torah and Talmud. I shared knowledge gleaned so long ago under the tutelage of Rabbis Lehrfield and Slae, and the Rabbi shared the tenants of Chassidut. Maybe in some small way we have served as teachers for each other.

When I arrived at the rabbi's house, his two daughters, then ages four and two, first peeked through the blinds, then opened the door with resounding happy cries of "Yisrael's here!" warming me to the core. I gave him bedroom sets and other items he needed and ran errands, shopping and schlepping for the congregation. As I got to know congregants, I helped them with their computers and other technical aggravations. The Chabad community engaged me and filled me with a spiritual joy for which I longed.

The rabbi also listened. He heard about my upcoming trial, my family, the highs and lows, frustrations and regrets of my life journey, as well as my plans to move to Israel after the trial. His perspectives prompted me to study Chassidic philosophy, what the rabbi sometimes calls G–dology. I began to see my struggles from a new perspective. The difficult road is capable of bringing forth the goodness in the world. Take Job's journey: He had a purpose in life, just as we all do. After losing his children, health, and wealth, he could have chosen to stay cloaked in despair, but despair is cheaply woven. It is nothing more than an excuse to avoid purpose.

The rabbi helped me recognize that when I cast off despair, I can begin to fathom my purpose. I had been shuttered in darkness through the divorce, the newspaper infamy, and the tremendous loss of my daughter, career, reputation, and material belongings, including the nostalgia that connected me to a loving, bright past. A spiritual joy was beginning to light the world, and I was eager to touch that world in a new way, to perfect or repair the world, as the rabbi explains the concept of tikkun olam. Would I have found this joy without such arduous experiences? Would I have found the rabbi? Chabad? The holy sparks that now light my world? Probably not.

꘎

October came and went. The trial should have been over,

but it hadn't even begun. As irritating as that was, I tried not to regret what could have been. Then, out of the blue, when I returned to the hangar one day, I discovered an eviction notice taped to the front door. John Gutierrez had sold the house and hangar in late summer and moved out of town. Josie knew the details of my situation. If Michael happened to be a day or two late on the rent, she never complained, just gently reminded. I thought it better that my son pay the bills because my mind still tired easily. Besides, the lease was in Michael's company name, Helena LLC. Grappling with trial details consumed my mental energy. As day dwindled to night, I often found myself unable to find words—anomic aphasia, it's called.

When Michael became embroiled in his own business turmoil, I took over paying the rent. For the past three months, I had mailed Josie a check, always by the first of the month. I called Josie, and she said not to worry about eviction, the lease went until January 31. It was only November. What neither of us realized was that Josie no longer owned the hangar. When she made the connection, she mailed the check back to me, not to the new owner, who was not so lenient. A few days after the eviction notice, this fellow not only locked the gate to the taxiway, he locked me out of the hangar. I texted Michael a photo of me sleeping in the truck.

No trespass

Locked out

I begged Michael to have Jeff Greenberg appear in court, but it never happened. So I went to court alone and gave a compelling argument before the judge, who, realizing that monies had been paid in good faith but to the wrong person, agreed to give me a stay of execution. I didn't have to move the next day, but I did need to move the next month. More tzuris (troubles) that I didn't need so close to the trial. I started my search for an affordable rental that could store all my property, a daunting task.

After viewing many houses, I found a two-thousand-square-foot single-family home with a fenced-in backyard for Maxi and within walking distance to the Rabbi's house. While cheaper rentals with more interior storage space were available, I wanted to return to being shomer Shabbat and walk to holiday and Shabbat services held at the rabbi's house. Rabbi Zimmerman had to co-sign the lease due to the IRS assault on my bank accounts and previous bankruptcy, even though it had been dismissed. He suggested hiring Abba & Sons Moving LLC, a company owned by a Chabad congregant. They loaded all the boxes, furniture, and other items and transported them the mile to the new house. Boxes were stacked from floor to ceiling, leaving one bathroom, a bedroom, and a narrow aisle in the hallway and kitchen. My bed and three-section desk squeezed into the bedroom, Michael Jordan's life-size cardboard cutout propped against the wall. Judaica filled the bookcase, and the microcalligraphy and the canvas photos of Elyse, Michael, and Josh hung next to it.

Although things began to settle into place two weeks before the trial began, life still felt hectic and unnerving. I read and reread all depositions and interviews. Michael had requested that he be excluded from any further involvement. Wanting to honor his request, I asked Jeff not to list him as my supporting character witness. The 3 Gorillas' attorney, Robert Fischer, subpoenaed Michael. Prior to Michael's deposition, I sent Jeff preliminary questions to pass on to Michael so that we knew what he was thinking and what he might say in court. He and I experienced the same events, but did we share the same perspective? Michael's answers were curt and relatively irrelevant. Fischer grilled him during a lengthy deposition in La Jolla. After reviewing transcripts, I asked Jeff to prepare Michael for taking the stand, but Jeff was so lackadaisical, I don't think he even spent thirty minutes with Michael. I wanted to speak with Michael before the trial, but this never happened. Some months before, the tone of Michael's communication with me changed. He had always expressed concern and inquired how he could help. Now he sounded angry and burdened. Yet, I couldn't get him to explain why. I could barely get him to talk on the phone for more than five minutes. His behavior baffled me.

When the Gregorian calendar flipped to January, the New Year inherited the same old asininity and insanity. Hopefully the trial would reset the year on a positive trajectory.

)(

The day before the trial, Maxi restlessly paced from bedroom to kitchen, through the narrow path, reminiscent of the path called the Siq at the entrance to Petra, the ancient Jordanian city. Maybe he picked up on the anxiety plucking my nerves, wound tight as violin strings. I loaded a hand truck and a half dozen bankers boxes filled with legal files into the Suburban. I wanted all records at my fingertips during the trial. Ironically, the hand truck was 3 Gorillas', left carelessly in the hangar twelve months earlier when they returned part of my belongings.

Siq of Petra

I took a seat at the plaintiff's table, Jeff on one side and the four-foot-high stack of boxes on the other. Troy and Arthur sat next to their lawyers at the defendant's table. They had proposed to represent themselves, but the judge overruled that idea and ordered them to hire attorneys. Matthew Schwartz and a cameraman were behind us. The defendants unsuccessfully had tried to quash the cameras. The rabbi also sat in the gallery. I had asked him to be present on the first day for moral support and G–d's blessings. The judge entered, we all rose, and the trial I hoped would restore my life commenced.

During the next two weeks, the true crime story unfolded. Depositions and court testimony obtained from former employees revealed that Troy Emerson and Arthur Back had a history of larcenous behavior, some of which Randy Downer had discovered in his investigations almost two years previously.

They had at least ten lawsuits filed against them and sixteen complaints reported to the Better Business Bureau. Their BBB ranking was an F, which Michael discovered a few weeks after contracting with the company. I had not had the presence of mind to check the rating before we hired them. That year, 3 Gorillas was the most complained about moving company in southern Arizona. Yet, the two cons managed to continue their nefarious activities under the 3 Gorillas corporate umbrella.

Last Name	First Name	Middle Initial	Birth Date
BACK	ARTHUR	D	12/25/1981
Gender	Height (inches)	Weight	Hair Color
MALE	71	190	BLACK
Eye Color	Ethnic Origin	Custody Class	Inmate / Detainee
BROWN	CAUCASIAN	MAX	INMATE
Sentence (yy/mm/dd)	Admission	Prison Release Date	Max End Date
005/00/00	12/01/2005	08/10/2009	07/07/2010
Curr. Absconded	Hist. Absconded	Release Type	Most Recent Loc.	Unit
--	--	COM SUPERV RLSE [info]	ASP - WINSLOW	
Community Supervision/ Parole	Last Movement	Commitment Status	Status
Y	08/10/2009	COMPLETE AND VERIFIED	INACTIVE

Inmate 200624
A BACK

The felon

When Troy took the stand, he admitted to selling my Disklavier piano on eBay. He also attempted to obtain approval from the Motor Vehicle Department to auction the Ferrari. When denied, he sold it to a private buyer. Arthur Back never was called to take the stand. In fact, he never showed up after the first day. As one of his witnesses, Jeff called Deborah Hall, long since fired by 3 Gorillas and dismissed as a named defendant—a smart move, as she wanted to clear herself of any wrongdoing and thus testified in my favor.

Michael drove to Arizona in a rental car at the beginning of the second week and testified for several hours. Robert Fischer's examination was brutal. Although Michael admitted to stopping payment on the deposit check, which was the basis of the countersuit against me, he really laid all the blame on me. His circumlocution and inconsiderate answers unsettled me. "My dad isn't able to manage his affairs, and I have to do everything." "I had to bail him out every time." "He cost me thousands." He sounded angry and refused to look at me. His accusations confused and saddened me.

When Michael contracted with 3 Gorillas, he knew that I was not capable of handling the details even though I knew what needed to be done. Shortly after the move, he texted me saying that if he wasn't in the middle of closing a deal, he would sue the company immediately. "Jeff and I are too busy to focus on this right now, so I intend to stall for the next week and sue them immediately upon closing my deal if they have not agreed to my resolution." Michael did not express any of this during the trial. He sounded far more frustrated with me, his father, than with the accused.

After his testimony, we met in the hall. Michael was in tears. He intimated that his life was over, that no one would hire him. At the time I didn't realize the seriousness of the business troubles he was experiencing. After he left for the airport to fly back to La Jolla, I called him repeatedly, worried sick about what he might do—he had sounded so utterly despondent—but he refused to answer. Now the one in tears, I called Rabbi Zimmerman. He said that he would try to talk to Michael and, if necessary, reach out to another Hasidic rabbi in La Jolla and ask him to visit Michael. Rabbi Zimmerman talked to Michael the next day. He relayed to me that Michael seemed to have calmed down and would be OK. I asked Matthew Schwartz not to include Michael in the upcoming segment about the trial. Matt honored my request and blurred the image of Michael testifying and did not mention him by name.

It was now my turn to take the stand. Testifying for two days, six hours per day, with a lunch break consumed by discussions of the trial proved arduous. Jeff questioned me. Robert Fischer insinuated all sorts of past criminal activities. Troy was not present. Jeff showed the slideshow that I had prepared, first of photos taken by Mike's appraiser before listing the house in the foothills, followed by photos of property delivered to the hangar. When 3 Gorillas' lawyer called me a liar about the cost of expensive items, insisting that the Peloponnesian urn was a cheap fake and the chandelier mere glass or maybe even plastic, I passed to the jurors actual Italian crystals from the chandelier.

I returned home each day exhausted but managed to stay awake to watch Matt's segment at 5:00 p.m. Commercials then promoted it until its re-airing at 10:00 p.m. The Tucson community could follow along, just as they had followed the reporting about my surgeries in the newspapers. This time, however, the truth was on display rather than inaccuracies and falsehoods.

Nightly news

On Friday, January 16, 2015, two weeks after jurors were selected, they received instructions and were excused from the courtroom to deliberate. Before that occurred, the judge summoned Jeff and the defendants' attorneys for a private consultation in his chambers. When I asked Jeff what happened, he said just the usual jury instructions—lawyer stuff. I kept asking Jeff about the Ferrari. Would 3 Gorillas be responsible for restitution? He said no, that would be in later criminal proceedings. This was not the first time that Jeff mentioned filing a criminal lawsuit against Troy and Arthur. Knowing Jeff, I was concerned about this plan and spoke with Randy about it, who then put William Walker on alert in case we needed another lawyer to handle a criminal case.

Jeff thought jury deliberation would take hours and even lapse over the impending weekend, so he sent me home. Few life events are as excruciating as waiting for a verdict. It's like family members in a surgical waiting room, waiting for the much-anticipated news. This was the culmination of several years of anticipation. No sooner did I arrive home than I received a text message from Jeff's secretary: the jury was in. I raced back to the courthouse.

Jeff and I stood. Robert Fisher stood. "We, the jury, find for the plaintiff . . ." In my exuberance I almost didn't hear the following: ". . . and set out the amount the defendant should pay the plaintiff for damages as one point seven million dollars." The jury also dismissed the countersuit. Joy and gratitude filled me. I turned and hugged Jeff.

The verdict is returned

I walked outside into the bright sunshine, the blue above streaked with a few wispy clouds. I raised my arms skyward and in Hebrew chanted, "Praise Hashem." Matt interviewed the jurors, and we talked about their unanimous decision. A few of the jurors expressed their sorrow and concern that

Michael seemed so hostile. Another said that all of them knew early on that 3 Gorillas was guilty of fraud and theft. I invited them to the deli for lunch, where we later raised chilled bottles of Dr. Brown's cream soda in a hearty toast to justice.

That evening, News 4 aired the scene in the courtroom, the back of my head, my kippah, my arms raised. Praise Hashem. Praise Hashem.

EPILOGUE

Aliyah

I would like to say that this was the end, that I received my $1.7 million that the lawsuit wrapped up nice and neat and the American justice system did its job. While he met with the judge in chambers, Jeff Greenberg ensured that would not happen. I never received one cent.

For reasons never fully discovered, he dismissed all parties to the lawsuit except for 3 Gorillas Moving LLC, a limited liability entity. Troy Emerson and his wife and Arthur Back and his wife were no longer liable for restitution. Had their names remained, I would have been awarded $1.7 million per entity or a total of over $8 million. Most likely, I wouldn't have received even a quarter of this amount, but I would have received something. Subsequent wages earned by Troy and Art would have been garnished. Maybe Randy Downer would have discovered where their illegal gains, including the $42,000 of cash from my safe, were stashed. Several fired employees discussed how the cash traveled north, confirmed by Randy's further investigations, but recovery of the funds became moot after the dismissal.

I reminded Jeff that he needed to recoup the replevin bond and the bond paid to the court before visiting the 3 Gorillas warehouse. He assured me that he was pursuing the matter—that is, until he stopped answering phone calls, emails, and texts. I repeatedly visited his office, but his secretary only said that he was out. A few months later, the door was locked with a For Rent sign on it. Randy Downer suggested that I take legal action against Jeff. I was not eager to engage in further litigation but saw little choice. I hired attorney Bill Walker and also kept Randy on the payroll.

Lawyer extraordinaire

After investigating for half a year, Randy concluded that Jeff, in keeping with his duplicitous nature, had forged my name and pocketed the bond money. Eighteen months later, we discovered that Jeff also inappropriately funneled a

$200,000 payout from 3 Gorillas' insurance company into his own bank account instead of mine. What a creep.

At least Bill Walker settled the lawsuit against Jeff, forcing Jeff's insurance company to pay the maximum amount: one million dollars. Jeff resurfaced during the trial discussions and promised to personally reimburse me, but of course that never happened. After paying Bill and Randy their fees and tithing a portion to Rabbi Zimmerman's Chabad congregation, I ended up with $300,000, a far cry from $1.7 million and certainly not enough to purchase an apartment in Israel. But I did venture to Chicago to visit my elderly Auntie Ettie and my cousin Sharon, and take Josh, in his first year of law school, to a Cubbie's World Series game.

Jeff Greenberg fell on hard times. He was arrested in his car with drugs. He also pleaded guilty to a Ponzi scheme and was sentenced in California to twenty-five years in prison. How many of those years he will have to serve, I don't know. During his trial, his young son was killed in a horrific traffic accident. He had my condolences and sympathy for the loss, but the tragedy did not negate or detract from his wrongdoing.

Following complaints by a number of citizens, Arizona attorney general Tom Horne filed a consumer fraud suit against 3 Gorillas in December of 2014, a month before my trial. Pima County Judge Leslie Miller found that, "3 Gorillas and [owner] Troy Emerson engaged in deceptive practices, misrepresentations, and suppression or omission of material facts in connection with the sale or advertisement of services." The judge ordered the defendants to pay restitution totaling almost $16,000 to seven customers, plus an $18,000 fine and attorney fees and costs, possibly totaling $400,000.

Unfortunately, Horne never included me in these filings. When I inquired as to why, his assistant told me I was omitted because I filed a private lawsuit. The one request the state made in its suit that was not granted was to prohibit the defendants from operating a moving business into or from Arizona. Troy Emerson and Arthur Back continue to do business under a new name and new location. I can only hope they don't destroy anyone else's life.

After three long years of investigation, I tracked down the Ferrari. The title had been in the red accordion file that Jeff Greenberg squirreled away in his office after the SWAT team visit to the 3 Gorillas warehouse. Either he or someone at 3 Gorillas forged my name on it and was complicit in selling the car locally. I visited auto dealers and repair shops around Tucson to try to gather any information and finally picked up the trail. The new owner had backed the car into a saguaro cactus at an upscale mall and brought it in for repairs. The shop's mechanic didn't initially want to give me the receipts listing owner contact information, but when I gently hinted of criminal involvement, the shop owner provided copies and photographs. By chance (Divine Providence?), I noticed those same photos of the car on CarGurus.com with a man's name listed underneath. CarGurus of New York refused to help me connect with the fellow, so I randomly called people in the New York City area with the same last name and eventually found the owner. By that time, however, the car already had been resold to someone in Texas.

I lost the trail until I saw it on the internet again, on the Beverly Hills Car Club web page, with a sale price of $35,000. Included in many photos of the car was my Schedoni leather luggage set containing about $200,000 of signed memorabilia worth more than the Ferrari. I called the club and told them the story. I talked to their attorney, who said he didn't realize it was stolen. "Hold the car," I said. "I'm flying out." I was inches away from reclaiming the car. When I arrived, the car and luggage were gone—vanished. Books, clothes, and electronics were all gone. The only information I could glean was that someone from Europe had purchased the car. As far as I know, the car is traversing the Alps or perhaps stored in a heated garage.

Sign of hope

It rained the other day. Water filled arroyos and puddled in yards. As the storm exited, a rainbow arced over the freshly washed desert. Saguaros and prickly pear, palo verde and mesquite, relieved of dust, boasted brighter shades of green. Raindrops lingering on their limbs and leaves glinted in the sunlight.

I, too, have been through a storm, a tempest with winds so strong at times that they pushed me backward. The repercussions were severe. I lost my wife and daughter, my professional reputation, my health, my material belongings. Like Job, I was tested. But why? Did Hashem strip me of belongings and leave me destitute so that I could see more clearly? Can anyone truly answer that question? G–d's intentions are not always apparent.

How did being the bechor of the family affect my outlook? What would my life have been like had I chosen a career in research instead of private practice? Maybe I should not have left the moving details to Michael; he was only twenty-four. I did not file correctly for disability insurance. I did not know about travel insurance. I trusted others to assist me. Some events were completely out of my control, like the doctor incorrectly prescribing blood thinner to my surgical patient.

Frank Goldstein died on the tennis court without anyone lifting a hand to help him. I do not wish for that. Job's friends and family, who had been estranged, eventually returned, consoled him, and offered tokens of affections. Josh calls me daily from Chicago. Michael sporadically communicates. I enjoy conversations with my cousins Liz, Sharon, Michael, and Gary, and of course, Auntie Ettie. The rabbi's family has embraced me. I spent various holidays with his extended family in Jacksonville, Florida, and Chicago and also flew to California for his brother's wedding. His children, now five in number, are like my grandchildren. Chabad congregants are my friends. I have relatives in Israel. New acquaintances and friends intersect my journey.

I still intend to move to Israel. I even took my pilot trip and found an apartment. Living there for six months gives me dual citizenship. The rabbi, however, strongly encourages me to remain in Tucson. He says that if moving has not yet happened, then it's not meant to be for now. I'm beginning to consider his words. As wonderful as Rabbis Slae and Lehrfield were, there is no rabbi like Rabbi Zimmerman. Perhaps six months in the homeland and six stateside would be fulfilling.

My plan is to sell The Beast, now in England under wraps, and give the money to the rabbi. His sights are set on a Chabad house in northwest Tucson. At one time, I envisioned driving it through Europe and ferrying it from Italy to Israel. But the VAT tax is now 75 percent of the initial sticker price. Plus, there are few parking spaces and drivers are as crazy as here. I would much rather relinquish ownership of the 220 and fund the Rivka and Chaim Moshe Bernstein house, a permanent Chabad house named after my parents.

G–d has restored my wealth, though not in the form of millions of dollars. Faith is my wealth. It fills my life and those spaces between memories of my dear parents and other departed loved ones, of sweet Elyse, of happier times with my now estranged brothers. It inspires me to be a better listener and to participate in the world in new ways. I set up classrooms for Rabbi Zimmerman's special programs, complete a minyan, and run errands for the rabbi and the congregation.

Will there be more forks in the road? I don't know. Who can say what Hashem has in mind for us? What I do know is that I am truly joyous, and like the mighty saguaro, I remain upright. Sometimes, after Shabbat, when the moon is waxing, the rabbi, his family, his guests, and I venture outdoors to the end of the cul-de-sac, where we say the Kiddush Levana, the Sanctification of the Moon that reminds us of G–d's magnificent creations. We tap our heels three times, and then, with gratitude and joy, we dance the Jewish dance of joy.

Author's Note

I am not inclined to be fully communicative of certain episodes in my life, those of disappointments and overwhelming emotional experiences. This reticence should be understandable, related to the following Jewish concepts and emphasized by considerations of Lashon hara, the Jewish term for derogatory speech—the speaking about another's indiscretion or shortcoming—literally, the evil tongue.[9]

We want life

Repeating innocuous gossip, also called rechilut, often

9 Rabbi Yisroel Greenwald, *We Want Life! A pictorial guide to the laws of Loshon Hora and Rechilus according to the Chofetz Chaim* (New York: Feldheim, 2017).

causes unforeseen negative consequences, while unfounded libelous gossip (*motzi shem ra*) is even worse. Words carry the potential of causing catastrophic harm, and I have tried to eschew such in writing this memoir, while following appropriate guidelines.

Finally, I have attempted to supplement and enhance my stories and anecdotes, with room for exaggeration, with Hasidic comments in these twenty-eight chapters. Twenty-eight is a significant number in Hebrew, as it stands for strength. The Hebrew language uses letters as numbers, and the letters are also words and concepts that can be used either literally or symbolically. So, the Hebrew letters *Chet* (8) and *Kaf* (20) together spell *Koah*, meaning strength.

Acknowledgments

Many thanks to the following:

Lynn Wiese Sneyd of LWS Literary Services and author Marilyn Pincus for their help in putting this memoir together.

The folks at Wheatmark who helped guide me through the publishing process.

Those in my family who have always supported me, including my Auntie Ettie, who reminds me of my mother with her grace and always-cheerful countenance, and my two cousins, Liz and Sharon.

Those who work at and own Eli's Delicatessen, for the wonderful food and for allowing me the countless hours spent there in writing and editing (and gently arguing) with Lynn over Moroccan Salmon, Shawarma, and Dr. Browns.

Rabbi Ephraim Zimmerman and his family, for the hours of study, inculcation of Chassidut philosophy of joy, and the never ending reinforcement that we are at the heels (Eikev) of Moshiach.

Rabbi Joel Lehrfield, for encouraging me to continue with Jewish Studies throughout Hebrew School, Hebrew High School, and Yeshiva, and for fostering my love of Israel.

Jay Leno, who thirty years ago tried to bribe my son,

Michael, to stop crying at the Pebble Beach Concourse. Jay was unsuccessful despite the wad of cash he offered.

To Bill Gates, for influencing new laws that allowed for so much car tsuris.

Frank Goldstein, Joseph Tarkington, and Anthony J. Raimondi, for encouraging me to be a skillful and ambidextrous neurosurgeon. I would facetiously and jokingly tell my patients that I was "equally bad with either hand."

My son, Joshua, for calling every day to threaten possible libel when he passes the bar and reads this memoir.

And finally, to my two younger brothers and my ex-wife, Jeanne—all of whom have been used by G–d to inspire this memoir and to teach me humility, patience, and perseverance.

Printed in the USA
CPSIA information can be obtained
at www.ICGtesting.com
LVHW070913041023
760083LV00016B/292/J